Fred Mitouer is a body-mind healer with great intuition and tremendous courage. Wounds into Blessings captures bo vortex and offers valuable knowledge and perspective on with clients. This is a must read for healers of all persuas body in the healing process.

~ **PHILLIP MOFFITT**, Author of *Emotional Chaos to Clarity* and
Dancing with Life

"Healing is the death of our wounded identity," says Fred Mitouer, master teacher and somatic practitioner. His work, Wounds Into Blessings chronicles his experience of more than twenty-five years playing and working in the interconnected labyrinth of mind, body and spirit. The wisdom springs off the pages with every story, especially his own. If you are intrigued with the idea that everything is relatedness....you will love this work."

~**TERRY PEARCE**, Founder/President, Leadership Communication

This is a rare book, and precious for the wisdom it opens to us. I am grateful to Fred Mitouer for opening truths that almost always are kept secret. To be able to enter the mind and heart of a true healer and accompany him in his work is a great gift. And to be touched by the intimate, vulnerable truths of those with the courage to persevere in their healing journey is a privilege and inspiration. In short, reading Wounds Into Blessings is a profound, deeply humanizing experience.

~**SHERRY RUTH ANDERSON**, Author *The Feminine Face of God* and
Ripening Time: Inside Stories for Aging Gracefully

Original and authentic. A wise, richly metaphorical and beautifully evoked twenty-five-year journey by a master healer and somatic therapist, revealing how his "disarmament" of "fertile wounds" knotted in the flesh can renew souls and revivifiy lives.

~**MARTY KRASNEY**, Executive Director, Dalai Lama Fellows

A game changer! Top down psychosomatic perception is turned on its head in Fred Mitouer's Wounds into Blessings; finally, the body gets to speak its mind. In eloquent philosophical reflections about his somatic practice, Dr. Mitouer gives us a gritty and graceful inside view of the humanity and rigor that real healing demands. From falling down and getting up, through disillusionment and redemption, to remembering the unity we forgot because of all the struggle -- there's something here for everyone.

~ **THE HONORABLE RUSSELL REDENBAUGH**, Former
Commissioner, United States Commission on Civil Rights

When someone who has achieved Mastership in an area and then writes a book about it, that book is always a must read. When Fred Mitouer presents us with this remarkable book that summarizes the past 25 years of his professional practice, then it needs to be a required reading. Wounds Into Blessings will deeply appeal to anyone who is even remotely interested in consciousness in general and the consciousness of the body more specifically. This book will be of assistance in your own personal process. This is not just a book about the human body. It is a book that expresses the accumulated wisdom of Fred Mitouer, a remarkable man who shares with us his journey towards Mastership. He transmutes the wounds that we suffer in our life into new and creative opportunities for personal growth and change as only someone can do who has transformed his own life into new and creative opportunities at every step along the way!

~ **HAL STONE, PhD & SIDRA STONE, PhD**, Authors of *Embracing
Our Selves, Partnering and Embracing Your Inner Critic*

Wounds into Blessings

10.19.16

For
Raquel

In Light
&
Love

How Healing Touch Evokes The Spirit
for a Passionate Life

by Fred Mitouer, Ph.D.

Author: Fred Mitouer, Ph.D.
Book designer: Blake More
ISBN number: 978-1-938166-983

The information in this book, though hopefully helpful in an anecdotal way for the reader is not meant to be diagnostic or prescriptive in general. The therapeutic work described herein was specific to the individual in treatment at that time. Readers should consult their own healers, therapists and bodyworkers within their respective communities before relying on any representations found herein. And if this writing stimulates more people to engage themselves in receiving hands-on healing work, the primary motivation for sharing my work here will be fulfilled.

© copyright
Flying Turtle Press
~~an imprint of Solano Press Books
Post Office Box 773
Point Arena, California 95468
tel 800-931-9373
fax 707-884-4109

for

two great spirits

Cheryl and Seth

my teachers and best friends

my wife and son

&

To all the brave warriors

and the wounded healers

who may be

so moved to be

a bridge

to the far shore

for themselves,

for another human being,

and for the world.

Wounds into Blessings

Blessures dans les bénédictions

Come, Come,
Whoever you are
Wanderer, worshipper,
lover of leaving,
It doesn't matter.
Ours is not a caravan of despair.
Come, even if you have broken your vow
a thousand times.
Come, yet again, come, come.

      - Rumi's epitaph

It feels as though I make my way
through massive rock
like a vein of ore
alone, encased.

I am so deep inside it
I can't see the path or any distance:
everything is close
and everything closing in on me
has turned to stone.

Since I still don't know enough about pain,
this terrible darkness makes me small.
If it's you, though---

press down hard on me, break in
that I may know the weight of your hand,
and you, the fullness of my cry.

Book of Hours 3,1
--Rainer Maria Rilke

Foreword

by
Meredith Beam

Fred Mitouer's personal investigation into the potential of people to grow into their full capacity and maturity as humans has been a life long inquiry. Through his own personal work and his work with clients and students, Dr. Mitouer has formed the basis of Transformational Bodywork, his pioneering practice.

For over thirty-five years, as a student and client of Fred's work, I have seen the evolution of how body based consciousness can be leveraged to transform one's life in unexpected and powerful ways. This book brings much needed attention to the interface of psychotherapy and psychological theory with the somatic practices of bodywork. Fred views body and transpersonal psychotherapy as inter and inner connected bridges between the once separated processes of psyche, soma and spirit.

Wounds into Blessings was first written in 1998 as an adaptation of his doctoral thesis, White Silk ~ Black Leather. Back then the field of Bodywork and Somatics was in its nascent form, not unlike the Internet. Since then, much has changed in our socio-economic world, especially in technology and in our scientific understanding of the relational dynamic between consciousness, molecular biology and psychological states of awareness. Yet with all the "change" in technological literacy and somatic awareness, one must question whether substantive transformation in the modern human's inner life is really possible without a sincere, dedicated intention to grow the full capacity of what it means to be human.

Fred wrote *Wounds into Blessings* to share his insights, the depth of his experience in the work and a desire to share his journey with his students and clients. As a result, a whole generation of body-workers and clients has been inspired to go more deeply into this amazing and artistic offering of Transformational Bodywork. For years he has shared this book with the increasing faith in the potential of the work along with a matching enthusiasm for the "better world" he felt could evolve through each person's embracing of their body wisdom.

In the last two and a half decades a whole language and field of inquiry has developed around body-based therapeutic healing work. And yet, the universal truths that underlie this work remain a constant, as one would expect. This book is an historical portrait of a healing artist as a young man who initiated an inquiry into how body based healing work uncovers a mysterious vertical pathway that is at the core of the perennial wisdom. This pathway spans the depths of the messy soulful realms of human suffering and the transcendental heights of redemptive spiritual valence.

The journey to legitimacy of somatic practices has been unsteady and challenging but, nonetheless, rewarding for those who have pioneered the proliferation of hands on healing. Certainly Fred's work itself has changed over these last two decades; and our society has changed as well in both awareness of, and interest in, Personal Transformation and Somatic Intelligence. Over the years the readership for this material has grown dramatically to include people of all walks of life -- from artists, academics, and business leaders to university programs and armchair philosophers and psychologists. The common theme that draws them to this work is the ongoing human quest to "lighten the load" of "what" this life offers up and further discover the right placement of one's life within the context of The Great Mystery that holds us all.

Fred continues this important inquiry. He is planning the release of a new book and a film that documents the continuing evolution of his discoveries, insights and wisdom about the human experience called – *Passport to the Soul: Using Somatic Intelligence For Personal Transformation.*

Meredith Beam
Anchor Bay, California
August 1, 2012

I am grateful

for the love and support of many clients, students, colleagues, and friends who have generously assisted me during the journey of assembling this material into its present form. I am honored to say "thank you" to: Agaja Enahoro, Rosamond Gumpert, Dan Beam, Rhonda Marin, Paula Sinclair, Marjorie Thomure, T. Rawlins, Marti Spiegelman, Carolyn Ingram, Cecile Cutler, Richard Kilday, Hallie, Mimi Buckley, JoAnna DeVrais, Robert E. Taylor, Ellen Rafkin, Kay Thompson, B. Kleinkopf, Connie Gerken, Gail Horvath, Mickey McGinnis, Teresa Glover, Helen Barrington, and Phoenix Hocking.

Special thanks to Victoria Fahey, Meredith Beam, Linda Ward, Dan Beam, and Cheryl Mitouer for their generous input on some very rough drafts. I am indebted to Dan Beam and Meredith Beam for their help in creating the graphic model of "The Transformational Journey," to Catherine Ingram for her professional editing assistance at a crucial time, and to David L. Schwartz, (and his good offices of Summit University of Louisiana) for his deep faith in me and my work, and for his assistance in translating my work into a doctoral dissertation. I also wish to acknowledge both Carolyn Ingram's psychological review and Bill Foote's psychiatric review of the manuscript and their personal support. In an earlier version of this writing I had the expert skill of Stephen Yafa who collaborated with me, and the editorial assistance of Bonnie Dahan. I am most fortunate to have had her knowledgeable input.

I wish to acknowledge my parents Regina Mitouer and Ralph Mitouer for their crucial roles in my existence and for the love I received in its many forms. I also wish to acknowledge my gratitude to the following people for their personal contributions: Abe and Dorothy Gerstein, Johanna Atman, Mark Wachter, Rebecca and Sam Keliihoomalu, Jessica Hirsch, Jasmine Hirsch, Tom Green, Deborah LeCover, Heather Myers, Anna Hawken, Matt Myers, Margaret Israel, Patty-Lynn Thorndike, Susan Shippey-Borski, Cherie Arnold, Randy Morris, Michael Horn, Tracey Coddington, Judith Fisher, Walt Thompson, Hal & Sidra Stone, Ilene Myers, Debbie Gunther, Jan Greene, Francine Baeza, Aurora Hayes, Del Potter and Gordon Smith.

And amore thanks to Blake More, for midwifing this baby of mine into its final form.

Contents

Foreword 8

Acknowledgements...10

Cocoon...13

Preface...14

Come to the Edge 20

The Fertile Wound 34

Figure A. Leveraging the Fertile Wound *48*

My Story 50

Battle's Over 66

The Only Way Out Is In 83

Awareness Exercise # 1 ....*84*

The Body Speaks Its Mind 95

Awareness Exercise # 2 ....*96*

Dragon's Brew..114

Zen Gardens 127

Awareness Exercise #.3 ....*146*

This Very Edge **151**

Epilogue **181**

The Transformational Journey **182**

    Figure 1. The Art of Personal Disarmament Transformational Map *183*
    Figure 2. Entrance to the Transformational Journey *186*
    Figure 3. Separate-Self Existence in Duality as The Wound *187*
    Figure 4. Core Life Force Expansion *187*
    Figure 5. Amoeba in Four States *188*
    Figure 6. Dynamic Tension *189*
    Figure 7. The Armament Ring *191*
    Figure 8. Unconscious Reaction to the Unhealed Wound *193*
    Figure 9. Splitting Time into Past and Future *194*
    Figure 10. Behavioral Effects of the Reactivity States *197*
    Figure 11. The Reactivity State of the Unhealed Wound *198*
    Figure 12. The Journey of Making the Unhealed Wound Fertile *200*
    Figure 13. Skillful Means *203*
    Figure 14. Mindfulness *205*
    Figure 15. The Healing Process *208*
    Figure 16. Disarmament *209*
    Figure 17. The Flow State *211*

Appendix **215**

    1. The Work *215*

    2. For the Client of Transformational Bodywork *216*

    3. Transformational Bodywork for the Healing Artist *217*

    4. Biography *220*

Notes **221**

Cocoon

A long a dusty road in India there sat a beggar who sold cocoons. A young boy watched him day after day, and the beggar finally beckoned to him.

"Do you know what beauty lies within this chrysalis? I will give you one so you might see for yourself. But you must be careful not to handle the cocoon until the butterfly comes out."

The boy was enchanted with the gift and hurried home to await the butterfly. He laid the cocoon on the floor and became aware of a curious thing. The butterfly was beating its fragile wings against the hard wall of the chrysalis until it appeared it would surely perish, before it could break the unyielding prison. Wanting only to help, the boy swiftly pried the cocoon open.

Out flopped a wet, brown, ugly thing which quickly died. When the beggar discovered what had happened, he explained to the boy, "In order for the butterfly wings to grow strong enough to support him, it is necessary that he beat them against the walls of his cocoon. Only by this struggle can his wings become beautiful and durable. When you denied him that struggle, you took away from him his only chance of survival."

Preface

Ten thousand flowers in spring,

the moon in autumn,

a cool breeze in summer, snow in winter...

if your mind isn't clouded by unnecessary things

this is the best season of your life

Wu - Men

"What the Caterpillar calls the end of the world,

the rest of the world calls butterfly."

a verse by Richard Bach

The human instinct of love is first expressed through the sense of touch beginning with the mother-child relationship—our primary bonding experience. When this love is present, health and a sense of wholeness characterize our lives. When there is a lack of bonding and nurturance, however, feelings of well being are, at best, infrequent. And if abuse, in its many forms, occurs, fragmentation will result and further diminish our sense of security in this world.

The absence of bonding, or the presence of abuse, creates a need for healing in a person. Through massage, and other forms of conscious touch, we are able to re-create a physical context in which love and trust can bond our fragments back into *wholeness,* which is both our birthright and, ultimately, our destiny. Conscious loving touch, in its many forms, is one of humanity's best hopes for transforming human suffering into the foundation of a more humane society.

In spite of all the bells and whistles of our technological society, the need for healing has never been greater. With all the talk of family values, people have never felt more fragmented and in need of real emotional security. Traditional religion, which has never been a great friend to the human body, has been replaced by a devotion to materialism that has neither improved the quality of medical care nor made the workplace more enlightened, nor helped educate us to raise children in non-authoritarian ways.

After all the so called progress, we have really very little to show as far as advancement in levels of human happiness. Each of us who cares deeply about a more conscious experience for human life in this society, and on this earth, must turn to the subject of healing and ask, "How can I bring about a positive change in my life? How can I find the compassion and courage to confront my personal demons, befriend their energies and re-awaken my aliveness?"

Healing work is about re-awakening; it is about self-remembering; and it is about listening to the body's dream of a better world. This book, *Wounds into Blessings*, is an invitation to you, the reader, to heal, to dance in the flow of life, and come into harmony with your body, your life path and contribute to this better world. As a longtime bodyworker, I have found that the keys to transformation lie within body awareness. This book is for both non-bodyworkers and for those who touch others; it is about the demystification of the healing process.

My perspective on healing has developed, over the past quarter century, through my direct contact with thousands of people, in all walks of life and of all ages, throughout the United States and in Europe and Asia. In my teaching and in my private practice I have continuously witnessed the common ground of all healing: our human need to bond into life, to give and receive affection and to make peace with our mortality.

Today, the new field of *somatics* refers to all the experimental approaches to bodymind healing and personal growth. These new body-based approaches are finding their way into the cultural mainstream alongside more traditional healing arts such as chiropractic, acupuncture, psycho-therapy and prayer. It is an exciting time for the healing arts because spirituality, ancient traditions and modern science are all converging into a new paradigm of the human adventure.

I call the work I do Transformational Bodywork (see Appendices) because it describes a process that can occur when several factors arise together within a healing context that manifests into a permanent and positive change of personal identity within a person. The work utilizes physical touch, breathing and focused intent and intuition to effect, in an individual, long-term change (transformation) as opposed to the short-term alleviation of symptoms—though such relief may be a significant aspect of each bodywork session.

It is understood that the major factor in transformation is expanded consciousness that grows within the client's direct experience. Complimentery to this basic understanding is the principle that transformation involves learning about the factors that have contributed to the circumstances that are present; and that, through this awareness, it is possible to develop more positive approaches to life challenges, create more and better choices about what goals are more worthy of our attention, and cultivate support to realize these goals in their fullest expression.

Healing is an organic process, like the ripening of fruit; and though it is simple work, it is not necessarily easy. What makes healing work difficult and challenging is that most of us do not know how to embrace our simplicity. The body reminds us. The body reminds us, by holding the pain of oppressive tension, that we need to make this healing journey.

Our minds, in contrast, have become conditioned by our cultures to be fearful, armed and reactive. This causes us to lose contact with our essential natures, which are naturally responsive. Because of this separation from our natural responsive state, defense and armament are erected to create the illusion of security in this world of duality. And in this pursuit of security, in an ever changing world, we hunker down into isolated realms dictated by old brain survival.

Healing is the return journey back, from duality, to the re-membered state of unity. In this book, the return journey is supported by a map, some awareness exercises and a few good stories. We don't want to get lost, on our journeys, in mental obsessions about our destinations or the rate at which we traverse our real or imagined paths. Nor do we want to identify with the significance of each rest stop on these journeys. The real question is are we taking this journey?

Many spiritual paths and religious traditions have characterized the journey of awakening as being long and arduous. By defining the journey in a hierarchical, cloistered and laborious manner, many potentially enlightened people have been discouraged from opening to the life of spirit. It is my experience that a precious gift awaits each of us in the heart of our difficulties and that by running from them we miss an incredible opportunity to grow spiritually. Healing is a new spirituality because soul does not get thrown aside nor does the body get left behind. Healing, naturally, begins when we put our attention on a wound.

What is a wound?

A wound is an energetic constriction of life-force energy. Wounds can be temporary or long term. When healing energy makes contact with a wound, a cleansing and rebuilding experience naturally occurs. This happens on biological, psychological, emotional and spiritual levels which mutually re-enforce one another. When healing energy cannot make contact with the wound, for whatever reason, the wound is isolated from a cleansing and no re-building can take place. The unhealed wound must then be managed.

Managing unhealed wounds becomes, over time, a life style characterized by coping behaviors and unconscious reactions. This state of woundedness is crippling to the spirit, depleting to the physical body and, sadly, is the source of humanity's spiritual malaise and social decay. But there is another kind of wound, or perception of our wound, that need not be crippling and that, ironically, is the source of great healing.

The difference between the crippling kind of wound and the wound that holds our passport for the healing journey is that, in the former, we identify with our pain and feel victimized; in the latter, feeling our pain tempers us, makes us stronger for life and shows us what we need to heal. In this way wounds, and the healing of wounds, assist the evolution of soul. I call these wounds *fertile wounds*.

Here's the choice. We can become fixated upon our wounds and be limited and run by them, or we can use our wounds as fertile soil for personal transformation. The intent of this book is to celebrate choice and free will and to encourage you to engage yourself in a fresh way with the aspects of your life that hunger and thirst for healing so that real healing occurs.

NOTE TO THE READER:

The organization of this book is designed to share with you, the reader, a non-analytic sense of the raw and amazing nature of bodywork that is transformational.

◆ In the client stories I share, there is a reflection of what I see happening along side what my clients self-describe as their own direct experience.

◆ In the chapter, "My Own Story", I share some of my personal path as a way of offering some ground and texture to my role as a healing arts practitioner.

◆ In the appendix, "The Transformational Journey", I share a more analytic overview which I have developed and use to help me understand the human condition with which I constantly am "in touch". I place this chapter at the end to spare you from engaging in the stories with an analytic filter that might buffer you from a more intimate engagement with the material, at first reading.

All the client stories have been freely shared by their authors with the express purpose of offering you a mirror within which to reflect upon your own journey into wholeness. These stories may evoke in you some unresolved emotions, repressed memories or, perhaps, your untapped faith. They are woven together as a psycho-physiological teaching that is intended to take you—not in a linear fashion to a specific conclusion but rather to a multi-dimensional awareness that can alter your perception of pain, grace, and creative personal growth. As you read about these different people, use their challenges as touchstones of self-perception. Look for the underlying patterns, themes and issues that strike a personal chord for you. Consider, as these chords resonate within your heart, the questions: "Am I ready to heal?" and "Do I want to heal?" and "What is stopping me from healing?" Sense your own edge as you appreciate that these people, like you and me, are learning to fly, land and take off again into whatever each moment delivers. I trust the insights gained will be useful to you as you embark or continue upon your healing journey.

Fred Mitouer, Ph.D.
Anchor Bay, California
Summer, 1998

Come to the Edge

"Come to the edge," he said.
They said, "We are afraid."
"Come to the edge," he said.
They came.
He pushed them.
And they flew.

Guillame Apollinaire

Though everyone is at some point called to their own edge, relatively few people "seize the day" and begin the journey, from that edge that takes us full circle into *the mystery* that holds us all. The gift of our painful difficulties is that, through them, we are humbled into surrendering our synthetic notions about our lives. For whatever reason you picked up this book, or it found you, we have now begun a journey that will remind you just how close you are to your own edge, your desire to fly, your fear of being free and your undeniable knowing that your very existence itself is, in one instant, awesome beyond belief and, in the next, utterly overwhelming.

What brings us to our edge?

All the inherited influences and all the environmental forces that shape our lives cannot compare with the karmic itch that takes us into our soul's calling. This itch in our lives serves a purpose, just as the irritating grain of sand caught in the stomach of an oyster eventually becomes a pearl. In every life there's an irritating itch that serves to motivate, to catalyze movement to some placement wherein our entire viewpoint transforms and a significant experience transpires. For me, my feelings of intense loneliness drew me into a life style in the healing arts. What began as a selfish need to be met myself eventually took me to a place of selflessness. In serving as a boatman for other people's crossings, I have come to see I was never outside the circle.

One of my best friends responded to an e-mail I sent her, describing a profound and painful opening I was going through, with this reflection:

"We humans are at once entirely fallible and yet it is our very failings that open the door to transcendence. I understand, and relate to your tears. Nothing comes without its cost, but the cost is also beautiful, fuel for our fires."

After reading this I walked out of my office into my garden, listened to the waterfall and felt such gratitude for my journey. What began as a lonely itch had evolved into a spark and then a fire, a fire that burned me to the ground and taught me that "What is to give light must endure the burning."

In the water garden I finally felt there was nothing left in me to burn and I just sat there, a bunch of ashes, looking into the koi pond, seeing the reflection of Kwan Yin, the goddess of mercy and compassion. I shook with the appreciation of the knowledge that our imperfections are perfect just the way they are. And with this total acceptance I came home. In this garden I had built from the grist of my struggle with loneliness, I arrived at my destination, which is precisely where I began my journey, a transcendent place that was at my very core—a place beyond all of my pain where faith never sleeps. And I sat there by the waters in my garden, in the home I built from these hands that are typing these words, and I recalled from my college days the words of the poet T. S. Eliot: "We shall not cease from exploring, and the end of all our exploring will be to arrive where we started, and know the place for the first time."

I could not write this book until I had died into the mystery at my own edge and truly accepted my imperfections as perfect; for what they taught me I could not have learned in any way other than the way it played. The poet Wendell Berry says, "The impeded stream is the one that sings." In building my water garden, I placed rocks as obstructions in the waterfalls to create that "singing." I am convinced that God has done this with us.

I have had many opportunities to meet my obstructions—my wounds and my shadow sides—and learn from them about fear and the alternatives to being afraid. My cravings and depressions and my rages have all haunted me at times and, until I learned to befriend these demons, they sapped my strength and made me crazy. But as fate would have it, healing work found me and had its way with me like no demon had. The *work* taught me to stop resisting what arises in me or with anyone I work with; it taught me to be still, with care, and allow what is so to unfold.

Once at the end of a meditation retreat I encountered some students of Buddhism seriously discussing the subject of suffering. I laughed very hard, I think, because we Jews have a rich heritage of jokes *about* suffering. (How many ways can you say "oy?") When my clients take their suffering *too* seriously, I give them the choice of either moving rocks on my property or telling me jokes at each bodywork session. Consequently, I have, over the years, heard lots of fabulous, dirty and stupid jokes and have landscaped a coastal mountaintop.

Through my experiences of wrestling with the issues that these clients bring to me, I have come to see that lightening up with humor and doing heavy labor or at least engaging in a physical work-out regularly, organizes the bodymind into a presence that is both light and strong. I remind myself and others that enlightenment means *Lightening Up*. Because this is easier said than done, I practice being silly and intentionally make time for play. When I erected a thirty-five foot totem pole on our land it was a soul statement, and everyone thought it was wonderful, but when the fire-breathing dragons demanded to be born, some of my friends were concerned about the affect mid-life was having on me. In truth I was experimenting with the esoteric meditation called "puttering."

There's an expression in the countryside: "If your chain saw isn't broken, don't fix it." It's actually good advice because fussing around usually creates a mess anyway and takes time away from the art of puttering. Fussing adds worry to things whereas puttering diminishes worry. So until something happens that merits our alert problem-solving abilities, we would do well to practice the ways of fun and play. Sooner or later, in one way or another, we will all encounter the mess of a very real situation; and then we will be challenged to shine our lightness upon these difficulties. At those times, we will be thankful to have within us the personal resource of memories when things were sweet.

Rubbing up against thousands of embodied lives from my box seat perspective, I have been fortunate to watch this dance of light upon darkness. Under my hands and before my eyes, I have witnessed many men and women who have met themselves at their edges and have moved their rocks with courage and dignity. This book is an expression of my gratitude for what I have learned through my practice in the healing arts with them, namely that human beings *can* realize "amazing grace," and that, through surrendering to the body's wisdom, we can all release our profound compassion, realize our faith in humanity and smell the flowers. I convey this "good news" not as some starry eyed, new-age optimist, but as a practical realist who has gone the distance, in the mess, with thousands of brave souls who have wrestled with the mystery and have shattered their illusions of what is real and what matters.

Everyone needs to know they are not alone and that someone else has experienced a crisis, perhaps worse than their own, and has come out the other side stronger and more loving. This book is written in that spirit for us all. I invite you to take a journey into the messy world of real healing. I ask you not to take the easy road for your healing needs but to take the practical road, the road that will take your soul to where it truly wants to go.

This is not a *How To* book. There are no twelve steps or ten commandments to follow but there is a clear message: You Can Heal! Many of my clients and students have asked me to share my perspective on healing. Because the nature of healing work is organic and messy, I have chosen to grow this story in an organic and earthy way that blends my personal reflections along with vignettes, from my private practice and school, to create an archetypal collage of the healing journey. I trust that the organization of these perspectives, teaching stories and awareness exercises will be, for you, a mirror in which to see your beauty, your opportunities, and your amazing grace.

In my twenty-five years of sculpting human flesh I have frequently seen this archetypal sight at the edge: At the very instant before a person leaps, either to his ego-death or instantaneously grows wings with which to fly, all that is unresolved in his heart surfaces to be met. Interestingly, those who have worked with the dying describe a similar phenomenon. Healing moments are, like death, turning points in our existence. Awareness and time become compressed and surreal. Caught between the desire to fly into, and with *the mystery,* and the fear of being swallowed up by the void, we seek answers to all that is unresolved in our hearts. Through my work with the human body, I have learned that we can only live into, and die into, the answers by loving the questions. In the following pages I will share a perspective that celebrates these questions and our relationship with them. But first things first.

What is in front of us all right now, if we can stand to look at it, is the transformation of our very perceptions about our existence and the difficulties and opportunities of being human. The way we *see* our world is quite conditioned by our beliefs about the way things are. The phrase, "I'll believe it when I see it," is actually a less accurate description of the way things are than this phrase: "I'll see it when I believe it." In truth, we do not really "see" anything that does not fit into our belief structures. With this subconscious mental selectivity we judge anyone, including parts of ourselves, who do not agree with our assessments about the world and our experience of it. Religious fundamentalists, for example, take drastic measures to condemn anyone who sees Christ, Mohammed, Moses or Buddha as different from what they think of their heroes. The violence in our world arises from this basic reaction of being against those who don't agree with our beliefs. It is evidenced in the way we treat other human beings and in the way we treat the rivers and the forests. The incredible wounds that have littered our personal and collective histories cannot heal until we humans are prepared to remove our conditioned belief filters, and *see* what is in front of us with fresh eyes. My experience has taught me that the body holds the keys to unlock this fresh perception, as this ancient healing story portrays.

There was a time, before history, when the wise elders of the original human race gathered together to discuss the fate of the human race...

All of the wise ones knew of the human capacities for mischief and were wary of offering them easy access to the keys of knowledge, for fear that they would exploit this knowledge and use it for ends that would be against the divine natural order of things. All but one of the wise elders argued against giving human beings another chance to have divine knowledge again. This wise one passionately told the assembled elders that he understood their concerns given the divisive racial history of human beings, but that it was in the interest of the divine order that each human being be given a chance to return home, to the *world of oneness*, by virtue of his own sincere effort.

The elders then remembered that this *was* one of the divine laws governing the *world of duality*. So one chosen elder spoke and said: "All right, we'll offer divine knowledge to humanity but we shall hide the wisdom where the mean and greedy humans will not find it...let's put it at the bottom of the ocean." Another elder, remembering the clever excesses of Atlantis, said "These humans will surely find a way to get at it there, let's project it out to space beyond the gravity field of Earth." After this was also dismissed for the same reason as before—namely that humans would create the means to travel anywhere to aggrandize their dominion over the natural world, the lone wise elder stood up to speak for the gentler side of humanity and said:

"We should place divine wisdom where no human being with less than divine intent will look. We will hide divine wisdom in the last place any exploitive human being will look. Because the exploitive humans are always looking outward for more to conquer, they will never look within. We shall hide the keys to spirit within the inner spaces of their own human bodies. In that way they will be brought to wisdom through their simple investigations of the mysteries of their own hearts, from where only good could flow." All the elders agreed that this was the most practical solution to their dilemma. And so the human body became the map for the journey home.

In general, it can be said that modern society has come between the human psyche and the mystery, and regards the mystery and the human body with suspicion and cynicism. Consequently, the keys to unlock the mystery are hidden and we live with little faith. In faith's absence, we do not perceive our uncomfortable edge places as transformational opportunities. Instead, we anxiously manipulate our perceptions into convenient dogmas and culturally correct behaviors, all to secure some buffer *from* the mystery.

In contrast, indigenous cultures are secure *with* the mystery. The ancient myths throughout the world describe dragons turning into princesses at the last moment. "Perhaps all the dragons of our lives are princesses who are only waiting to see us once beautiful and brave," the poet Rainer Maria Rilke writes. "Perhaps everything terrible is, in its deepest being, something helpless that wants help from us." Perhaps we humans can awaken from the consensus trance that tells us that the best way to live is to get comfortable and avoid pain at all costs. Perhaps our terrible dragons and our deepest sufferings are present in our lives so that we *will* investigate the mystery and, out of necessity, find for ourselves a passionate and exciting life at the center, well worth the pain we encounter at the edge. Our dragons are both leading us to our greatest treasures and challenging us to be brave enough to meet our fears and, in so doing, reveal the faith we never lost but just forgot.

We have had a lot of help forgetting who we really are. With rare exception, spiritual traditions and religion have viewed the human body with disdain and have socialized our relationship to it in adversarial terms. To the extent we perceive the physical world as a dimension that should be transcended or rejected, we exploit and pollute the earth, we abandon the wisdom of our bodies and we exist with "unresolved heart," continuously encountering the messiness of our human condition.

And just what is that condition?

Simply put, it has been about separation, scarcity and survival. *A better world is possible.* It could be about unity and inclusion, and abundance and joyous living. Standing at millennium's edge, we humans, as a species, *can* choose to embrace co-creation with the laws of nature, and find harmony within this physical world, *or* we can continue to manipulate our realities so that some people can survive well while violence, poverty, oppression and environmental degradation characterize the majority of human experience.

If we are to evolve into the harmonious former view, we will have to transform our perceptions and look at the life in front of us with fresh eyes and see the incredible opportunity that awaits us. To do this we will need a new kind of spirituality—one that does not leave the body behind. With the body's wisdom aligned with our true heart's desire, we *can* heal our wounds and experience the real lives we came to live—the ones we remember when we come to the edge.

I was young when this healing work found me. I had to grow into it; but even in the beginning, the massages I gave often became transformational healing experiences that taught me much about how belief structures imprison all of our hearts and minds. The more I did bodywork, the more my hands took over my brain cells, and in one simple, quantum moment *the mystery* that holds the heart's resolution found me.

In one instant, I was overwhelmed by the profound pain that I was seeing in a client and in the next instant I saw how perfect the pain was in causing a transformation of perception to occur. So simple; *the mess was the message.* There was no problem anymore, only a project. With this shift in perception—from overwhelm to awe—everything became interesting. I didn't need to have the special skill or know the right answer. I could just hang out in the question and massage my client's body with love and tell the person "I don't know." And in that *don't know* space something opened. I watched the painful difficulty transform into tears and then laughter and then quiet breathing. Without overwhelm there was nothing to fix; with awe everything was perfect just the way it was.

After this revelation everyone who drove up my driveway was the perfect person for each moment. Each client brought the issue I had just worked with or was about to open up to. Every student asked the question I had been contemplating, and every worker on my land became a philosopher. One of my local clients on the coast where I live asked me what I did with all the shit people brought me and I said, "Your shit's my compost."

The premise of this book is that most of us have similar areas of emotional vulnerability locked or stored in the body, what I call *wounds,* and that by revisiting the source of these wounds in a safe and non-threatening context in bodywork, they can be healed. In these revisitations, if we are allied with compassion, the "shit" does become "compost", the imperfect becomes perfect. For me, personally, though it took a long time, I became grateful to my father for his neglect, for in the vacuum of his abandonment, I learned how to show up for myself.

Imperfection leads us through what doesn't work into awareness of what needs to happen. We suffer, but for an important reason: our soul's education. So, if our soul's learning is inevitable, and our lessons arrive often through bumping into what doesn't work, we may as well learn to enjoy our suffering, get the message from the mess and refine our lives accordingly by putting into practice what we've learned. Because the body is the library of all this *learning,* it leads us to our insights through its callings. Our angers call us to our learning about our forgiveness, our fears call us to the places where we lost our faith, and so on and so forth. Ultimately these callings take each of us to whatever place there was, in our past, where we split from our wholeness. We find there, in that split, both our innocence that preceded it and the survival mechanisms that followed. Because so many of these "breaks from wholeness" originated in our formative years, we find in our revisitations, a sometimes shocking reunion with our scared and tender parts. And this meeting is sacred and it is inevitable.

Culture and traditions aside, too many parents—usually because of their own childhood pain—are not mature enough to guide children into socially appropriate roles and behaviors with gentle hands and kind hearts. Instead, they rely upon shaming, withdrawing love, intimidation and outright violence as methods of coercion. The long-term consequences are often disastrous in that feelings of betrayal, repressed rage, nervous fear, and grief color our life experiences in deep and painful ways. Children grow up defending their emotional vulnerability by doing what all animals instinctually do to protect themselves from hostile influences in their environment: they become hostile in return, run away, or pretend that they are invisible. Defense, just like in the rest of nature, comes in the forms of Fight, Flight and Freeze.

Each of these forms of self-defense may provide temporary solace, but carries with it heavy baggage that is ultimately self-destructive. For example, children who freeze—lose touch with their own emotions—tend to grow up not knowing what they really want or need and instead feel obligated to become caretakers for others. That dynamic in a relationship frequently fosters lingering resentment. Running away or fighting whenever tensions arise doesn't work either; they're both inevitably non-productive approaches to personal conflict because the underlying problems remain fixed in place.

Included in this writing are some stories from men and women who have tried variations of these tactics for managing the pain of human wounds. We'll also learn from their personal accounts how they finally became alert to the messages of their bodies and began to explore an alternative approach that actually uses emotional pain to transform the energy of wounds into a positive, creative life force.

Fundamental change is never easy, no matter how rewarding. It takes determination and faith to explore the unknown—and also a little help. The people who come to receive my help and work on themselves venture with me into uncharted areas where emotional pain has constricted and sometimes even physically crippled them. They trust that they'll find their way out, stronger, more capable and more vital than before. And when they do, their sense of liberation is exhilarating, like a breath freely drawn for the first time in memory. It's the essence of the pure joy I am lucky enough to share with my clients.

The process goes something like this. We get hurt—wounded—early in life by a rejecting parent, or by any number of genuinely painful relationships and events. To survive, we develop ways of reacting to these wounds that will at least allow us to function adequately as we go about our daily business. We learn to get by, but our reaction-based behavior paradoxically contributes to a deepening sense of discomfort and unhappiness in us that no amount of worldly success can rectify. Many of us react to early wounds by wrapping ourselves in a "survivor identity". We ultimately come to know ourselves through our pain rather than through our joy. Others of us react by identifying ourselves primarily as victims, going through life unconsciously waiting for the next aggressor to do us harm.

In our culture it is often thought that if we don't have pain, we lack depth. Compounding this is the intimacy dance wherein people demonstrate their comfort with one another by bonding through the ritual of sharing their stories of woe. We have all, at one time, mistaken intimacy by sharing our unhealed wounds with others and thinking this to be our place of depth.

Though there is truth to the adage *misery loves company*, it does not mean that in sharing our loneliness with others we are being truly intimate, for intimacy is really about meeting in unity, not the sharing of our pain in duality.

By knowing ourselves primarily through our pain we build an identity around remaining unhealed. Our mental bumpersticker reads: "I hurt therefore I am." And our physical dashboard is filled with the warning lights of sore throats, chronic fatigue, stiff joints, digestive problems, and any number of stress symptoms. Subconsciously, we become intimate with these physical and mental realities in a way that gives us a sense of relationship through the dualistic split in consciousness. By fragmenting into at least two parts, we are able to both feel our hurt *and* give solace to that part which hurts. In this ironic way we bond to our existence in an addictive way through an intimate clinging to our pain and become afraid that if we heal we might die.

The fear of death felt by our wounded part generates a self-protective instinct called *defensive armament;* it's based upon withdrawing from the real world. The armored wardrobe we don may be as cumbersome and unwieldy as a knight's creaky battle garb, but we trust it to keep us safe from further injury. We go on like this, day after day, until one day our bodies get tired and whisper to us with quiet dignity or shout with burning resentment, *"I can't do this anymore"* or *"Is the war over?"* In truth, healing *is* the death of our wounded identity, but in the wake of our wounded identity's absence, our essential self, and its connection to Grace, enters. These moments are turning points, times when self-destructive emotional and spiritual constrictions begin a transformation from *unhealed wounds* to *fertile wounds.*

We have all made adjustments in our lives when we bump and re-bump a cut, bruise or blister. Inner wounds are no different. They prevent us from freely going about our business but are more pernicious in that they hide from plain view behind our well-constructed armor. Sometimes they unexpectedly reveal themselves when we over-react to an innocuous comment that penetrates through a tiny chink in our defensive armament directly into the raw vulnerability of our unhealed wound. This usually drives us into upgrading our armament and its maintenance. This can become a full time job but should not be confused with loving ourselves "warts and all". This kind of wound management is really about loving the warts at the expense of loving ourselves.

In contrast, the *fertile wound* does not freeze us with inhibitions nor make us react in addictive ways; rather, it opens a door in our hearts, turns on a light in our minds, and invites us into the juiciness of the life we are here to live. My approach in helping a person drop his addiction to his unhealed wound is first to help him recognize where it has taken up residence in his body. Working with a client, my hands make contact with the constricted area and probe to find out why the clenched muscles are working so hard and what might happen if they weren't. It's an intensely non-verbal exchange, skin to skin and soul to soul. I cultivate this intensity through focused breathing, subtle energy work and by manipulating the muscular armament of the client. It's my job to create a safe space for the man or woman to let go—literally to unclench. Once that difference is felt at the deepest levels in the neuro-musculature, a new awareness and/or emotional release almost always accompanies it, for the physical sensation, emotional state and mental awareness are all facets of the same psychic crystal.

Clients of transformational bodywork have an opportunity, at long last, to perceive their struggles for what they are: sometimes the ongoing relationship with a genuine trauma, but often they are a means of both gathering solace for their vulnerable part and generating the adrenaline necessary to get up for work on Monday. That's the source of the addiction. Unhealed wounds can often be perversely energizing in the short term; if we separate from them we fear we might run out of fuel. Over time, however, like any artificial stimulant, they ultimately exhaust us. When people are ready to heal, their bodies send out clear signals that the game is up; pretenses drop away, bodies soften into relaxation as muscles that have been held in a constricted state for much of a lifetime begin to yield.

This yielding, this disarmament, can be thought of in organic terms as a soul ripening. Like underground bulbs, planted in the dark soil of late Fall and emerging in the early Spring, fertile wounds surface to remind us that this mysterious universe keeps offering us endless opportunities to learn humility and evolve, through healing, into more gracious creatures. Through these openings, we discover some new ways of being ourselves. We stop depending on our suffering for our energy, and we stop confusing the "depth" we previously attributed to our pain with the spiritual solace we deserve.

It's easy to understand how as children we defend and arm ourselves out of instinctual necessity to remain safe. As adults, however, safety often comes to be equated with protecting ourselves *against* intimacy. Once our wounds transform from unhealed to fertile, a remarkable physical and emotional receptivity seems to present itself. We open up to truly intimate relationships with others, and it is within these relationships that real healing takes place.

The kind of healing I practice, and that I share with you here, takes place where mind and spirit directly interact with the physical body. Historically, it is the place toward which Shamans direct their energies; it is also the place where individuals go either in crisis or in meditation to re-connect with their truest selves. In my view there exists a developed consciousness within each of us, a spiritual witness, that guides us toward wholeness and grace. For want of a better term, I call it our oversoul. I would describe this oversoul as a gardening teacher for the spirit, an ally that exists in each of us who understands our essential life paths and is connected to the deepest part of all humanity. Our oversoul can be the champion and guide we need, and the gardener that cultivates our lives into fruitful harvest. And since the oversoul is also connected to the deepest part of the collective human unconscious, it delivers to us the universal lessons of the human adventure that inspire compassion and empathy for others by serving as a bookmark to the source. Perhaps there is no more profound reflection about the Tao, or "the way"—this subtle and delicious realm where healing happens—than this excerpt from the *Tao Te Ching*, by Lao Tzu.

Empty your mind of all thoughts.

Let your heart be at peace.

Watch the turmoil of beings,

But contemplate their return.

Each separate being in the universe,

Returns to the common source.

Returning to the source is serenity.

If you don't realize the source,

You stumble in confusion and sorrow.

When you realize where you come from,

You naturally become tolerant,

disinterested, amused,

Kindhearted as a grandmother,

Dignified as a king.

Immersed in the Wonder of the Tao,

You can deal with whatever life brings you,

And when death comes, you are ready.

Recipients of transformational bodywork, experience a version of this subtle and delicious flow in their bodies and with it a deep acceptance of the *Tao*. Within this flow state, perception shifts and they can clearly see the hidden costs of maintaining their unhealed wounds. This shift in perception begins the transformational process that elevates the unhealed wound into the fertile state where the soul's learning can occur.

The taste of the flow state's "ease with life" is strong motivation for embracing the healing process, but there is another kind of motivation that can evoke the process of transformation. This secondary motivation is felt as fatigue or exhaustion; "I'm sick and tired of being sick and tired." The carrot (of flow) or the stick (of fatigue) can catalyze the transformational process, but will ultimately fail unless a person is ready to see his wound as holding, within its core, a great gift, namely the long lost fragment he needs for his soul's journey home.

In transformational bodywork, dynamic tension, is not oppressive tension; it is natural and serves a practical purpose. It respects healing as an organic process, like the ripening of fruit on the tree. The work evokes from the body's wisdom a healing resolution to a person's wounded state of affairs. The body contains vital messages that, once understood help us to heal. Like breaking the code of the Rosetta Stone or Mayan glyphs, information that has always been unavailable suddenly surfaces and we see ourselves clearly. Before our shift in perception, our emotional states appeared, at the experiential level, laden with contradiction and complexity. With the code broken, biological and emotional language are conversations between soul and spirit. At this deeper level there exists a paradoxical simplicity. All light and all heat require friction. As the eighteenth century German philosopher, Friedrich Nietzsche, said: "You must carry your chaos, and fashion it into a dancing star."

It took me most of the twenty-five years I have practiced this work with others to finally give in to my own depth healing. It has been a painful and educational journey filled with profound insights and tumultuous periods of uncertainty and inner chaos.

In my work, I've learned to guide men and women to embrace their chaos and help themselves by taking advantage of their bodies' emotional intelligence at every stage of the process. The body's awareness, once engaged, can be a most trusted ally, especially for those of us who have made an elegant game of getting our needs met either by manipulating other people or by not really "showing up". This engagement of the body's wisdom remains the simplest yet most profoundly effective way I know to repair the kind of deep emotional wounds most of us carry about through our daily lives. Our bodies often know more about us than our minds, but that knowledge will remain unavailable until we become adept at deciphering its content. Once understood, our body's "cellular language" holds the key to emotional and spiritual health. Learning to tune in to its messages and to become emotionally healthy as a consequence—truly at peace with ourselves and our world—is the essence of spiritual and soulful healing work.

The purpose of this book is to first share with you an overview of the transformational process in healing bodywork. Second, it is to share stories about people that will help you identify some of your own healing issues and third, it is to offer you some practical tools for releasing the hold that unhealed wounds may have upon your life. Reading about bodywork cannot be a substitute for receiving it. Nevertheless I trust that, through this exploration, you will find within the heart of your own personal healing challenges a gift that will nurture you through the difficulties of your *edge* times and will help you to celebrate your own life and path with a free and passionate spirit.

****

The Fertile Wound

"Any idiot can face a crisis. It is this day to day living that wears us out."

Anton Chekhov

"Life is a sexually transmitted disease that is always fatal."

Jack Kornfield

The felt pain of the fertile wound reminds us of the inevitability of suffering. In realizing, through our vulnerability, our humble connection to everyone and everything else, we are brought face to face with the hurtful, real, but sweet secret: none of us escapes unscathed. Too bad, but there it is. Or maybe not too bad, for it confirms to us that we're not alone. We don't need suffering to be reminded that we exist, but neither do we need to fear it. In fact, the capacity to transform woundedness into insight, and ultimately into service to others, is one of the noblest adventures human beings can have. All it takes is your life, and a commitment to embrace life *as it is*, with all its paradoxes, contradictions, and tensions.

The great dividend for our efforts is that once healed, we can allow ourselves to have our real feelings. Our feelings no longer have us—we're safe to be ourselves. No longer at the mercy of our emotional systems, we can fully invite our feelings, with all their richness and diversity, into our daily lives. That's a lot different from trying to stay in control. It's true acceptance, and our bodies love it; a limberness in the muscles and joints develops and we feel relaxed and alert, with energy to spare. But the moment we begin to fake it again by holding our pain at a distance while pretending we're relaxed, our bodies respond by showing symptoms of illness. How perfect — our body as best friend.

Our bodies are basically Republicans no matter what our political persuasions. They're conservative; they prefer stability and a regular routine over sudden impulsive behavior. They generally take only calculated risks and prefer not to foolishly expend their resources. They pride themselves in being predictable and dull, even. Sober. Efficient. Utilitarian. There are few if any stand-up comedians among them. That's why our bodies can be trusted as barometers for our psychic and emotional states. They are centrists, not comfortable with extremes of constant change or with participation in long-term deception, because in those circumstances they break down.

Feelings, on the other hand, continually rise and fall like waves at sea, but they arise from sub-conscious mind states. By comparison, they're hopelessly mercurial and capricious. Our task is not so much to subdue our feelings, but to ride them without fear of drowning, using their power to get to the far shore.

Our wounds present a similar choice. We can become overwhelmed by them or fixated on them, or we can use our wounds as the impetus for personal growth. Engage yourself in a fresh way now as you read about wounds and their healing. Give your overactive mind a rest and simply observe its ornate rationalizations and convoluted justifications as you would hear out a bright but confused child, for healing is a hot button topic that evokes defenses and a fast search for convenient answers.

Real healing invites contradiction and is never convenient. It acknowledges the tension between the spirit's hunger for more than what *this world can offer* and the soul's thirst for the roiling waters of *real stuff-of-life experience*. In the body, spirit and soul forces are in a continual relationship, often characterized by struggle. Spirit invites us to soar, to scale mountain peaks, to transcend our daily mundane chores and merge with the various states of enlightenment. The individual human being feels this invitation of spirit as an upward calling to the physical body to get organized, clear and lighter. When we feel spirit at work in our lives, we walk through our life experiences as if we are lifted from above, like a marionette, with "higher-self" strings directing our actions. Consequently, sensations in the body feel diffused, transparent and of the floating kind. Since spirit speaks to the greater Self, the galactic explorer, its teachings warn us to be wary of earthly emotions, "lower body" sensations and "personal" memories that may blur our cosmic vision.

In contrast to spirit, soul thrives on direct and, sometimes traumatic, subjective stuff-of-life experience. The gardener, for example, breaks a sweat in the compost heap and exults in the sinewy contraction of biceps lifting shovelfulls of fecund earth. The body, like a loyal worker, will give us another hour of hard labor if we deliver on our promise of a cold lemonade or beer. If the soul is deprived of this kind of fully engaged relationship with the body and the body's yearnings, passions and appetites, it will shrink and wither. Learning how to heal involves a coming to terms with the dynamic tension that inherently exists between spirit and soul. If we choose one over the other it leads to the kind of folly in life where there is more talk than walk and the garden is full of weeds.

This journey we are on goes directly into the heart of our main mental absorption: sex, death and money, and the body-based drives they evoke, namely: desire, transcendence and security on all levels. Unconsciously or consciously these core aspects of our existence motivate us to act and react in basic ways that we often see in the animal kingdom: fight, flight and freeze. Though we humans fancy ourselves beyond the gravity of basic animal survival instincts, our bodies remind us, to the contrary, of our inability to really relax into our lives.

But what does that mean?

As a long time bodyworker, someone who massages muscles and tunes up the energetics of the nerves and acupressure meridians, I continuously notice how bodies suffer the tension that results from a certain ignorance of how polarities exist in this universe. Lao Tzu, the Chinese sage and writer of the *Tao Te Ching* (or the way of changing), implies that, "only ten percent of the people have the wisdom to accept both life and death as facts and simply enjoy the dance of existence." What Lao Tzu infers is that ninety percent of the people are reactive to their existences, with the fight, flight, freeze instincts of animals.

These fear based reactions to life and death are broken down, by Lao Tzu, into thirds. The first third "love life and fear death"; they're the fighters. The second third "prefer death and avoid life"; they flee. And the last third of the people "fear both life and death"; they're the frozen ones. Naturally, there are different situations in our lives in which we experience each of these different reactions. In this brief distillation, we see that only one out of ten people is really ready and able to *flow* with life—or "dance with existence," as our Chinese sage would say. This book is addressed to those people who are tired of surviving and want to join the ten percent that can live simply, as dancers in the flow.

You'd think, in today's "material" world with all its general disenchant-
ment, that people would be lining up to transform their basic orientations
from surviving to living simply. In reality, however, this transformation
involves a de-conditioning, much like an addict that commits to a new life
of freedom. Like any addict, the survivor is hooked on the body's own
hormonal pharmacopia. Unhooking from this vicious cycle of generating conflict and then reacting to it is the subject of this exploration. The
de-conditioning necessary to accomplish the unhooking is developed
through awareness. The first thing we become aware of is that our bodies
have minds of their own and have inherited unconscious memory banks of
reactive instincts that sometimes serve us and often do not. We notice this
either in crisis or in the stillness of experience. Since most of us have not
cultivated stillness to a great extent, we've relied mostly on crisis to show
us how we "do," rather than "be," ourselves.

Our ancestral heritage of survival is a familiar story we meet every day
within the cellular biochemistry of our bodies, as we biologically and
emotionally experience the tension of our existences. Hooked into reacting
to this tension with the hard-wired survival mechanisms of more primitive
times, we attempt to relax into life but find the body has its own program-
ming that lies deeper than volition.

Our frustration in being run by our unconscious, instinctual lives, and our
attempts to cultivate new and fresh ways of being with ourselves is very
humbling, because we meet the parts of ourselves that do not necessarily
feel safe or happy. And we can be sure, as we begin to de-condition, that
our primitive, little minds will be waiting to start another nice little war,
because survival is the primitive mind's prime directive. Conflict, "me
versus you," or "us versus them," or "me versus myself" thinking—is the
addictive fuel of the primitive mind state, and it lurks in deep personal
or collective unconsciousness, awaiting activation from almost any little
stimulus. The outcome of this meeting is far from certain, but, without
awareness and effort, it is clear that our sad and scared parts will never
surface for a healing. Peace and relaxation will elude us, and we will be
left with the familiarity of our ancient human struggle.

It's been said that peace is difficult to come by because it's boring compared to the physiological rush initiated by real or imagined fear and danger. Peace making efforts are usually born out of a strong need to transform a mess. It's the messiness of things that motivates a better world.
When King Arthur defeated other warriors, he gathered them all and
demanded that they surrender their arms and vow allegiance to him. Then
he told them to look around at the devastating mess all around the country.
In those days, like today, soldiers raped and pillaged the defeated enemies.

The pillaging usually involved the burning of the fields so that the suffering from war was very often felt as starvation. King Arthur said to all of the survivors: "The wars are over; now go to your homes and plant your gardens, for the cultivation of the soil is the first art of a civilized humanity." All the defeated warriors agreed with Arthur's vision and, for a time, a peaceful kingdom prevailed.

Today, it is our time to create a new, peaceful kingdom—*within and without*—by gardening ourselves. But first we need to acknowledge the messiness of things or motivation will be weak. This acknowledgment requires a shift in perception and doing so will take some effort. Just as we train a pet to behave or we suffer the undesirable consequences, we must do the same with the education of our survivalist minds. So if you're wanting to "go with the flow," like that Chinese philosopher, kiss off any hope of getting through life without a little mess.

The Mess of it All

Gautama Buddha, about 2500 years ago, was born a prince within a loving family, enjoying all the benefits of wealth and power. Even so, he made a strong philosophical case that things are not very satisfying here on earth for us humans. He observed and named three basic qualities of existence. The first is *dukkha*, which means that ultimately nothing ever satisfies because, even when it's all great for a moment or two, pleasure just doesn't last; then we suffer. This suffering—and our aversion to it and our craving for that lost moment of satisfaction—is the mess. This mess happens because of *annica*, the second aspect of existence, which states that nothing is lasting or substantial; everything is constantly changing, causing us great insecurity. (*You just can't depend on anything*.) But there's some consolation in the third aspect of existence, *anatta*, or selflessness, which states that nothing is personal because there's no lasting entity behind this mind and body we call "self."

Oy! This existence thing is a real pain. What can I do?

A better question is: "How can I be?"

There appears to be two kinds of approaches to this "existence thing," reacting or responding. Reacting to life has the philosophy "get a grip" and ninety percent of the people unconsciously grasp for this method of resolving discomfort. The second approach involves responding to life's events rather than reacting to them; the philosophy here is "go with the flow". Ten percent of the people, at most, consciously choose this approach. The difference between the two is that reacting does not require any reflection or much awareness while responding always involves choice, responsibility and free will. Physiologically, the two are characterized by adrenaline and endorphins respectively.

Go with the flow is the "way of life" Lao Tzu describes in the *Tao Te Ching*. In fact, the word *tao* means "way." (*Taoists* are those who follow "the way.") The thinking behind this can be seen in the metaphor of a river. If you go into the river you can float along with it—and in it—so that you are moving along with (and in) the changing nature of things. There is a relative security in going *with* the changing nature of things. The mind state of the ten percent of the people who choose this experience is faith. Faith allows us to greet the next bend in the river whether it be a waterfall, a swamp or, ultimately, the ocean with a spirit of equanimity.

Get a Grip is not about equanimity. It is the fear-based survivalist thinking of ninety percent of the population and is the result of lost or non-existent faith. Sometimes *Get a Grippers,* co-opt Flow speech and behavior to camouflage or overcome their reactivity; but more often *Get a Grip* is typified by a hunkering down, fortress mentality. And like the walls and armament of the historical Crusades, the human body armors its musculature and becomes hyper-vigilant in its attempt to create a synthetic security in this world of impermanence. Within this biological rush of creative coping, sex, death and money become tainted by fear and the cravings and aversions generated from this fear. In its extreme, intimacy is perceived with suspicion. Death wishes, killing or escapism lurk between each breath and scarcity consciousness reigns supreme; there is never enough food, land, influence, love or money. Pretty grim, really. In the less extreme circumstances exist thoughts of "I'm not good enough, thin enough, smart enough." Angst, angst, angst.

There is a better way.

Most people know this in their bones and feel frustrated by their gripping reaction to things, wishing they had accessibility to a "way" out of their suffering, their *dukkha*. Where is this way out? Is it in therapy, in a meditation practice, in positive thinking or in mind control? Should I go back to school, leave my marriage, travel to Nepal, find a new drug, join a community, become a vegetarian, have a love affair, plant a garden or...?

It has been noted in therapeutic circles that severely disturbed people receive help more easily than those "normal neurotics" (most of us) whose negative behaviors are less obvious. We normal ones, therefore, are more able to deceive ourselves into thinking that "things aren't really that bad after all." In reality we all need help in exposing our vulnerabilities, (feeling the mess), so that we can journey deeper into the unity at our core. The Buddhists would say that this core unity lies in the realization of selflessness, *annata*; and that detachment from the illusion of our separate-self existence, which is the cause of all our suffering, is realized through meditation. Assuming this is true, appreciate the paradox of a person wanting to "gain detachment", in other words *spiritual materialism*.

Enjoy the spiritual materialism in this description of an early evening in the synagogue after all the students and worshippers have gone home to their families. The custodian is sweeping. The Rabbi comes into the sanctuary, depressed about his lagging enthusiasm for everything as of late. "I am nothing, I am nothing," he laments to the holy ark as he humbles himself in quiet tears. He sits down as the Cantor comes into the sanctuary, also despondent from his disappointments with his recent teachings of the Bar Mitzvah students. He confesses to God about his failings, "I am nothing, I am nothing," and sits next to the Rabbi. Meanwhile, the custodian who has overheard these learned men humble themselves, goes up to the holy ark, and feeling deeply his own limitations—wishing he could have worked harder, had more time to pray and be with his family—passionately wails out "I am nothing, I am nothing!" At this point, the Rabbi and the Cantor look to one another and say: "Look who thinks he's nothing?"

"Spiritual materialism" describes how egoic strivings covered in humbly divine cloth can be just another reaction. These strivings are not about *fighting* reality or about *freezing,* holding our breath until things calm down. Instead, it's a *flight* into light. "Look mom, I'm enlightened," as if there would be an *I* left to care. It seems that we just can't get to core unity by trying to get there. If we get trapped so easily by our conditioned minds, is there another way we can get unhooked from its tenacious grasp? Is there another way we can really let go?

As a bodyworker, I have found the body's deep capacity for healing and re-programming to be much more than just physical; the body also has the ability to transform our lives by harmonizing our personal life forces with the universal energies that surround and interpenetrate this field of experience we call the "self." Like the simplicity of meditation, the different forms of loving touch, either from another person or from one's self, are not panaceas to suffering, but are opportunities to transform and transcend our separation—our loneliness—and experience the flowing integration of unity consciousness, even for a brief time.

Loving touch can provide the ground of unity wherein an individual can work through their blockages, their sense of isolation and their negativity. Just as a negative is required in photography to create a positive print, we need to acknowledge our felt isolation, and work with it, to realize our unity. When one's heart is open, even negative experiences can grow positive consciousness; compassion is often learned through suffering. Skilled, loving touch can truly shift the felt experience of dualistic isolation into the felt experience of unity consciousness; but because there has been so much taboo about the human body—pan-culturally and throughout history—we have yet to really experience the spiritual gifts within the body. In truth, body based taboos have created so many moralists who are faithful out of duty and so many promiscuous rebels who physically pass through each other's lives without essential contact of heart and mind that loneliness, isolation and further wounding characterize much of what passes for relationship today.

We can do better.

The growth of respectful and loving touch can provide a way for people to connect with one another with dignity and humility. Loving touch has the capacity to open hearts and the wisdom contained therein. This opening can release the dammed healing waters that, once moving, can and will erode the shame based taboos about the human body that have inhibited the healthy relationship between matter and spirit, here on earth.

This is the transformation. Just as the body contains spiritual energy, the human body's energy is itself contained within the seamless "unified field"—a term Einstein coined. Simply put, when the body relaxes, awareness expands and deepens, and we lighten up. This "enlightening" is not a state we acquire; we relax into it and discover that it *is* our natural state. In this way duality keeps evaporating and our lives become our meditation.

Sounds great but what happens once I relax?

The harmonizing process just described can, at times, actually be messy, because when the body feels safe to relax, the stuff it has been holding onto is released. Like a crimped hose being freed, our waters begin to move, at first with a jerk and then with a more even flow. It is just this way when we are lovingly touched by someone who is comfortable with, and accepts, discomfort, imperfection and struggle. We subconsciously give ourselves permission to free up our waters—be with ourselves with our messes. We don't need a crisis to push us or pull us. We can choose to open to our pain, meet it, and in this meeting find an acceptance that allows our anxieties to dissolve and our awareness to become more subtle. By allowing our bodies to be loved impersonally as well as personally, we can locate and then glue our fragments back together again and become whole. This loving touch is what a compassionate universe has given human beings to offer one another as compensation for the pain of being born into duality, often in difficult circumstances.

For those who were unbonded at birth, for those who were born into war zones and for those who were shamed, neglected and abused, loving touch can be a bonding into *Life,* a letting go into *Life,* a form of divine intervention that transforms despair into faith. And with faith, all things are possible.

So let us do whatever is necessary to find our lost faith. Perhaps we left our faith behind somewhere, along with our lost soul parts; perhaps they both disappeared through some break of our hearts. Let us decide, right now, to do the work of retrieving those parts of ourselves that left us, or were sent away for safe keeping.

If our faith has not been lost but has become weak and smaller through our pain, let us decide that today we will begin to cultivate our hearts and minds and make them bigger than the pain. Then we can feel our pain because we will have learned that nothing lasts; then we can own and feel our stories, because we know that by doing so our stories stop owning and feeling us.

We can outgrow "story" by allowing it to arise and pass on. We do not have to transcend our stories through some flight into light. We can complete them and feel the freedom of "selflessness," *annata,* as the old scripts dissolve. In the dissolve we can experience the beauty and the direct immediacy of this present moment. We can be free to see the mess, be with the mess and still kiss the ground and dance just because we want to dance.

So, we have a mess....
.....so what!

Zen thought tells us that in reality nothing is wrong with us and that we suffer because we don't understand that everything works perfectly. Because we buy into the belief that we're not okay (orignial sin and all that), we become very attached to various processes of becoming okay.

I want to be okay and happy but it is this wanting to be okay and happy that causes my unhappiness. What am I to do?

Who I am and what I have just doesn't cut it. Something's missing. That's why I'm not okay. This is the bottom line of dissatisfaction, *dukkha*. I'm expecting something else, something more—maybe "the real thing." And then, with these thoughts, I go off into any number of pastel new-age retreats—a dolphin swim or tantric exploration or whatever— where "I" and "the real thing" will merge and then I won't feel like I'm outside reality, whatever that is.

This "outsider" feeling, this sense that something's missing, is so core to the human experience that we hardly question its validity or benefit. We take it for granted. This is really quite dangerous because, by not questioning this almost cosmic myth that we're not okay, we further support the consensus trance that there is a "normal" that can be a standard that we use to define our mental health and the mental health of other people. This normality masquerading as mental health, I believe, actually permits most people to fall asleep, to become puppets without real human freedom. Being part of the normal majority characterized Communist Russia and Nazi Germany but today's normal majority has a massive devotion to materialism; and this too doesn't deliver "satisfaction." So we should question authority and challenge everything. As the saying goes: "If you meet the Buddha on the road, kill him."

I am definitely one of those people who wanted to be okay. I felt the dissatisfaction of my life. And I did all the cool things, including the dolphins and "designer drugs," and it didn't help. Frustrated with my frenetic attempts to relax into the "real thing," I found myself in a session with a very sweet and wise shrink—the father I never had. How could it be any different! He said to me: "Fred, I've got good news and bad news." Of course I asked for the bad news first which was this: "No guru, designer drug, lover or experience will make up for what didn't happen with Mommy and Daddy during those early days." I heard that and agreed and then asked for the good news. The good news, he explained, went like this: "No guru, designer drug, lover or experience will make up for what didn't happen with Mommy and Daddy during those early days." I naturally asked why this was such good news to which he replied "Now you can stop looking for it."

Stopping the search for "okay" is like breaking a bad habit and it takes a kind of unlearning, which is one of the reasons why people meditate. In Buddhist meditation we don't meditate to seek more knowledge or wisdom. We sit and become still in order to allow the knowledge and wisdom latent within us to emerge. *Where does it emerge from?* Lao Tzu would say that all things emerge from the *Tao* and dissolve into the *Tao*. And, in our calm relaxation, when the *Tao* merges with us, we discover that we're already okay; we just forgot. Ironically, there is nowhere to go because there is no need to go anywhere.

There's a Chinese proverb that says, "When the mind is still, the whole universe surrenders." The process of surrendering into the universe is inevitable for all of us in our death but we can experience little ego deaths by relaxing our mental grip on life, by giving into the laws of nature that resonate within our bodies—the breath and the heart beat, for example. Some meditation is devotional and is based upon the belief that you become what you meditate upon, implying that you don't meditate upon your story but upon God.

The laws of nature flow through all things. When we can relax into our bodys' rhythms—when "natural flow" is unimpeded—inspiration and grace permeate our experiences. Aldous Huxley tells us, "We are helpless without grace, but grace cannot help us unless we choose to co-operate with it." When flow is impeded, we experience blocked energy in the form of tight muscles, repressed emotions and strained organs. Excessive amounts of energy are required from the person who is in resistance to flow. The resulting body tension motivates some of these people to seek out massage and bodywork. When I touch these people, I sculpt away the excess and reveal the essence of that person. It's an art project for me. As the strain, the blockage and the tightness is chiseled away, an innate being is revealed. I love Michelangelo's response when asked why he chose a particular piece of marble to carve the *Pieta* (Jesus and Mother Mary). He said, "There is an angel in it and I want to free it."

In our own growth and healing we similarly sculpt our lives from the rock of our circumstances—awareness and compassion being our hammer and chisel. This artistic rock work we do on our selves is much more fun than the rock work of the Greek God Sisyphus who had to endlessly push a huge boulder up a mountain. Self-revelation is an odyssey of coming to know and to co-operate with the law of grace. After all, when all the chunks of rock have been chiseled away, what's left?

It's a law of nature that when we're in relationship with Grace, all earthly matters find their natural placement in our consciousness; and then our preoccupation with issues of security diminish accordingly. But Grace does not come to us unless we open to it. If we do not have a wisdom tradition with ritual opportunities to help us create an opening, we must rely on crisis and pain to break us down in order to give us a break-through. So this is the gift of our wound. At the very moment we crack open, Grace is there to meet us and help us become free. When we finally decide that it is okay to feel the pain of our separation from Grace, Grace finds us. We never visit our wounded places alone.

Let's proceed now with some basic understanding of how the pain of the mess gets us going and how that going proceeds.

Inevitably, when a very painful experience happens, we often fragment out of our bodies because the experience is too intense to remain present within. We then create life styles that adjust to this partial fragmentation; generally, we don't think about it too much until we experience intimate contact with another person or feel a yearning to re-connect with our selves in some spiritual or artistic pursuits, or feel inexplicably blocked at work or find ourselves in repetitive patterns that don't serve. These experiences often activate unhealed wounds—the fragments that have existed on the periphery of our hearts and minds. This activation is often painful and edgy, like the feeling of blood returning to a leg that has fallen asleep. Circulation of heart energy to our fragmented parts awakens our sleeping wounds and then the edgy pain becomes interesting.

Some of us have noticed a curious phenomenon in relationships: when we finally feel safe enough to be ourselves, we test the relationship. Although it's probably safe and okay, a fear of intimacy arises to meet the opportunity for intimacy. Our wounded identity, which has worked overtime to guarantee our security from any potential rejections, judgments or abandonments feels threatened. After all, our wounded identities have been our best friends ever since the "dark days" of childhood (or perhaps even other lives). Now, suddenly here's an opportunity for real bonding with another human being, and this opportunity activates everything—our yearning for union, our abandoned soul fragments, all our fear reactions, our saboteur that is ready to destroy any deep relationship, and lastly, our karmic itch that tells us we need this love no matter what.

By surrendering into this karmic knowing we grow beyond the co-dependent friendships we've had with our wounded identities and retrieve our lost parts. This journey of soul retrieval is the essence of depth healing and it can only happen when one is truly *ready* to make this journey back to the scene of the original fragmentation. Life itself makes us *ready* for this inner journey in ten thousand ways.

Fruit on the tree is ready to harvest because an organic process has brought it to a certain point. Over ripeness is a problem caused by missing the harvest and life is certainly filled with the grief and regret of missed opportunity. In healing, there is also a time for our wounds to mature into a fertile state. Where we used to feel sympathy for ourselves, we begin to feel empathy. A turning point happens; a realization dawns; something tells us that we *can* heal and that the time is *now*.

This is our time to heal; we're big enough to perceive our difficulty as a gift and we realize that going inside does not mean that we'll get stuck there, like in our youth. Perhaps the unhealed wound was catalyzed by a failed marriage or the death of a parent, by a spiritual opening or the crisis of a friend. Whatever the entry point, when we're ready to heal we seize the day; we give up our addiction to the false benefits of the wound because we're ripe.

And we've been here before.

We may be ripe but we're not ready yet to see the gift in the wound. The beauty of karmic law is that we will continue to receive painful opportunities to get the messages from our messes until we *are* ready. This is not punishment from a cruel world but is, in truth, the surest sign of a compassionate universe. We come to our edges over and over because we are still learning from our inability to really alter our perceptions. We are still using the persistence of our wounded state to erode us further. Besides, the saboteur has its own agenda.

Don't give me this "gift in the wound" talk.

We're talking resistance, avoidance and denial. In addition, there are some attractive false benefits inherent to the unhealed state. These false benefits occupy opposing walls between which an individual runs back and forth. On one wall is the adrenaline we get from our reactions to the wounds as we bang up against them. On the other wall is the relationship we get with our spiritual depths as we lean against the wall in spiritual exhaustion, feeling supported long enough to catch our breath. In a perverse way, a part of us gets energy and another part gets solace by reacting to our unhealed wounds. If we heal, these parts of us cannot exist any more. This threat of annihilation drives the desperate, wound-licking parts of us to sabotage our best intentions. My job is to help reveal the nature of these wounds to the person's consciousness and let the natural laws of karma work unimpeded by self-sabotage. I usually cannot do this until there is a degree of deep yearning or spiritual fatigue and dissatisfaction.

Feeling this dissatisfaction *is* necessary to the transformational process in healing. This dissatisfaction—*("I can't get no sat-is-faction")*—is accompanied by feelings of disillusionment. It is a sad time and a joyous time.

46

Illusions dissolve (disillusionment). Finally, we get to see things just "as they are." We simply witness our bodily felt experience of *the way it is*. We simply stop making effortful attempts to fix, improve or manipulate our reality anymore. We simply surrender to what is in front of us. Period. Simple.

Just because it is simple does not mean that it is easy.

Au contraire. This is the point where the plot thins. This is where we go to work at not working things anymore. Our illusions are burned and we are just here and it's okay. This disillusionment is good news from the soul's view point. The illusionary veil dissolves, like a cloud bank lifting. Suddenly, we see reality without the filtering of our conditioned minds. How exciting! How terrifying!

Bodywork can initiate a kind of altered state perception that can facilitate this unveiling. It is interesting that this shift in perception can be felt as an initiation. It can also feel like grief for some people, in that we say good-bye to a relatively naive view point, much like we felt when we grew beyond our childhood innocence.

Initiation always marks a turning point in which there is no going back to sleep. We realize that tight muscles, security gates, or black leather jackets may temporarily assuage our symptoms of anxiety, but eventually, we will meet the root causes of our insecurities and recognize them as our addictive states of woundedness. In this expanded awareness we can truly see that real healing for this wounded state of affairs lies only in our capacity to go inside ourselves, like the silkworm within its cocoon, and find there a mystery beyond the rational mind's ability to conceive.

Within this womb, duality ceases as we see the wound and its very healing as two halves of a whole. *The wholeness of consciousness is recognized within the core of our suffering.* From a fourth dimensional view point, this three dimensional world appears as a karmic staging ground for spiritual lessons to be learned. Just as we see, on a Hollywood film lot, two dimensional painted facades held up with two-by-fours, so do our bodies and relationships act as constructs for our spiritual home movies. *Shifting awareness and then accepting that awareness into our bodies is precisely the goal and challenge in depth healing and spiritual evolution.* The power of unveiled awareness to heal our wounds and grow our souls is immense; it is illustrated by the diagram that follows (see next page).

Awareness leverages the unhealed wound from the "underground" to the surface of consciousness—where its power to sabotage is neutralized by awareness itself. The fulcrum that leverages awareness is our pain and suffering. We need our pain for leverage. The fruit of our harvest is our soulful spirit.

Figure A.
Leveraging
The Fertile Wound

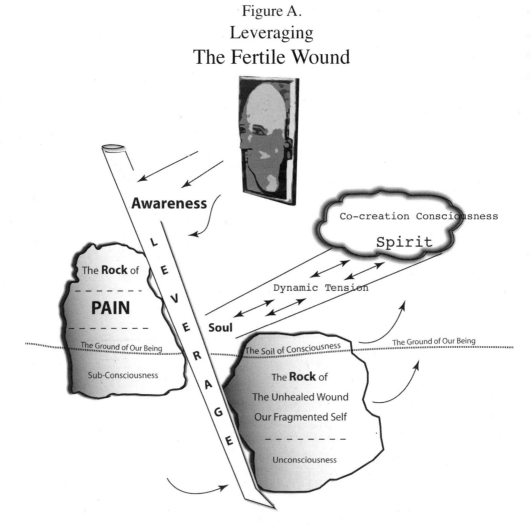

Each of us has what it takes to leverage our parts into a whole and to wake up to life. It's really very simple. The journey of awakening is about making friends with ourselves, completely. It is about full self-acceptance, not just acceptance of the parts we like. We must make it safe and loving in our own hearts for the parts we don't like too—to come out, to come up, and to come home; and no one can make this happen for us. Perhaps this is the real journey of self-realization: *we must singularly circle around our own being in ever increasing inclusion of all that we*

are, until there are no parts, only a whole. When all the parts of self are realized, an alchemy occurs in which selflessness results.

The word "whole" comes from the Greek word *helios*; it is the root for "healing." It is healing work that brings about wholeness. So when we speak of healing and self-realization, we are speaking of the same thing. In this light, ironically, the wound becomes a sacrament.

So our journey of self-realization is a circle and all of us are somewhere on the circle of life, cycling through our experiences and learning our lessons. Some of us cycle continuously over the same terrain visiting familiar psychic landmarks over and over until we find that our "selves" have become synthetic "self-images" with redundant story lines that reduce perceptions and experiences into tired cliches. But for those of us who choose to heal and explore the mystery, the journey cycles with increasing refinement as we learn our lessons. The radius of our circle decreases as we climb higher in spiritual understanding or sink deeper into our soul's calling. Through all this travelling, we come to a still point where we realize that we are "nobody going nowhere" and that we are co-creative with the divine. To quote the Indian mystic Ramana Maharshi's paraphrase of the Greek philosopher Empedocles view of God, and the circle of life: "the true self, [God], is a circle whose center is everywhere and whose circumference is nowhere."

Most people's stories are really variations of a few basic plots; it's just that some character development is a little more extreme and some settings are more harsh. But just because most of us are learning similar lessons does not mean that our souls' curriculum is a casual matter, that we ought to just jump to the chase and transcend our "story."

My bias in healing work is that the body holds the story and that before the story can be transcended, it must first be known, felt, accepted, owned and then transformed, otherwise it will surface in another form until we *get it down and get it right.* All people bring their unique twists to the universal story plots of *"Who am I?" and "Where am I going?"* It is our unique privilege to *live* the answers to these questions. If we prematurely disidentify with our story, we miss the opportunity to create a *self* as a gift to God in our surrender. And it is within the containment of this crucible of self that we are able to transform our wounds into blessings.

****

My Story

Do not imagine that he who seeks to comfort you now lives untroubled among the simple and quiet words that sometimes do you good. His life has much more difficulties and sadness and remains far behind yours. Were it otherwise, he would never have been able to find these words.

— Rainer Maria Rilke

The life I had before moving to the Mendocino coast was filled with two careers and one major personal issue. The first career was the life of a public school teacher in Mill Valley, California—a trendy and progressive town, where my interest in massage therapy flourished into a practice just shy of a day job. Teaching and healing work made for interesting and exciting times but the real powder keg of experience came in the form of my relationship to my wife, Cheryl, and her powerful need to have a baby.

One unseasonably hot and still summer night in 1975, Cheryl awoke at three a.m. insisting that we take a walk and talk about having a baby. She was inspired and totally convincing, perhaps knowing that I could wait on this kind of commitment. Nevertheless we made sincere attempts and after each monthly period, a little disappointment grew into a growing concern. We went to an endocrinologist after nine months of trying to get pregnant and, after examining my semen under a microscope, he told us that I had NO sperm.

I went home feeling hollow throughout the core of my body, wondering about the deeper implications of this reality while staying practical enough to make an appointment with a "holistic nutritional doctor" who could assist me in creating sperm. If I had a low sperm count I think I would have felt quite different, but the "no sperm" report threw me into deep anguish. As a result of this news, Cheryl and I spent the next two years getting our bodies squeaky clean with herbal regimens, enemas, special hormone and vitamin shots and psychic readings, just to top the list. We got to know each other very intimately through this ordeal. Surviving this episode in our relationship was due, I know, to divine intervention.

In our early years, Cheryl would frequently get exasperated trying to get me to show up and argue with her. As a child I had built strong walls around my feelings of vulnerability; I would transcend my emotions and act aloof while discussing the subject at hand with an intellectual tone of superiority. This infuriated her to no end; and then the infertility issue came into our lives landing our relationship dynamics into very present and honest terms. Subsequently, the quality of my teaching and the depth of the healing work I was doing changed dramatically.

It was a painful journey; it lasted seven years and it brought me to my knees many times. I am grateful for the suffering I went through because it cracked me open. I can still get arrogant when I'm insecure but the humility I've learned has helped me to stay focused in my heart.

After exhausting all the biological avenues to bring a child into our lives, Cheryl and I opened ourselves to artificial insemination. This saga was loaded with new and surprising emotional twists which could easily be Cheryl's best seller. For me, it was just the next step for us to take in fulfilling the "movie" of having the ideal natural child birth Cheryl hungered for and was rightfully entitled to pursue. My pursuits were aimed at getting us into a rural life style away from the wonderful distractions of the San Francisco Bay Area.

Cheryl finally got pregnant from artificial insemination. We left the Bay Area in a state of joy, so excited to at last get on with the family life of raising children in the country. We moved into a small house on the bluffs overlooking the ocean; we unpacked, set-up our home, and breathed deeply for the first time in years. The respite was short-lived. After four days,

Cheryl began to bleed. We went to the local medical center. A miscarriage was possible. We needed to lay low and just relax. We had no phone. We knew no one except Cheryl's brother, sister-in-law and niece. The days which followed the visit to the doctor were spent meditating and talking about what we would do with our lives. I played house maid and walked by myself on the cliffs studying the waves for any sign that would give me back my fragile faith.

On the fifth morning Cheryl awoke with very painful cramps which culminated in a miscarriage. The aborted fetus symbolized all the relationship work, the dreams we shared and mostly the exhaustion of persevering for so long in our attempts to create a new human being. Suddenly the balloon had popped and for many days the sound of the ocean was deafening. Then after about a week everything suddenly became very quiet, as if a bell had sounded to silence all of my chattering.

And then the dreams and memories began.

I awoke about four a.m. unsure whether or not I was dreaming:

I am standing at the edge of this plane of experience, not yet born into it; in back of me are seven elders who are responsible for facilitating my impending incarnation. They are very wise and caring and they are concerned that I may have invoked too much sensitivity into my new life for the worldliness I wished to address. Their conversations created background noise for me as I scanned this experiential panorama of my life (this life) to be. One of the elders came to my side and touched me. We both were shimmering. His deep blue eyes kindly penetrated mine telepathically asking if I had any questions. I looked back at him and said,"Will I be loved?"

There was a pause in which I sensed all the other elders in the room telepathically joining; then the one elder smiled at me with moist eyes and said,"Yes, you will be loved."

It would take me another fifteen years or more to realize that the real challenge was to disarm myself enough so that I could open up enough to let the love in.

That morning after the dream, as I walked along the beach, I felt very calm. All the private pain of being infertile as a man suddenly softened. Cheryl's incredible need to be a mother had tweaked my father issue with all the dormant pain of being my father's son. But in the calmness of that morning walk, with such beauty and freshness coming from the ocean, everything seemed manageable, maybe even easy.

My emotional sensitivity had threatened my father's buried emotions. *So what!* He shamed me for my tears and derived an eerie satisfaction out of toying with my vulnerability. *He couldn't help himself.* The salt air must have expanded my heart and mind because I was so full of forgiveness. I could see my precious wounds as just a small price to pay for a box seat to my wonderful home movie now playing on this glorious beach.

The euphoria was short lived and I went back to hating him and feeling sorry for myself again. I needed my anger and anguish as fuel in my life a little longer. A few years before his death from a stroke I had forgiven him completely. It would take me a lot longer, as it turned out, to forgive myself for all the reactive behaviors that emanated out of that father-son wound.

The lack of male bonding and the female world of self-absorption that existed between my mother and sisters left me lonely and isolated, yearning for belonging. I desperately wanted to love and to be loved as I unconsciously remembered being promised. The depth of my need felt unfathomable. I remember seeing the world around me two-dimensionally, like those Hollywood set props, while I walked through the scene in multidimensional loneliness.

Loneliness became my best friend. I found solace in it. It was masked on the outside by a strong personality as a pleaser as I attempted to serve others and thereby cultivate interest from them in return. When closeness occurred I became both excited and cautious, for I didn't want to scare anyone away with my neediness. My personality developed manipulative tendencies as it grew more sophisticated, and I found that I could satisfy a whole range of secondary needs, often forgetting the loneliness I felt at the core.

In my childhood, during the first rains of late autumn, I would lay by the fire, sometimes poking the embers, inviting the loneliness to arise. I would take out my loneliness and hold it close, always ready to hide it in an instant if someone were to disturb me. It would come to me in the form of melancholy at first, its sweetness the most intoxicating experience I knew. I fondled it. It nurtured me back. My loneliness gave me my self. It connected me to my depths. I felt intimate and integrated within the bubble of my solitude, so much so that intimacy with another person was seen as a threat by my cocooned, solitudinous self.

My relationship with my loneliness was pervasive, fragile and subterranean. I could not be the real me because it was not safe. In my teenage years, I started meditating. Often, during these times, my father would interrupt and yell at me—coarse sandpaper on a delicate nervous system. Once, while I was meditating in my room, he barged in and yelled at me. Incredible rage surfaced. I exploded in a loud, quavering voice all the feelings I had harbored behind my veil of pleasing. My mother attempted to quell the confrontation and I turned on her, ridiculing her wimpiness. I stormed out. I had spoken the truth. No apologies were expected and none would have been forthcoming. I found a self-respect through that unexpected confrontation. On the surface, my life at home was easier, yet underneath I had unleashed a killer. So much for meditation.

My meditations were unsettling after that, but I sat regularly nonetheless. I did not know what to do with these angry forces I felt inside. I realized that inherently I was always angry yet too afraid to express it. When I softened into my loneliness after this episode, I felt the depth of my self-bonding tainted by anger and betrayal—betrayal toward a universe that doesn't keep its promise of providing the love I needed in which to play? I didn't know then that I was supposed to create it. I was sixteen years old.

At sixteen I am making my way by car, driving eastward from Venice Beach across a maze of freeways toward downtown, to the Los Angeles Zen Center. Burt is driving; Joey is in the back seat. I'm sitting in the front passenger seat, window open to the warm evening breeze as I watch the wild and familiar scenery of Venice, my high school community, change into L.A.'s more established neighborhoods.

We've all read some of the writings of Alan Watts and Aldous Huxley. We're cool. We know about altered states of consciousness and Buddhist meditation practice. We have our driver's licenses and a car. We're almost out of high school and we're musicians; after graduation we'll drive up Coast Highway One to the Monterey Jazz Festival. We're off to U.C.L.A. in the Fall, we're ahead of the curve.

The beach front community of Venice during the 1950's and 1960's has been my home since birth. It hasn't yet become gentrified; in fact, it's still a kind of multicultural ghetto filled with ancient—to my eyes—Eastern European Jews, my father sometimes among them, who sit around the Venice boardwalk speaking Yiddish, playing checkers or chess with each other and always eating some borscht or piroshki while arguing passionately with their hands.

When I was eleven years old I'd take the Number 8 Ocean Park bus, transfer to the Number 1, and walk through colorful ethnic pockets of Black, Mexican, and Filipino mini communities on my way to the synagogue for Hebrew lessons. I'd always stop and eat at one of the crowded taco stands and listen to the jazz musicians who congregated around these various debris littered sections of my walk. They were playing long saxophone riffs while smoking marijuana and collecting spare change. Each week I'd pass the same winos in their usual borrowed doorways, go past the Catholic school, with all the kids in uniform, and then descend the staircase into the dark and pungent bowels of the synagogue, entering another world.

The cantor's gnarly hand, knobby with arthritis, would move the "pointer" over the Hebrew characters of my bar mitzvah torah reading. I would feel and smell his warm garlic breath next to my ear uttering the sounds I repeated with my cracking voice. I would notice the numbers tattooed on his wrist, numbers which were not new to me because some of my relatives also had them—concentration camp identification tattoos from the Nazis.

Driving East with Burt and Joey, away from all these colors and smells including those coming from the polluted Venice canals, I feel myself leaving my world behind. I'm venturing forth from it, but not to seek out the lights of Hollywood or the glittering fast life L.A. has to offer. I'm heading East to a monastic dwelling where people come to do nothing but sit—not sit and think, even...but rather to just SIT and not think. They meditate, in the company of other sitters, all under the watchful eye of the great sitter himself, Zen master Roshi.

If this adventure does not neatly fit in with every adolescent boy's idea of a good time away from home, it's hardly surprising. At sixteen I'm about as atypical of the breed as a spotted zebra. For the past six years, since age ten, I've begun to notice that I'm different—not different simply in the way all adolescents feel themselves to be—"My God, is there anyone anywhere who could possibly ever *understand* me!" I am truly weird, at least by my parent's definition of how to live a normal life, or gauged by the things I see and hear my high school locker mates saying and doing. I'm nothing like a James Dean outsider, hunched and defiant and yearning to be envied and misunderstood. Actually I can enter almost any social group for a brief time without ever belonging to any of them. I play trombone in the school jazz band without being in the musician's clique; I'm not studious enough to be part of the intellectual crowd but am friendly with some of the top nerds. I'm on the gymnastics team but, at five feet six inches, I'm hardly jock material, especially at L.A.'s most integrated Venice High School—which has as tough a locker room as any nice Jewish boy would wish to hang out in. And then there's the social crowd of cheerleaders and club members with their color coordinated presentations. Palleeeze....

I am simply Fred, fascinated by something called spirit that I know more about than I can explain. At most high school gatherings, conversations about spiritual quests are like outbreaks of acne; everyone pretends not to notice them and silently prays they'll simply vanish. Mostly I keep my spiritual interests to myself; they're jumbled with feelings of confusion and anguish about the Holocaust, inherited from my father, and include a strong dose of rampant heterosexual unfulfilled horniness. At times I reach for divine inspiration and grasp, instead, an imagined pair of firm, heaving breasts. I'm a mess, but a reasonably earnest one—gifted, or cursed, with an inquiring mind and a restless need to explore the unknown dimensions of enlightenment.

It's that quest that propels me, in my senior year of high school, across Greater Los Angeles to the fabled Zen Center, accompanied by Joey and Burt, my nerdy musician friends, who are even more odd than I by Venice "Gondolier" High's home room standards. We bonded over the trivia of the jazz world, quoting obscure reviews in *Downbeat* magazine like other kids would memorize baseball statistics. Zen Buddhism was the logical extension of our interests in jazz and poetry of the "beat" generation that had filtered down to our high school minds because we were all so.... weird.

Now as we're entering a courtyard surrounded by well manicured trees and a Japanese style fence, we're cordially met by a soft spoken man with dark brown eyes. He hands to each of us an orientation letter which we read immediately, and then we're ushered into a hall, where we are told to sit on a bench in a kneeling posture. That's it. Sit.

I could be sitting in my room back in Venice, but that would be simply sitting. This is *sitting*. This sitting comes with basic instructions: notice the breath; when your mind wanders come back to noticing the breath. That's it. After fifteen minutes the silence and the pain in my legs have become quite intense. I'm beginning to wonder if coming here was such a smart idea after all. I have no idea how long this will go on. Maybe I didn't read that orientation letter carefully enough. I've read stories of Buddhists sitting for *months* (surely not with *this* pain)...HELP!! But what else can I do? I'm here. So I sit.

About half an hour into it, I start planning my departure and fantasizing about food and girls. Sometime later a bell is rung. Everyone gets up and silently walks around the courtyard slowly—either looking at the ground or straight ahead. To me they look like zombies. I try to get Burt's attention but he's already looking at the ground. I catch Joey's eyes with a *what's up?* look but he looks down at the ground. I want to bolt for the big gate we came in through before any more strange events happen.

Instead, the bell rings and we follow the group into the hall and, again, we sit. I'm agitated by now, sure that I'm trapped and powerless to rebel. I start counting my breaths as a way of settling down. I came here for love—boundless love, Buddhist style, a longing instilled in me by favorite writers like Alan Watts and I wanted it now! Not *this* --sit 'til your knees fall off. Hello?..........*excuse me*. But as I sit, waiting for my brief audience with the Roshi—as a brochure for this public event promised, I stop judging myself and everyone around me and begin to notice how quiet the room is.

I have an odd thought. This *is* the atmosphere I've always craved within my own home, a feeling of safety from interference. I notice my breath has become even and that I'm feeling lonely again—that constant, lifelong gnawing feeling—only now my loneliness has company. All these other people are also sitting in their own experience of loneliness, or solitude. I'm lonely, but no longer alone. Something about this realization produces a comforting, engulfing sensation in the base of my spine, as if I'm sinking down into a tub of warm, soapy water...and I stop resisting.

After another hour, including a courtyard meditation walk and another quiet sitting of breath watching, an attendant, dressed in a dark robe with brocaded orange trim, taps me alert and escorts me into a waiting room where he instructs me on how to bow. He tells me that the Roshi will interview me shortly. I sit there, now very much in awe of this silent community, sinking deeper into my breath and becoming gradually aware that I have to piss badly. I attempt, with little success, to focus my mind on my breath; my mind only wants to calibrate just how full my bladder *really* is.

"The Roshi will see you now," the attendant announces. As my mind screams, ("How 'bout peeing?"), I walk in and bow as instructed. Roshi Joshu Sasaki, the venerable Zen teacher of the Los Angeles Zen Center, orders me, with a thick Japanese accent, to "Sit up, please!" Posture lesson number one. I look up to find a bulky Japanese man, bald and smiling broadly. He is sitting on a large cushion with a bell in front of him. The room is adorned with elegant reddish tapestries on the walls and is dimly lit from above. A blaze of candles illuminates Roshi's face; the room can barely contain his presence.

"What is your name?"

When I tell him in a nervous cough-cleared voice, he looks at me and smiles again, but with an edge. He then asks in a thin, high pitched, inquisitive voice: *"Who are you?"*

A puff ball celebrity quiz show question! Easy!

With a winning grin I answer that I am a human being named Fred, that I go to Venice High School and like jazz. But the Roshi stopped smiling.

"No, No, No! Who are you?"

Now his chin has jutted out, his eyes burrow a hole directly through mine, and his eyebrows rise in consternation as if I've suddenly vanished.

"Who are you?" he demands again.

I plunge headlong into a scrambled history of my unexceptional life up to my early days of high school. My voice sounds as weak and hollow as a little boy caught in a lie. The Roshi listens silently, while casting a withering look my way. I'm clearly not telling him what he wants to hear. What's he got in mind? He keeps interrupting me with that "No, No, No" eye response. I end out of breath, more agitated than at any time since I've arrived.

There is silence in the room and not a comforting kind.

Finally the Roshi speaks: "Fred? That's it, just "Fred." He then stares at me for a long time and says, now almost in a kindly way, "Who *are* you, Fred?"

Not that again!

I take a deep breath, stalling, grasping for mental footing. *"What can I say? What does he really want to know?"* Being ever persistent, I try once more and give him what, to me, is a self-portrait that emphasizes my most heartfelt, idealized image of myself complete with numerous acts of generosity and kindness that any saint would die again just to be remembered for them. When I finish, the Roshi just sighs and looks me up and down like Sandy Koufax wondering why he should waste his fastball on a no-name rookie. I want to speak clearly and long enough to tell him I'm sorry for taking up his valuable time. But I don't. I discover I have enough chutzpah to just sit there across from this powerful, deeply intimidating teacher, and look back at him in silence. Then I lose it.

I suddenly find myself unable to focus on anything or anybody, as if in a swoon, and at that moment the Roshi shouts at me, thunderously: "WHO

ARE YOU!?"

I'm so unnerved now, so drained and harried that I rise on my wobbly legs and shout right back in his face, "I DON'T KNOW!"

Shaking with fear and confusion, I am ashamed of myself. The Roshi gestures calmly for me to sit down again on the pillow as if I've just entered. As I do he breaks out into a wide, expansive grin. His eyes light up and he says with genuine and penetrating warmth: "Good, Fred. Now we can begin."

I drove West back to my childhood home, very relaxed but unsure about what I had begun. That night I slept more soundly than I ever remembered and awoke the next morning very calm, as if an angel had whispered into my ear: "Don't worry, it's all going to be alright."

****

So there I was, after the miscarriage, walking the beaches in the mornings while having rich flashbacks—one of which was the sensation of deep, viseral calm after my initiation with the Roshi. The waves echoed in my brain a whispering mantra, "Don't worry, it's all going to be alright." In the afternoons Cheryl and I had long heart to heart talks about our marriage. Though I loved her with everything in my heart, I had no energy left to pursue adoption or to continue with artificial insemination. I had quit teaching, withdrawn my retirement fund and, for the first time, faced an array of new choices. Perhaps, I thought, Cheryl would be happier with another man, someone with a greater affinity for home, hearth, and children—someone who could provide her with a child. I felt a tremendous urge to put everything in storage and hop the next plane to Tahiti, where I would lie on the beaches and shake for about a year. Then, and only then, would I be able to discuss what to do with my life. As things turned out, Cheryl agreed to put the child issue on the shelf for at least a year while we looked anew at a life together unencumbered by the sticky, neurotic and painful scenario of trying to have children when you can't do it naturally.

We could not imagine going back to Mill Valley. We had started teaching massage and had just a little money to live on before we would need to find work. Cheryl did not want to sail off to Tahiti without some home to come back to; she suggested that we sell our Marin house and buy one on the Mendocino Coast. I was ready to burst into the unknown. The thought of setting up a new domestic scene was repulsive.

"Look," I said, "it's either Tahiti this afternoon or we agree to find a piece of mountaintop and start over together." We both cried for a long time and then began devouring the Real Estate section of the local paper. One month later we found an incredible piece of land—nine acres of ridge top with great weather, an ocean view and a well. We daringly bought it with lots of borrowed money and a ridiculous notion that we could make a living teaching massage. We now recall this period with amazement, humor and affection. Both Cheryl and I took jobs teaching challenging classes in the public schools. I worked half-time there and half-time developing our land for construction. As we had only one car, I hitchhiked back and forth. People were very helpful to us—trading design consulting and blue-prints for massages. We lived in an 8' by 24' trailer on our raw land with our dog, Sunshine.

House-building in the country brought us right into the community. My first day of construction was very manly—a right of passage. I was nervous about going to work with the guys who did this for a living. I would pose in front of the mirror in our trailer with my leather tool bag strapped just so. Cheryl laughed at me on her way out to teach, but for me it was not a laughing matter. I really needed to be accepted by the construction guys. I was tired of the heady world I had been in but I was even more tired of the vulnerability that had permeated my life for so long.

I walked up to the construction site, excited and anxious. One of the guys came right up to me and shook my hand, saying, "Good morning, Boss!" In a low, contained voice I said, "Good morning," back, and in the next couple of hours I settled into a warm, masculine camaraderie.

The house-building project became for me a secular Bar Mitzvah, only I was now thirty years old. In my childhood home few tools existed and basic home maintenance was left undone. I craved interaction with my father in sports or making things, but he was unavailable. There was no positive side of doing to compensate for the negative aspects of being. Here I was, now doing and being in my masculinity and thereby healing a huge wound of inadequacy that went much further back than my inability to produce sperm.

The memory of my interview with the Roshi was a great liberation when I was walking those beaches, confused. As freeing as it was to *not* know who I was then, it was just as liberating to become someone who was empowered and respected by other men. The ancient loneliness receded into the background during the house construction.

The house was beautiful. We decorated it sparsely. After Cheryl left for work in the mornings I would read a novel on the back porch, in the sun. There was no more construction happening; my school teaching days were over. My second cup of coffee became a ritual time of reflection. One day I unpacked a box of old photographs and found three of them in classic oval frames; one was of my grandmother as a child and two were of my great grandfathers, as old wise men. I hung the pictures on the wall above the fireplace. My maternal grandmother was a loving matriarch who commanded respect from everyone and had a home full of large, happy gatherings with delicious aromas from exotic foods. Both great-grandfathers had been rabbis, one in Hungary and one in Latvia. I derived great strength from looking at these photographs.

I remember the large family gatherings when I was growing up in the fifties in Los Angeles—often at my grandmother's but also at our home and at the homes of cousins, aunts and uncles. Some of those relatives had numbers tattooed on their wrists. As a young child I innocently asked one how he or she got that tattoo. The room suddenly became hushed and my mom said, "I'll tell you later, Freddy."

Six million Jews were exterminated in Nazi Germany during World War II. To grow up Jewish after the war was to know an existential shadow whose effects were felt in the relatives one spent time with. I asked frequent questions about the Holocaust, to the point of exhausting other people's interest. I don't know why I was so obsessed with the Holocaust; perhaps it was that I wanted to know what human beings were capable of. At one point I remember crying about it. My father said I was too sensitive. I suspect he was quite sensitive about the subject too, but a man of his generation often had to suffocate strong feelings. My father's role, he thought, was to toughen me up for the world and he did it well with name calling and shaming. How sad, the idea of toughening someone up for the "real world". No wonder the "real world" is so tough?

I would look at those photos of my ancestors and gaze out the window over miles of virgin redwood forest to the blue blue ocean and I would feel them wanting to be free in this world. And they came, or their children came, to America, like so many persecuted people had, looking for a life of dignity and opportunity. For them, if for no other reason, I thought, I would be happy. I felt connected to my roots in this desire to open my heart to a free and happy life. And I sat there in my new living room, feeling my ancestral gene pool and accepted the fact that the genetic heritage in my body stopped with me. I was the end of this genetic line. And I stopped feeling sorry for myself and found I could be happy because it would make my ancestors happy.

In present time, I touch into painful memories of my clients and though I am affected deeply, I have found a strange tolerance for hearing their stories of personal tragedy, and an even stranger capacity to help these people re-write and transcend their stories. In this vein, I like Bennett W. Goodspeed's reflection: "The difference between a comedy and a tragedy is that in comedy the characters figure out reality in time to do something about it."

For me, any rendition of my inner journey as a healer starts with that lesson learned at the Roshi's knee. In that moment I discovered the terror of not knowing who I was, and the paradoxical freedom of not having to know. In fact, after that incident it seemed to me that I finally had been given permission to just be who I was, and not someone struggling to fit a mode or find a group, or conversely, cultivate my strangeness as a perverse lifestyle.

Looking back, after working with thousands of people, I understand even more profoundly what a gift I was given by the Roshi: wounds—the kind this book addresses—are often created by the lack of permission we get to be ourselves. Those wounds I developed close to home as a child—from the persistent experiences of shaming and ridicule from my father—were in actuality the motivating forces that unconsciously propelled me to seek out the Roshi. In a real sense, my wound brought me to a healing that I was ready for even if I realized this only later in life.

My earliest memories are of my father sticking out his lower lip in a pouting mimic of how I appeared to him when I cried. I would break into tears, which was what he wanted; and he would break into a giddy laughter at the whole scene. This set-up and ridicule was tolerated by others. My tears were not Pavlovian as I suspect he believed but rather an expression of my yearning to be met through my emotions rather than have them be toyed with or used as evidence for my being "too sensitive."

Most children are born with exquisite sensitivity. My karma was to have this sensitivity adjacent to a human assault force designed to test my limits. My father, Ralph, derived great pleasure from eating and defecating. After I passed through early childhood stages of fascination with feces, I was amazed that he was still hooked on the eliminative process and bathroom humor in general. My father was a playground bully in our house that no one could stand up to. One day, when I was about four years of age, he put our little dog Friskie in a burlap bag and violently shook it and swung it around, freaking Friskie out so much that he growled when approached. After that, for a good week, I did not feel safe to be physically close to my puppy for fear that he'd bite me. One evening, shortly after this incident, I went out to the back yard, unhooked Friskie from his chain and threw tennis balls at the brick wall until Friskie was so exhausted from chasing them, and I couldn't see in the dark anymore, that we both collapsed on a chaise lounge in the garage. Friskie was panting with exhaustion and I had tears rolling down my face. I was so sad for him and angry at my father for the way he treated my dog that I told Friskie that I had the "father from hell." Friskie licked me. I felt safe. He felt playful. We both spent endless hours, after that evening, developing our throwing and catching skills together. As a little boy, I bonded with "life" in a way that allowed me to see that fear can be assuaged by loving attention. Something else happened that night. I put my tears away.

I felt guilty that I had such rage toward my father who I was supposed to love. There must be something basically wrong with me, otherwise he'd treat me with kindness. Little kids want to be cuddled and feel safe. My little boy body was confused by the impulse to run away or numb out further and by this deep inexplicable yearning to be held by my father and feel loved. I hated myself for having this yearning, for being needy, for sitting on his lap and having him pat me like a dog.

All these childhood memories and wounded feelings came up as I dug into the earth of our new mountain top home and planted my garden. I placed my spear into the earth, I watered the tomatoes, I weeded my mind. As fate would have it, a phone call announcing the possibility for adoption came just as our house had truly become a home.

On July 6, 1981, our son, Seth, was born. We held him in the hospital room when he was eleven hours old. I did Jin Shin Jyutsu, a form of acupressure, on his little body to assist him in letting go of his rejection from his birth mother while Cheryl held him. It was a joyous and blessed time. We all went home to a wonderful and amazing time of gardening, "chopping wood and carrying water" on all levels. *Chop Wood/Carry Water* is a classic Zen Buddhist reminder that before enlightenment you chop wood and carry water; and after enlightenment you chop wood and carry water. Very very simple.

Three years later my father passed on from this world and I delivered the eulogy. It was one of my finest moments. Without my exposure to Buddhist thought, I am sure I'd have gotten lost in my self-absorbed confusion. Immediately after the funeral I felt enlivened, ventillated and grateful. Cheryl and Seth and I returned home to the coast. I lit a memorial candle and said kadish for my father and performed my sitting meditation more consistently. Kadish is a beautiful Hebrew prayer for mourning that sanctifies God without mentioning death at all. I would sit with a candle into the wee hours of the night, softly chanting the prayer, rocking and grieving, and being the grace of new beginnings.

Life deepened; more memories surfaced and always there were physical opportunities to express myself. Afterall, it is not everyone who has the good fortune to homestead a moutain top. Appreciating this, I cleared land, developed irrigation systems and immersed myself into the reality of making organic compost from the waste products of our kitchen, and metaphorically from my heart.

The high road I took to the grave site was appropriate but my body still hungered for a fight it could never have. Though my father was a bully, he was an *enfant terrible* we all had to tolerate. In my youth, I continuously wanted to lead a revolt, scream at the top of my lungs and set things right once and for all. But I could see that no one believed the effort would be productive. My sister Debbie said it best in describing my father as a person "one enchilada shy of a combination plate".

She was correct.

My father was mentally and emotionally compromised by what years later would be called "Fragile X" syndrome—a genetic abnormality that later surfaced through others in my family. As an adult looking back at my childhood it all makes sense because my father was, in truth, not playing with a full deck. If he were a sweet passive type, life would have been quite different, but my father was an "in your face" extrovert who delighted in being the center of attention regardless of the circumstances. But understanding this mentally never quite assuaged my visceral issues of anger about the unfairness of it all.

In my growing up years I had no idea my father suffered from anything; nor did anyone. Intuitively we all just tolerated his excesses because we felt futile in any attempt to reach him. And also, I wanted a father I could love and respect. So I tempered my angst and maintained my illusions of normalcy about my father and our family throughout my childhood. My tolerance allowed me to function adequately enough but I consistently had sore throats and a congested chest from all the repressed screams and tears I held back. I finally cleared this condition by manually opening up my own throat and screaming at my father.

It wasn't until the mid-morning of my mid-life, that my muscles quite un-expectedly released the unexpressed rage they had been holding back for decades. I was assembling a jungle gym and hit a stubborn underground root, for the umpteenth time. Every tool was a drama and on one attempt, a slow motion vibration arose out of the impact of metal against root. When the energtic wave travelled up the post hole digger into my mid back, a volcanic rage exploded out of my body and for twenty minutes I threw every tool in the meadow, and I swore at the top of my lungs, "my father never did anything for me". Shocked and relieved by my outburst, I realized that my body was full of my incomplete story and that pretty soon Seth would outgrow the wounded child in me if I didn't get current and let go of my painful cellular memories.

I enrolled in a meditation course, found a new therapist and bought a new car, determined to be happy but not pretend. My journey in coming through painful places has given me strength, perspective, humor and an ability to help others get through many themes, including father-hunger and some of the related father-issues like authority, success and power. I have my scars from the journey and there are times when I feel I am still on this healing adventure with no arrival guaranteed. Gaining comfort from the discomforting thought of there being "no guarantee" has, itself, been a great teacher.

Battle's Over

Pictured here is a metal sculpture entitled Battle's Over. It portrays a knight, during the Crusades, dressed in full battle regalia, with open arms—having dropped his shield, his spear, and his sword. He is the warrior who has chosen to disarm. His open arms are capable of giving and receiving love; and he represents all of us who hunger for love and are ready to make peace.

Beneath and within the skin, written within the *cellular memory* of each person, is a story. As rich and complex as a human life can be, each story is really quite simple; each of us will always be vulnerable as long as we live in a body. Each person's story, therefore, revolves around relationship to vulnerability and the means of creating security in a world of uncertainty.

Brenda came to study with me in 1987. She had short hair, muscular arms and walked with a strut. She worked in a lumber mill in Northern California and she knew how to take care of herself physically. She carried herself with strength and dignity, and with considerable attitude. Brenda's eyes had a hard and tight presentation, cautioning anyone looking at her to be careful. While Brenda was on the massage table, during the class, I looked into her eyes and sustained soft eye contact; eventually she looked away.

Later that week, I noticed Brenda's eyes soften as she listened to another woman's story of sexual repression and a version of "The Transformational Journey." Her eyes relaxed and they revealed a sad and vulnerable child. She spoke to the class, one evening toward the end of the week, of her lesbian life style and how she had been estranged from her father for the past twelve years because of his inability to accept her sexual orientation.

All of these years she had felt wounded by his rejection, and so prideful in reaction to it, that she had built a tight wall between her vulnerability and the world. As a child she had felt close to her father. He was a sensitive and artistic man and, perhaps, had scripted himself to be the loving grandfather of Brenda's children. Whatever his pain was in relation to Brenda's sexual orientation, his behavior was to turn away from his daughter and, coincidentally, his art.

During the practice month Brenda drove to see her father. A desire to attempt a reconciliation had developed within her new softness. She gave him a massage and, afterward, they talked about it. She asked him to make something for her; she left and did not hear from him until just a few days before the second part of her massage training. Brenda received a phone call from her father asking her to stop by and pick up a box. In that box she found the metal sculpture: *Battle's Over*.

Brenda arrived with this statue and presented it to Cheryl and me with a story of the healing between her and her father. It was the loving touch Brenda brought to her father that allowed him to reconcile his feelings, make his peace and unconditionally love his daughter again. And, in opening his heart, he once again embraced his art. This is a simple but profound story; but we find, in healing, that simplicity is the most powerful force in the universe.

****

The hypothalamus is situated at the center of the underside of the brain, below the thalamus and above the pituitary. It is connected, by many nerve tracts, to the brain and spinal cord and acts as a translator between the endocrine system and the brain. It functions automatically, monitoring and regulating the autonomic nervous system, and the state of the body's metabolism, thirst, and temperature controls. In addition to sex-drive, the controlling of the female menstrual cycle and fight-flight reactions, the hypothalamus has two sections adjacent to one another that are relevant to our investigation. The dorsomedial nucleus controls aggressive behavior and the dorsal area is thought to be the human "pleasure center."

Sexual expression is influenced by cultural and psychological factors just as much as by instinctual drives. Today research demonstrates that, "Body pleasure and violent behavior have a mutually inhibiting relationship. The presence of one inhibits the other. When the brain's pleasure circuits are on, the violence circuits are off, and vice versa."[1]

Anthropological studies clearly indicate that physically affectionate and nurturing human societies are also unlikely to be physically violent. An American study of child abusers found that "Parents who abused their children were invariably deprived of physical affection themselves during childhood and their adult sex life was extremely poor."[2] My own research on this subject came in the form of incest survivors being referred to me for healing bodywork. The individual cases pieced together became, in my mind, a profound indictment of our culture's moralistic denial of the body's natural pleasures. The depressing upshot of this denial can be seen in our culture's general tolerance for films exhibiting sexual violence while, in contrast, exhibitions of human Eros where lovers truly meet in delicious and respectful ways is hardly ever given much play.

There is something very real and very important for us to understand about this realm of sensual pleasure and pain. If we don't find a way to "return to the garden" of our true sensuality and discover what respectful and loving touch is about, we will continue to repress our life force (freeze), transcend it by running away from intimacy and relationship (flight), or worse, act-out on others in destructive ways (fight). To flow lovingly within our bodies is noble; it makes love possible in a world tired of violence in its many forms.

Learning a reverential way of being embodied is our challenge. The present shame based paradigm of craving and aversion has stripped us from our bodys' desire to dance and play. Truly, the erotic and creative force is a sacred journey into the heart of our deepest human yearning—the desire to experience oneness within this world of duality. Unfortunately, for most of humanity, this pleasurable dance is too threatening to the consensus trance of mainstream consciousness. And so, as I mentioned earlier, we seem to find our motivation for change more in our crises than in our yearnings for spirit or in our aspirations of the heart.

I hope the following story will prod you, through its pain and suffering, to wrestle with your view of the wound of abuse as an opportunity to heal some very real parts of yourself. Many of us, at one time or another, have felt betrayed by a parent, a best friend or even ourselves; we've all been unskillful with ourselves and with each other. When we see the shadow side of our lives, we must be careful to honor the learning that happens at the edge of our boundaries. We must not judge ourselves or others too harshly—for the "mystery" has outrageous ways of teaching what needs to be taught when we're open to being students of life, even when shadow and instinct are all we have.

****

Like the nasturtium winding itself around the deck post outside my treatment room at my home, the route North along California Highway One hugs and weaves up the rugged coastline, reminding the driver to *pay attention*. It's also a long drive, 2-3 hours for most, full of peaceful farm land, sandy beaches and breath-taking panoramas. By the time most of my clients get out of their cars on Fish Rock Road, they have been in solitude with their driving meditation in full process.

Bob Taylor arrived nervous. He knew I could help him in some deep and powerful way. He also knew that the work we did together was going to be difficult for him because of the magnitude of damage that had been done to him. When Bob made the appointment he told me in a nutshell of his incest memories and all the therapy he had experienced. Despite the reclamation and the processing of all his abuse memories and despite his amazing progress in the areas of forgiveness and self-esteem, Bob still carried the trauma in his body; and it showed itself in his patterns of relationship. Bob realized that if he was ever going to completely recover he would have to journey into the wound of his incest through bodywork. I encouraged Bob to write his story, and I will freely quote some passages from the book[3] he wrote—inspired by the work we did together.

Bob writes: "I was shy with my body and uncomfortable with touch. I yearned for physical closeness but was never at peace when I had the-chance for contact. I could, however, be physically close during sex but only in a manner that was animalistic, intense, passionate, and short-lived. Immediately after orgasm, I felt revulsion for the person and had to withdraw. I knew that there was something unhealthy about this revulsion, and so I fought against it and was able to stay physically close for a little while after sex, but the closeness didn't feel good. I always felt dirty and guilty after sex, as if sex were something cheap and degrading. I could be a good friend to someone as long as I wasn't attracted to the person, and I could have passionate sex with someone but not be their friend: and so I had friends, and I had sex partners, but I didn't have anyone who remained both for very long.

Sex and alcohol were compulsive. One night Bob bottomed out after drinking to excess. It was a spiritual event. "It was," he writes. "as if a voice from outside of me spoke to me and said, 'Bob, you can't go on like this any longer;' and I just said 'Yes.' I don't know to this day whether that voice was my voice or the voice of my pain or the voice of God. But from that moment on, I stopped drinking, got involved in a program of recovery, and worked hard to get better."

Bob entered therapy for the eighth time hoping that without alcohol in his life he would be able to access the pain that haunted him and molded his life. A friend, an incest survivor, wondered whether Bob, too, might be an incest survivor but at that time he had no memories. His parents caused him pain; his father was an alcoholic and his mother had emotional problems. Bob pondered the incest possibility and then one day bolted up from the sofa, packed his boxes, arranged for a Realtor to sell his house and arranged for his attorney to represent him at the settlement.

Bob left a college professorship in Boston to move to San Francisco and explore what was beneath his pervasive feelings of being like a stranger from another planet. He felt like an impostor most of the time and though he had worked long and hard in therapy, and had uncovered deep feelings and much of his history, the really important events in his life *never* surfaced. Bob just wrote himself off as a mental case. In his words: "I would just have to play the really bad hand of cards I was dealt the best I could."

Traditional routes of therapy had not worked. He knew his path would have to be a spiritual one and in San Francisco his inner voice came alive guiding him to study Sanskrit and yoga. His consciousness shifted into another wave length. Vague emotional echoes began to surface. Bob began to have weekly bodywork and he read Louise Hay's book, <u>Love Yourself, Heal Your Life Workbook.</u> One assignment in the book is to write a letter to someone with whom you are angry. He went into a semi-comatose, semi-awake state. He got scared and put the book away for several weeks. During this time Bob repeated two affirmations continuously: "I love myself and approve of myself," and "I release the past and forgive everyone including myself." He writes: "these affirmations were the immediate trigger that released to my consciousness the most important events in my history, events that had been enveloped in a shroud of amnesia for over thirty-seven years."

With the initial surfacing of vague memories Bob developed a urinary tract infection, the third in the past year. Also a rash appeared on his groin, penis, and testicles at this time. Sadness and anger would surface during and after taking a shower, leaving Bob disoriented and wondering whether he was losing his mind. Was this a nervous breakdown or was this perhaps a breakthrough? Bob came to understand that his anger had to do with his father but still he couldn't recapture the full memory complex.

Bob would get angry that he was still angry with his father. He laments: "It didn't seem fair. I had been a good person all of my life, and all I had known was suffering and pain. I had been sober for almost ten years and had worked my recovery program hard and had sought help through therapists and other sources, and still I was a mess."

"My anger increased the more I thought about these things. When would this pain and anger cease? When would I begin to feel like a normal person, whatever that was? I was tired; tired of all the work, tired of all the pain, very tired, tired of the depressions, tired of the recovery. It seemed hopeless. Nothing had worked—and nothing was ever going to work. I began to scream these things out loud and to think of my father. I started to ask myself 'what happened to me to wind up in this condition after all these years?' I knew now for sure that something really terrible had happened. People don't get into this state naturally; they aren't born this way; they don't feel this way unless something is down there in their history that is unresolved and powerful."

Bob became obsessed with knowing what it was. Sleepless nights, spontaneous crying jags, high fevers, and then suddenly things would appear normal temporarily. Bob began to feel like hurting himself. He had castration fantasies and was afraid he would act on these impulses. He knew these impulses went back to his childhood and that also, despite his exhaustion and death wishes, a part of Bob knew that he had to stay with these feelings; he was at the edge of a major shift. At this emotionally poignant time, Bob decided to get his nipples pierced. He remembers, "The experience was cathartic and I sensed afterwards that I was changed somehow, and that something was beginning to be released."

During the subsequent week Bob felt like he couldn't breathe, that he was smothered and trapped by some dark figure and without any means of escape. He knew that these suffocating feelings of terror had to do with his father but he kept searching for something tangible to surface. And then Bob got his first memory.

After a particularly difficult day, Bob stepped into the shower, repeated his affirmations, as was his habit, and then he started to cough and gag and became dizzy. Bob writes: "I felt tiny and weak, sitting in the tub, and then as if through a thick, foggy haze, I saw my father burying my head in his groin. He had his penis in my mouth, or he was trying to get it in.

He had his hands on the back of my head and neck. I was in pain and was being suffocated. I felt like I was going to die if he didn't stop and let me breathe."

Bob's father incested him many times during the ages of five and seven, almost always drunk. Bob writes: "He would enter my bedroom at night, come over to my bed, and talk nicely to me. Then he would start touching me, still in a nice way. When he first started to do this, I liked it. I liked being close to him; I craved his touch. He never touched me usually. He never kissed me or hugged me. So at first I was glad that he was doing this. But as time went on, he became rough and started to hurt me. I didn't understand and was frightened." When Bob initially called me, I basically got from our interview the gist of what has just been described.

Bob arrived on Fish Rock Road a little disoriented. We talked briefly and then began our session. Bob is a large man with intelligent eyes. He had on a black leather jacket, had an East Coast accent and short red hair and beard. He said he was very nervous. I knew the work of the "psychic healer," K.C. Cotton, who had referred Bob to me. There was no need to talk further as far as I was concerned. Letting Bob's body speak its mind was my direct goal. After Bob got situated on the massage table, I simply asked him to relax and breathe.

In the course of our preliminaries I noticed gold rings pierced through his nipples and two tattoos, a phoenix rising on one arm and a dragon on the other arm. I asked, naturally, for Bob's interpretations of these tattoos, and he explained that the dragon was a symbol of the strength and enlightenment that he had felt in remembering his history and that the phoenix symbolized his rebirth. Bob explained that he was repossessing his body through these tattoos and educated me, saying: "In primitive tribes people were tattooed to mark the entrance to adulthood, to indicate graphically that they had matured, to let the world know that they were sexual beings in complete possession of their bodies."

Bob recalls our first meeting: "I intuitively sensed that Fred was a shaman, a wounded healer who was able to heal and who was called to heal through his own brokenness and wounds. I was immediately at home with Fred and sensed that he was a strong, gentle, loving and supremely spiritual man. I opened up to him completely and told him my story. I realized immediately that he was psychic, because when we discussed a particular incest scene after I told him about it, he mentioned details from the scene that I had not told him. He also included some details that I still had not remembered, and this helped me piece together more of what had happened to me. I realized by now that the only way for me to let go completely of what was done to me was to know as fully as possible what was done to me. I couldn't totally let go of something that I didn't consciously know about."

[When I originally read Bob's words—*psychic, intuitive, and spiritual*—describing me, I felt embarrassed and considered re-writing his perceptions of our relationship in order to "stay humble." But I think it is important to realize that the healing zone is often filled with the energetics of positive spiritual transference. People need to be held by someone, or force, that is BIG. (Therefore, I include my client's writings, along with the complimentary perspectives on our working relationship because they reveal the intimacy of this work and the heart-felt characterstics of "positive bonding.") Also, from the conventional mode of perception, and in particular when a person is seeing through a window of childhood trauma, healing work is, and appears to be, quite magical and profound. It is; but from my experience of working within the domain of this healing zone, much of what is seen to be extraordinary is very straight forward and practical. Therefore nothing special is really happening beause you are just looking at what is in front of you, scanning the situation for information much like any electronic scanner we see in markets or offices these days. I believe that telepathy and clairvoyance are core parts of our racial heritage and that we have just lost our natural relationship with these faculties. Through giving and receiving healing work, of all kinds, I am convinced that these atrophied modes of consciousness and perception will revive, and thus transform our lives. In addition, there is the *mystery*.]

Bob had a big wound inside him that needed to be cleaned out and a bunch of smaller ones that had never healed properly. Together we shared five two-hour sessions over a period of five months. We went into the wound, cleaned it out, worked the residue out of his body, closed the wound and put a healing salve on it. Bob reflects: "Finally, after all these years, I began to heal deeply from the inside out. Transformation then began to take place in me. But for this transformation to take place, I had to die and be reborn on Fred's table."

During our first session, I began with back work. I located the area where Bob was storing all his pent up rage. I pressed deeply into the tissue and Bob began to lose it. He lost awareness of the room and went into a dreamlike state and felt this tremendous pain begin to surface and move in his back.

He wrote later: "the pain traveled inside my body from my back, into my chest, to my throat, and then to my mouth. Suddenly and uncontrollably my mouth opened wide and I screamed out long and hard the pain and rage of thirty-eight years. Fred coached me and even physically assisted me to open my throat and mouth wider. He repeatedly yelled, 'Let it go;

let it all out!' It was out—finally, after all those years—and I began to cry intensely and long. A lifetime of anguish and outrage blasted out of my body. Afterwards, I lay there totally spent, and then this new, warm, pulsating energy flowed into my body, and I felt a peace and a calm come over my body that I never remembered feeling before.

Bob turned over, and while talking to me about what had just transpired, he mentioned that he felt a stirring in his left leg. He had been feeling these jumping sensations ever since the memories had returned. I began manipulating the leg hard and deep. Bob went in and out of a trancelike state as his left leg became both more energized and at the same time out of control.

Bob was having flashbacks to one of his incest episodes. He was resisting his father's advances on him. Bob's left leg kicked his father in the chest as hard as he could; his father, quite tipsy, fell backwards against a dresser. His father looked down at Bob fiercely and said that he was really going to get Bob for this. He told Bob that he was going to go down to the kitchen and get an ice pick and put it in Bob. Bob blacked out and was reliving the sheer terror of blacking out again, on my massage table, while expecting his father to return.

Bob and I bonded in that moment. I reminded him where he was in real time and that he could anchor his consciousness to the present moment by focusing on his breath and on my physical contact with him. Bob's leg was twitching uncontrollably and in his flashback, his father had returned to his room with the ice pick in his hand and put it into Bob's penis while trying to penetrate Bob's rectum with his penis. Bob was about to black out on the table from the sheer intensity of the recall and I yelled at Bob very loud: "Kick him! ...Do it...kick the son of a bitch."

Bob resisted at first. He looked totally defeated and in complete terror. I immediately realized this was the moment he needed to claim his warrior. Bob's eyes pleaded for me to stop this painful madness; yet I knew we were at a point of no return and that I must have conveyed that urgency because as soon as Bob got that he was not alone in this, that he had an ally in me, something beautiful and terrifying occurred.

Bob's eyes changed color. Time slowed down. I heard my own voice urging him on: "Let go...do it...kick!" A powerful energy swept through every cell of Bob's body as his leg came up flexed and poised for one killer strike. Bob kicked with such a force that the table broke and with it a spell that he had been under for most his life.

This session was one of the most powerful ones I can recall. When we completed, I went into my Japanese garden and shook for a long time. Bob also went into the garden to collect himself for his drive home. Bob and I knew and agreed that the way out of the pain was through it. We knew there was more to explore, yet after this first session, we knew that an evil spell had been broken and that together we would certainly prevail.

****

Beth came to her first appointment with me a little pissed off and edgy. In our phone conversation, previous to this appointment, she said that she was in a lot of pain, tired of talk therapy and her intellectual defenses toward her therapist. At thirty years old, Beth functioned just fine in the practical world but in relationships, just when things looked most promising, she would sabotage her happiness and find herself heavy in a depression. Her therapy felt like a skipped record.

She writes in her journal: "The more 'talk' therapy I did, the more armored I became. The closer my therapist would get to my wound, the more 'intelligent' I became at saying just the right thing to protect myself. I could actually see myself doing this but could not change my behavior. At some point I began to wonder, 'What good is this doing me? I'm here because I'm trying to access my feelings, not become more detached from them'".

Beth quit therapy, had a crisis and thought, "Now I'm ready to really talk." She went back to the same therapist and played her same game and didn't get to where she wanted to go. She was spending tons of time, money and gas "not getting there," so she quit again and just "did" her life with relative comfort until, about a year ago, she entered into a relationship with a man that she "really came to love."

Beth writes:"Underneath this layer of positive feelings, I found myself in pain. I couldn't help but be shocked by this dichotomy: love causing excruciating pain." Beth was sure these strong feelings could be sourced to her childhood, and once again she thought of doing therapy, but with a new therapist.

Beth was apprehensive about a body-based approach, knowing that she would be vulnerable without the armament of her quick mind and facile tongue; but she had come to a point of desperation. She wanted to deal with this "stuff" inside her that would bubble up in unexpected moments, uncontrolled and uncontrollable. Most of all she did not want to destroy her valued relationship by sabotaging it.

Beth came to "break new ground," as she said. She came to work with me because she didn't want to "get off easy," meaning that if she wanted to change as much as she professed she did, she would have to work for it. She knew that my role was to facilitate her in this and that if she was going to be successful, she would have to accept my help.

The one thing that had been missing in her other therapy settings was trust. Bodywork is different from talk-therapy. Rather than confronting Beth, which her other therapist had done in a desperate attempt to "get through," I simply pointed out what I saw her doing, and gave her time to reflect and really 'see' that her apprehension and anxiety about our work together was a natural part of the process. In fact, I told her that her process would be to observe her body having all this resistance. This permission allowed her to sink into the vulnerability that was bubbling up out of her body as she told her story.

As she was laying naked on the table with a blanket covering her, I noticed that her breathing was hard and uneven and her jaw quivered a bit. The body so quickly reveals the underlying forces at work in a person's life that sometimes just observing and sharing my observations with a client can activate a full blown release of their reactive material. Beth looked exactly like an angry and confused four-year-old.

"Tell me about your memories at age four," I said.

The pivotal event in Beth's early life was the death of her mother when she was four years of age. No one in her family ever talked about it; Beth dealt with this denial by devising numerous coping mechanisms and sub-personalities to "handle" her life, which she did quite well. In fact, it was her very strong abilities to cope that were now the problem. When love entered Beth's life and promised more than coping well could ever provide, her little girl wound became ripe for the healing.

Through a combination of bodywork and Voice Dialogue techniques[4], we located that four-year-old living inside of Beth's belly. Beth remembers how our session went: "We talked to *her* (Little Beth) gently, in a nurturing way, like no one else had ever done. *She* (Little Beth) was very touched. *She* felt safe and validated in the way 'we' (both Big and Little Beth) felt—which was afraid, alone, uncertain, shut out, unloved, and uncared for on an emotional level."

After Little Beth had really been heard, we explored some more to see if there were other voices that wished to speak. In her shoulder girdle we then found a very defiant personality who seemed about eight years old.

That 'person' was fully convinced that she could take care of herself and didn't need anyone else's help. It was then that I introduced her to Little Beth. Rather than challenging her independence, I asked her if she would befriend the four-year-old so she wouldn't have to be alone. They could be like sister-friends. The eight-year-old agreed and so did the four-year-old. For Big Beth it was like watching a movie about two orphans who find each other and fill each other's need for companionship.

After watching two of her selves bond and agree to look after each other, Beth felt more at peace. We did three more bodywork sessions where we integrated Beth's inner voices with her body sensations and emotional memories—very important work. Beth's intellect had protected her from feeling the pain of her deep woundedness but she had reached that point in her life where protection was an obstacle to love and intimacy.

Beth's initial resistance to our work was her attachment to her relationship with her reactive behavior. When she got stressed, which happened a day or so before our sessions, she often reacted like a four year old—even defining her behavior that way. She would feel a different life force enter her body in those moments. She writes: "It didn't feel like me. I think it was really a part of myself that I had fragmented off because the time period was such a painful one."

In the past, when Beth's defenses were down, this grieving, fearful four year old would burst forth and take over Beth's life. After our work together Beth's four year old had a friend. She has learned how to listen to her four year old with discernment and respect, and both nurture her and define clear psychological boundaries to her little one. In integrating her, Beth cares for her and gives her a rightful place in her life; but Beth calls the shots in her life as the responsible adult she has become.

Her metamorphosis freed Beth to take more risks in life and to truly open to her relationship. She has married the man she fell in love with and has relocated to a foreign country where she has established a life there energized by creativity and commitment.

****

A four year old losing her mother is painful. When people around the four year old go on with their lives as if nothing happened, it is crazy. Naturally, a wall of protection goes up to protect that little child. Beth abandoned her sensitivity to mute the pain of her loss, and enlisted her "left brain controller" to create a whole array of interesting mental distractions so that she wouldn't have to feel her pain.

Walls are good for keeping pain away but they fragment off a part of us that yearns to return. When will that time be? The original pain is an historical chapter in our lives, but the reactions to the pain become our lifestyles. People spend their entire lives wondering when their time will come. I like Ashleigh Brilliant's "pot shot" philosophy card: "Inside every older person, there's a younger person, wondering what happened."

All around us we see people living out reactive home movies and then we watch ourselves get into our own as we get into relationship with these other people. Our problems stem from relationship, they get played out in relationship, and reactivity often grows stronger through relationship if one doesn't integrate their fragments. Those fragments could easily return, like filings to a magnet, if it weren't for those walls.

There are many kinds of walls. The healing path begins somewhere between the lands of divine inspiration and total disgust, but it leads directly, and precisely, to one specific wall — your wall; and behind that wall there is a very sensitive person wondering: "Is it time?"

****

Esther came to our massage course as a very overweight middle aged woman. The minute I saw her, I was touched by the courage it takes to show up at a massage course with that much fat; and then I learned that she had lost 120 pounds within the previous three years. At one point her weight was very close to 400 pounds. Esther confided to me that her parents had died, that there were no family members still around that she cared for, and that she had tried to commit suicide three times before she made the commitment to face whatever ghosts were living behind her wall of fat.

Esther lived in this prison of obesity since she was six months of age. The first five years of her life she was forced to deal with the deaths, from polio, of her younger brother and sister. Esther's mother had an emotional breakdown from the loss of her children, and this ignited the surfacing of her mother's own abused childhood.

Esther was sexually abused by her mother; and Esther was obsessed over by both her mother and grandmother. Her father took the position that Esther was her mother's child, not his; his child was the dead sister. It was a brutal home filled with grief and rage. What passed as physical and verbal discipline would, today, be called abuse.

Esther remembers her father's form of discipline. "At the age of nine," she writes, "I was 'fired' from a job at home because I failed to do it one week." Her father tore into her, ranting and raving about how stupid she was and what a complete failure she was. For the next five years, from that night until Esther's parents separated, Esther had to bring a dictionary to the table. Her father would impossibly challenge Esther and then go berserk, shaming her to no end.

Esther writes: "Meals were always a nightmare for me. I would open my mouth and throw the food down my throat so I could get away from him. At the age of ten, Dad caught me picking at food while I was clearing the table one night after dinner. He took the leftover pasta from our meal, which was in a large mixing bowl, physically held me down and took large handfuls of the pasta and shoved it down my throat until the bowl was empty. He was going to make sure I was full. Afterwards I had to go into the living room and apologize to our company, telling them I was a pig."

If Esther cried at all during these periods of outrageous discipline, he would scream: "Stop crying or I'll really give you something to cry about." Esther not only learned to stuff food down her throat, she also learned to stuff her feelings. This foundation of always stuffing her feelings has ruled Esther's life. There was very little self-expression except for lots of tears and the words: "Don't touch me, please don't touch me."

When Esther's parents divorced, she felt freed, joyous beyond belief. The nightmare of her father came to an end but the uncertainty of her mother's life brought Esther into new fears, all justifiable. Her mother and Esther moved into a logging town, where alcoholic friends of her mother lived. It was a rough and tough place to be. Esther remembers: "I was so afraid of where we lived and the people we lived with that I did not sleep in the house. Instead, I slept in the shed on the back porch of the house—no heat, no locks on the door, only bunk beds, cold, worn-out linoleum and rough wooden planks for walls. It was safer there than in the house. At the age of fourteen I stood watching while two men had a shoot-out over my mother in a rural area. No one was hurt; my mother and I were terrified. She grabbed my arm and we ran out of town. I was so confused when she would not tell the police what went on. Weeks later she got back together with one of these men—more confusion for me."

Esther had no religious background but her mother dumped her in a Catholic boarding school after the shooting scene. Once Esther adjusted to being in the school, it was a beautiful year; the chapel in the convent became a spiritual sanctuary for Esther. "I felt I was safe and had come home," she says, "but it lasted only a year."

Esther's mom pulled Esther out of the boarding school, and they both moved in with her grandmother. She describes the experience: "It was a three year period of living in hell. My mom and grandmother hated each other; lots more abuse, but in essence they are repeats of the earlier years. I was always afraid of my grandmother's verbal abuse; her mouth was more powerful than a fist or a kick."

"Throughout my entire childhood and adult life I have been fat. It was the only way I knew how to protect myself and my terrified inner child. I became a workaholic with my career, building two successful businesses and had little time for relationships; the ones I did have mirrored the abuses of my parents. I did not know how to have any other type of relationship. Periodically the pain inside of me would become so unbearable that I would reach out for help through various forms of therapy. When the pain would subside, I would get on with my career and put the personal back on hold."

In the three years since Esther decided to heal, she surrendered 120 pounds of her protective armament and decided to nurture herself with loving touch. She came to massage school with the hope that by giving and receiving love, in a safe and healing way, she could come out of hiding from behind her prison walls of fat.

In the deep bodywork class Esther released an immense rage that was stored in her gut. She writes: "I'll never forget the first time my rage surfaced. I screamed in pain uncontrollably from the very depths of my gut several times. I sounded like a wounded animal, and felt like one. I could no longer keep the pain inside me."

"After the incredible release of energy I felt fragile and sensitive; the experience was like being reborn. I was this very small young girl lying on the table. I was scared and shaking; I didn't know what to do. I stayed with this young girl on the table and allowed myself to be nurtured by the other bodyworkers."

"This experience opened up so much inside me. I finally found the person who has been hiding inside my body. Meeting her has freed me to trust again, in myself and in other people. Being on this healing path has calmed me; when my 'little girl' gets scared, I let her know that it's safe to live now, by opening myself to skilled and loving touch."

In private sessions Esther and I worked out a great deal of her anger and fear; she also is supported in her healing process with regular "talk therapy." A transformation has been going on with Esther. Her body is now softer to the touch. A large hump between the shoulder blades is gone and the electrical charge around her body has balanced out.

Esther writes: "There is still more weight to lose; and every five to ten pound weight loss causes an entire set of emotional issues to come up and be dealt with, either through transformational bodywork or other alternatives. But there is confidence now, there is hope and trust, and I'm committed to continue the process of healing, part of which is to reach out and help others. "My whole life I was told to go on diets or I would not be socially accepted. I spent a lot of years crying in frustration, feeling like I had failed. I realize today I never failed. I was protecting myself from a world of abuse and pain as a child. Today I am excited and scared about my future and what is in store for me. However, I am not hiding behind my prison walls of fat anymore."

****

Let's pause and take a deep breath now. This would be a good time for you to reflect on any personal healing issue or theme, such as forgiveness or lost faith or some sticky attachment in your heart and mind. Let this issue or painful memory be a mirror or distance marker as you continue reading. Be aware of your own "stuff" as we proceed. This will help you to open and appreciate a simple fact: we're all imperfect—always were and always will be.

Since there's no hope of perfection, we might as well just relax and be with our scars and our wounds that are healing. Our life experience has left noticeable traces, of course, and this, too, is acceptable. In fact, it makes us aware of our humanity.

Now our pain can just be our pain, not badges for having gotten really deep nor scourges that prove we couldn't cut the grade. If we just stop our mental manipulation of our experiences, we can simply feel into the beauty of what is right in front of us—this moment.

So just look deeply into what's true for you right now and appreciate that none of us need to flaunt our flaws or be embarrassed by them; nor do we need to love our pain or be afraid of it. By relaxing with ourselves in this way, we begin something very sweet.

****

Footnotes:

1. Lionel Gambill/review of James W. Prescott's *Pleasure/Violence Reciprocity Theory*. Published by Living Earth Crafts Volume 1 No. 3: January-February 1985

2. Original publication of this material in *The Futurist* /April 1975

3. *Journey Through The Tunnel: One man's story of Incest and Survival*, by Robert E. Taylor

4. *Voice Dialogue* is an internationally acclaimed approach to the psychology of selves created by Hall Stone Ph.D. and Sidra Stone Ph.D. The balancing of sub-personalities through an aware ego is the primary focus of this approach to mental health.

The Only Way Out
Is In

Relax........

We're going to cultivate calmness in a meditation.

The word meditation means "concentration." For many people "concentration" is a problem solving mental focus. Actually, concentration does not need to be mental at all; it can be the simple awareness of an autumn leaf twisting in an afternoon breeze or the watching of a kitten play with a ball of string. By concentrating awareness on just that experience, our mental preoccupations naturally diminish and we can see through the water of our minds into the depths of our experiences. Without calmness, our busy thoughts—like pebbles being dropped into a pond—create disturbances on the water's surface preventing our perceptions from penetrating deeper.

The goal of meditation is to break addiction to thought and thereby experience "real life". Real life is only happening right now. Thought takes us into fantasies of the future and memories of the past, into unreal realms that are far from what is happening in our lives right now. Because the body lives in the present moment, it is an excellent focus for attention.

In the awareness exercises of this book, you will be given an opportunity to tune in to aspects of your bodily felt experience. This world of experience may hold subtle information about your healing challenges and opportunities. This book is a "field guide," so feel free to read a little, put the book down, *see the sights* of your personal experience, and then pick it up again and continue to explore the possibilities.

Read through the following Awareness Exercise once completely; then read through it again slowly. The italic writing is instructional, the normal writing is reflective.

Reflection is like a sigh. It is helpful to experience meditation, like an artist who sighs before placing anything upon a white canvas. Then after something is placed upon the canvas, there is another pause for reflection, and so on and so forth. I love T.S. Eliot's perspective on this: "Teach us to care and not to care, Teach us to sit still."

Awareness Exercise # 1

Take about twenty minutes for this exercise. Read slowly.

Cultivating the Witness

Come sit with me, allow your eyes to slowly open and close several times. Relax, and ask yourself, gently, "What needs to be healed?"

Notice how your body feels just sitting.

Perhaps the posture could be more supportive or relaxed.

Now become aware of your breath; the rate of inspiration and exhalation, the sensation of the air moving through your nostrils.

Notice how, as you concentrate on your breath and sensations, your conventional mentalities subside. Notice what is in the mind below the surface and what you are feeling.

Of course we could compile a mile long list of all the human complaints about life in the body, life in the mind and life of the spirit. Let us not do that here. Instead let us just sit for a while.

Relax.

It is because we are uncomfortable with our feelings and their accompanying mind states that we dream of the future or relive past memories over and over in our minds instead of being with what is in front of us in the present. When we sit with ourselves on a regular basis, we find that the confusion and chaos of the *reactive mind* subsides. In the calm that enters we find ourselves in contact with our hearts and, with this opening, life is deep and full.

Breathe into your heart ten full breaths.

Real freedom, truth and healing never arrive through an outside source such as a guru, a lover, a book or some physical object, but rather they arise when we finally stop grasping for them and enter into the silence and simplicity of being within our own hearts. No healing or great teaching can ever reach us until we open to our hearts.

Breathe into your heart ten full breaths again, and be silent and receptive. Open to yourself.

So here we are, you and I, sitting together; you reading and I writing. Perhaps we can visualize this 'sitting together' in a quiet room next to a garden. We are sitting on meditation pillows and we are aware that, though we are separate individuals, we are united by our commitment to investigate a mystery together.

As you sit, relax into your experience without distraction or striving. There is no goal or agenda. Rather see this time as an opportunity to just *be with* what surfaces. This simple allowing of what *is*, sets in motion a healing current that carries deep seeds of peace and affinity with the *creative intelligence* that people call by ten thousand names: God, higher power, Christ consciousness, or Dhamma (Dharma), to name a few.

This healing current that meditation sets in motion can bring consciousness to areas of your life that have long been asleep or, perhaps, have been tormenting you with emotional tension. Some of these places that are yearning for the healing current to arrive are places of profound wounding or places of guilt or shame at having wounded another human being, intentionally or unintentionally. Sitting with yourself is an exercise in humility and honest self-confrontation.

Sit quietly for five minutes and allow your heart to speak to you about what needs healing in your life.

In practical ways, a person who cultivates awareness through regular meditation finds life characterized by impermanence and frustration. Rather than seeing this reality as a problem to be solved, a more open perceiving arises that allows us to accept difficulties. This more open perceiver is what I call the witness.

When ego-centered mind dissolves, great spaciousness and fresh air permeate the mind and one is able to see without looking for anything in particular. Insight arises naturally because a space of total freedom prevails.

Allow your breath to calm your mind like a gentle breeze coming through a window. Sit quietly for five minutes and allow your heart to speak to you about what needs healing in your life.

There is no goal to our sitting here together, since having one creates more effort and defeats the purpose.

Notice that in just sitting here in meditation, together, there can be awareness without concept. Take five more minutes of just quiet sitting.

It is this quality of mind, free from conceptualization, that reveals subtle layers of consciousness. As you become more experienced at observing your thoughts and feelings without any goal, judgment, or strategy, you find deeper levels of relaxation and simplicity. You become increasingly self-accepting and ultimately self-transcending.

Who is sitting here now? Who is breathing? Let this awareness be the expanded perceptions of an inner witness in your life who just calmly observes and knows.

Body, breath, emotions and changing awareness are all part of the meditation experience. Like all things, the cultivation of awareness is a process. Within the direct immediacy of experience in the present moment, the part of the mind that plans, evaluates and categorizes recedes out of benign neglect, and you will become more sensitive to your emotions before they fully arise.

By observing your emotions in their incipient phase you can *witness* your attachments to them and begin to break emotional habit patterns. Witnessing your emotions without reacting to them, reduces anxieties and awareness becomes more subtle. In this way, what needs to be healed presents itself for healing, in its own time, as this Oriental classic illustrates.

When one finally stops grasping for what one wants most,

What one wants most comes unexpectedly

In ways one cannot know.

When the mind becomes still,

The whole universe surrenders.

Breathe and smile and sit and let the mind go...

****

Healing only happens when you are truly ready for it. And you are never ready until you stop judging yourself for not being ready sooner. Readiness to heal is felt when the shields and weapons, that once created armament, feel burdensome to carry and the sense of self, that once afforded the comfort of identity, feels like a wall that separates and fragments us in so many ways: us and them, me and you, I and thou. Healing is the process of dismantling these walls, dropping the shields and the swords, and calling home all the fragments.

Healing work is like self-sculpting. Healing work is ancient, it is tribal, it precedes religion and has, in the native cultures, served as a bridge between this manifested world and the world beyond. This "beyond" world is the domain of the shamans, and it is also the world of the "ordinary" person who visits himself at his edge. I've been inspired by the courage and wisdom that flows from the depths of people's lives when they meet themselves at their edges—the crucible where wounds finally open to the healing they contain. What started out as a clinical practice in stress-reduction became, over time, a window from which I have seen a side of human spiritual development that, rather than being written in religious verse or in devotional song, is sculpted in human flesh.

Healing bodywork can stimulate the body to secrete abnormal amounts of specialized chemical hormones, (opiates, beta-endorphins, nucleopeptides), that alter our physiological experiences in ways that allow high-frequency subjective states of consciousness to predominate for a time. During this time of accelerated awareness, insights arise regarding our lives and the forces which govern them. This is true for meditation as well. The difference is that in meditation the body resonates to a calmed mind, and in bodywork the mind resonates to an energetically coherent body. In both contexts, a shift in awareness occurs; and with this shift a life can be transformed.

Anything less than this transformation needs to be thought of as a cure, not a healing. A cure manages or eliminates the painful symptoms of an imbalanced body or life. It does not, in contrast to healing, break through symptomatology to the core of a person's imbalanced energy. Healing, and language that describes true healing, is inherently of a spiritual nature.

Many years ago, one of my oldest and dearest friends died a painful death of AIDS. My experiences with him and his family, especially in the weeks following his death, led me deeper into the understanding that healing is a redemption into oneness. Though he was not cured, my friend left this earth a healed soul because he accepted his death and gracefully came to terms with his life. In contrast, I know of others who have been successfully cured from painful diseases yet never received a healing. They were unable to disidentify from their stories, and "die into" the *soul life*. This disidentification is a kind of dying and learning to do this gracefully is an essential step in healing work.

Healing is about wholeness, or oneness. To be healed, therefore, means to *be* one again. Oneness means that all the fragments have returned home and have been fused together again. So if a person is cured of symptoms temporarily, but does not unite his fragmented parts together again, then a healing did not happen.

The Western medical model, which has some real strengths, is sadly lacking in its vision of what real healing is about. If one keeps attempting to eradicate painful symptoms, the wisdom of the wound, and the teaching it contains, will find another way to deliver the healing opportunity. This is why medicine and therapy must be viewed differently from healing. Healing is not about the eradication of symptoms but is instead about fulfilling an original life purpose. Healing is also not about understanding your life-story better by identifying with it, it is about finding a life beyond story through a resolution of heart.

Touch therapy gives the human body a chance to communicate true and unfiltered information to both the practitioner and the recipient in a way that embraces the mystery. When we surrender into our healing process, our awareness grows and we get more proficient at co-creating with life. The mystery is demystified at one level but at the same time a deeper mystery is unveiled. Such is the healing path. The work revolves around a simple premise: *We are spiritual beings having a human experience on Earth.*

****

People seek transformational assistance because of deep commitments to personal growth and because of a biological need to be more comfortable in their bodies. Transformation, as a motive for self work, usually develops in a person after the healing work has well begun. Though today's healing marketplace is full of incredible and diverse opportunities for healing, it is one's readiness to heal that most determines the success of the healing opportunity.

Caroline came to her bodywork sessions already a veteran of the healing path. She is a psychologist and student of bioenergetics—a type of bodywork. She describes herself: "I had worked on healing my wounds and freeing myself through therapy, spiritual path taking, and increasingly nurturing health habits. I had worked with insight, intuition, experiential exercises and feelings in my commitment to personal growth and a more loving world. Yet there were some areas where I felt little change, little progress. I experienced these unchanging places in several ways—as numbness, as a tendency to escape through busy-ness, *staying beside myself rather than inside,* by extraverting my basically introverted nature, and as low-grade depression." From the beginning our bodywork was powerful. Numb spots on Caroline's back elicited deep sobs. Caroline had no idea what content had been touched upon, but she knew that "something very profound had happened that had bypassed insight.

Caroline is very cerebral by nature. Having a history of sexual abuse, it was very easy to leave her body; and having grown up in an alcoholic family, it was easy for Caroline to take on the responsibility of any relationship. Years of self-work taught Caroline to integrate her feelings with her mind, but she still needed to inhabit her body in order to stay present to herself in a loving way. Our bodywork sessions helped Caroline to achieve this integration. They also have allowed her to develop her own observing self.

Through skilled touch and the use of focused breath, Caroline's bodymind eventually entered a *flow state.* A *flow state* can feel like an energetic river that carries memories and the emotions associated with those memories. Rivers that are damned by tight muscles hold back emotions that are considered dangerous to have, and impossible to express. Tight muscles are often the expression of a child that couldn't trust, and Caroline was no exception to this. As her musculature softened, memories arose and were released into her flowing river of experience. As they floated by Caroline's "inner witness" observing from the river bank, Caroline came to feel a loving neutrality about her life. She could see things differently after these flow state experiences. As her perception shifted, her identity as a victim and survivor diminished, and a compassion for others and herself developed.

The strengthening of Caroline's observing self directly facilitated her ability to freshly perceive her reactive patterns and to see that she could *choose* to reprogram her cellular memory banks. In our bodywork sessions she could feel herself "moving back and forth between familiar fear-based cellular patternings and healthy responses within the loving neutrality of our work together." The body became, for Caroline, a theater for her to re-educate her mind to respond differently to the world. "It feels so deep—like a plant's tropic response to sun or water." Caroline's strengthened observing self effectively helped her to overcome fear-based reactions and to begin to actually enjoy life from within her body.

The working relationship with Caroline was central to her healing and ultimately was the vehicle for her healing. Relating to men, because of her alcoholic father and the cousin who molested her, was always problematic. Critical to her healing was working through her distrust and her blocks to being able to be appropriately vulnerable. These blockages were emotional in nature but had very specific physical manifestations. Her back, for example, had one completely numb point that when skillfully addressed became the treasure chest which she had stored all of the grief and sorrow she felt for her unlived childhood. When this grief and sorrow were accessed and brought into our working relationship, she was able to let go of her protective fears and as a result, move fully into her present life. The numbness left Caroline; her breath deepened, and her emotional life nourished her with joy and humor because the darker emotions, from her childhood, no longer were threatening. She could now live in the present.

Being present to *what is happening* sounds pretty simple but, in fact, basic bodily experiences such as whether we are cold, hungry or tired, can go largely unnoticed. Wounded people transcend life in the body for the life stories they script for themselves. When they outgrow the script, anxiety runs supreme. A great many people suffer the stories of their difficult childhoods more than the actual difficulties themselves; this is why, when the body itself tells the story, there is a basic honesty without the frills of egoic attachments. Caroline detached from her own story through our work together, and became attentive to her bodily felt emotions, her physical sensations, and the continuity of her unfolding consciousness. Through this intentional process of paying attention to "what's happening," her truth revealed itself and Caroline began to trust herself.

The reactive mind scripts experience to conform around predetermined, usually unconscious, goals of security. Caroline's armor was elegant, her antennae exquisitely tuned, and her persona refined—right down to her eye contact and voice inflection. After all, she was a psychologist. Caroline describes herself: "I was chronically exhausted from fight or flight reactions to the world; I sort of used adrenaline like caffeine as a substitute for real energy. This was a sane response, when I was a child, to a world from which I could expect violence and abandonment. I needed protection."

Caroline had crafted a hyper vigilant nervous system that was part of her shield, her childhood heroic response. The bodywork explorations afforded her nervous system some unexpected choices, and Caroline chose to give herself a rest. In subsequent integrative work, Caroline came to see that her adrenaline driven persona, with its need for approval, could now relax and make way for her true heart space to emerge. "I don't have to get hyped up on adrenaline anymore," she writes, "I can lower my response-threshold to allow ever more subtle and loving aspects of life to enter my awareness. Because of the bodywork, there are trustworthy levels of *knowing* that I never had before."

Caroline's work with me was tested when she was diagnosed with breast cancer. Previous to this diagnosis, Caroline had made great strides in embodying her life through our bodywork sessions. Despite her remarkable progress, she was always in resistance to me, personally—a replication of her trust issues with men. One day, after a chemotherapy treatment, Caroline arrived for her session wearing a wig and a weak smile. I knew she would be scarred and scared and I held my heart open to her for something sacred to happen. Her face quivered trying to hold back tears. Pride and grief and embarrassment all played with her chin, lips and nostrils. I told her she could get this part over with quickly by just taking off her wig and showing me what the surgeon's knife had done. Caroline's eyes locked onto mine for quite some time. In this silent gaze, some transmission of mind occurred between us and an inner trust threshold was crossed. Caroline immediately took off her wig and undraped the sheet to expose her wound, herself and her soul. She burst into tears as I gently placed one hand on the incision and the other on her heart.

For quite some time she lay there as wave after wave of emotion came crashing out of her body into the room. I think every unshed tear from her childhood, her mother's death and all the disappointments of a lifetime came out then. And then she spoke eloquently of how good it felt to be so vulnerable and trusting. At one point she referred to her lymph nodes as "nymph lodes." I caught the slip, and laughingly pointed it out. Caroline, in a Zen flash, caught the entire depth and beauty of the moment and burst into hysterical laughter and tears.

On one level, her work with me was to heal enough to embrace her juiciness, her "inner nymph." Suddenly in this moment, at her edge, she saw that the removal of the lymph had opened the door to her nymph and that she could now totally embrace her life knowing it was hers to enjoy and hers to share. I kissed her bald head and left the room knowing that Caroline's wound became fertile. Her pain was harvesting this blessing in disguise. And Caroline knew this too, and the light emanating from her entire body was testament to this truth.

This deep knowing is the fruit of flow state awareness. Like quiet joy or true happiness, it does not require an outside observer to judge its value. We recognize it as truth. When we stop manipulating reality so that we might have more preferred moments and fewer unpleasant ones, we are able to simply merge with what is happening. Caroline, a master of complexity confronted her mortality and in this meeting found her simplicity. The prospect of death levels our field of consciousness of all extraneous matters. That which truly does matter is revealed with elegant simplicity, and we are able to open gratefully to life and embrace what is happening just as it is. We don't have to work everything anymore. We and "what's happening" with us are seamlessly contained within a whole. What we observe and the observer within implode into a unified field of observation that always exists and awaits us at the edge of our life and in all of our kinds of death. Simple.

This wholeness, or "unified field of consciousness", is possible for most people to achieve, given adequate opportunity and guidance. Sustaining this field is a little trickier, especially if one is forced to attend to unhealed wounds. This is why healed people can sustain flow state awareness even amidst the natural conflict that arises between two or more sub-personalities.

The energy that had been used to manipulate experience around the wound is, in the healing person, available to mitigate the friction that naturally arises in normal life situations. This natural friction needs to be acknowledged and worked with, and there are countless ways to do it; but one thing we can count on is that the work is never done. There has been an unspoken popular illusion in many "new age" pursuits that once we become aware of integration and flow, we've completed our "work" and deserve to be *happy*, at least most of the time (whatever that means). In truth, we have to choose *in every moment* to wake up, be mindful and behave consciously with ourselves and others, and learn to forgive ourselves and others when we miss the mark.

The word *sin*, incidentally, is an archery term; it means *missed the mark*. We miss the mark sometimes. We're imperfect. *To err is human, to forgive is divine*.

Instead of trying to succeed in life, a person in flow brings the harmonizing power of compassionate awareness to his or her imperfect and difficult moments. When we consciously embrace the unfoldment of our experiences, we meet each moment with restraint, kindness, compassion and patience. To do otherwise is unproductive or potentially harmful. What we see when our hearts are open is whatever needs to be loved. Therefore, a person who enters Flow State awareness becomes a nurturer, someone who extends loving kindness in all directions, and is receptive to loving kindness from all directions.

When we cultivate loving kindness and nurture what we touch, then all experience that flows from this intention is imbued with healing qualities. We are in tune with this energy and it comes back to us from unexpected sources. Realizing, on a cellular level, the interdependency of all life, an ecology of the heart develops, and love becomes our spiritual gravity.

Love is still the answer. Without love we will never have the strength to meet ourselves at our edges — the place where our wounds humble us into receptivity and the place of accelerated insight where our spiritual growth curves originate. Our awesome meeting of ourselves at the edge, whether it be to heal a wound or to explore the big mystery, is always an exercise in humility. Humility generates a larger opening through which healing light may pass. After enough of this, there is little egoic identification left, unless...an ever more subtle wound appears just to make life interesting.

The endless humility of healing work describes our co-creative relationship with the divine. For after we have healed and all we have are scars to remind us of our journey, there are other sentient beings who need the support of loving kindness. While serving on this "Transformational Journey" we become aware that it is not the destination, at all, that qualifies our experience, but rather it is the way we meet ourselves and others along the path.

Healing work is our spiritual gravity. Healing is endless, and enlightenment is ongoing. Healing, thus, is the ongoing process of gracefully loving and serving from unity while living within duality and its inherent tension. The grace to do this is available. Opening to this grace is our greatest struggle and our sweetest blessing.

And it is all "perfect" just the way it is.

The Body Speaks
Its Mind

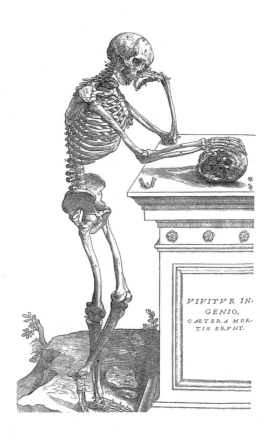

VIVITVR IN-
GENIO,
CAETERA MOR-
TIS ERVNT.

When we open to healing and have cultivated our witnesses, our perceptions change. Before that, when we felt afraid for example, we would experience the sensation of fear and say, "I am afraid." By bringing our awareness to the feeling of being afraid, we perceive the sensations and say to ourselves, "There is fear." This takes the "I" out of the experience. When the observer steps into the equation, fear moving through our bodymind is perceived as energy in motion, or E-motion. The sensation of shaky electric coolness, that characterizes fear, moves through our body;

because it has the quality of movement, we know—from our studies of impermanence *(anicca)*—that it too shall pass. So we transform our awareness once more and say "Fear is leaving me."

Without awareness we react to fear and feed it, making it greater than it ever was. With awareness we feel it arising, dis-identify from it and see it passing out of our bodies. With this liberating awareness, we co-create our lives. We take responsibility for our experiences by cultivating self-discipline with our awareness and our perceptions. "We see what we want to see" is an old saying that describes it all. If you want to see fear, there's plenty to see, but if you want to see hope, there's that too. By wanting freedom and happiness we prepare ourselves to see the subtle positive signs that the universe is truly capable of delivering the goods.

Our bodies are willing to present these signs to us, even though their presentation is often overwhelming and chaotic. Geological awareness has helped us to see that even though earthquakes are disruptive, a tectonic rebalancing results releasing the stress in the earth's crust for a period of time. Our bodies speak their minds in this same way, transforming psycho-emotional stress in ways that permit a realignment with the laws of nature.

Let us do another awareness exercise that can help us harmonize our perceptions with natural law. This exercise will help you to *sense* and interpret information that your body is giving you regarding your personal healing work.

Awareness Exercise # 2

Sensate Awareness

Since I am a touch-therapist and am sharing my perspective with you through words, it would be most helpful if you could become more familiar with your body's sensations as you read. The body yearns to reclaim its natural placement in your consciousness. Hopefully, the language of your breath and your awareness of your body's sensations, will be as interesting to you as anything I write.

The healing journey is messy. Sometimes we read more quickly or gloss over material that evokes in us our own unfinished business. Also, as you read, you may be able to identify your particular wound, and the healing for it, more easily by noting sensations such as heaviness, or electric heat or coolness.

Sit quietly for five minutes, with your eyes closed, as we remember doing in Exercise #1.

Notice how deep your breath goes, how the muscles around the entire rib cage feel as you breathe and how the diaphragm muscle, above the solar plexus, feels as your lungs expand against it.

The breath is a key indicator of how our emotional life is being managed. Dynamic tension exists in the musculature throughout the body, not just around our respiratory system.

Imagine that your awareness could be microscopically reduced to a single cell and that you, as pure awareness, could travel through your entire body. Observe the energy and terrain of your body from this perspective.

Sit quietly for ten minutes and travel through your body from head to toe, noticing areas of tension, blocked areas, cold areas, electrically charged areas and areas of heat.

You may have noticed in this brief journey through your body, certain zones that fit my descriptions. You may have noticed other experiences as well. The more we scan, impartially as a fair witness, this inner terrain of our human bodies, the easier it becomes to *know* what healing needs we have. Remaining a fair witness in this exercise is not as simple as it sounds. Often when we *sense* an inner wall, we lose our objectivity and find ourselves in judgment or analysis. We may even quicken our scanning and jump to another part of the body. Let's explore this process.

Again, sit quietly for ten minutes and travel through your body from head to toe and notice again areas of tension, blocked areas, cold areas, electrically charged areas and areas of heat. When you get to a particular area where you sense a reaction, stay there and just notice your breath and any sensations that arise for you. Don't interpret or make a story from these sensations...just allow them to present information.

When awareness is brought to the body in this meditative way, we are able to see deeply into our unconscious personal histories. Actually, through meditation, we make the unconscious conscious. The meditative mind combined with healing touch are powerful tools for a person to have on his healing journey. When the aware mind lingers at a charged or blocked area in the human energy field long enough, something very subtle and incredible happens.

It is as if our awareness, like a lascr beam, had the power to melt an inner wall, and from the wall's breakdown we could see revealed a dynamic tension that the wall was holding back. If we calmly explore these inner walls, we may sense their corresponding relationships to aspects of our "defensive personalities." This "Aha!" experience is referred to as insight. It arises unexpectedly in our quietude and "lands into" the empty space we have cultivated in meditation.

Once again, sit quietly for ten minutes and travel through your body to the one area that calls out to you most prominently at this time. Invite the wall to dissolve and "investigate" the energy that lives there. Is it a running energy, a frozen energy or a fighting kind of energy? Just notice the quality of energy; resist creating a story around it.

The psycho-somatic energy that exists behind this dissolved wall is the very material of your unhealed and unprocessed emotions. These disarmed energetic tensions usually express themselves in this way: Tingling electric heat signifies anger-based feeling and has to do with FIGHT. Heavy, slow, contained, and dense energy signifies grief and has to do with FREEZE. Cold, rapid pulsations usually centering around the spine or solar plexus, signify fear and relates to FLIGHT.

Most of us are stuck in the linear prison of our personal historical identities, defined by "what went wrong" and "how we coped with what went wrong." The evolution of our egos can be seen, in fact, as a defense to real and imaginary wounds we incurred growing up. Most non-Western people believe their defenses and related "stories" are carried over from past lives as *karma*—the emotionally charged material that seeks resolution of some kind.

The ego structure is a "story-wall" that we create as psychic armament to contain feelings that might otherwise overwhelm us. The armament children place around their pain may be necessary. However, the illusion of security it provides the adult who maintains it is too often bought at a price far greater than most of us would pay if we knew the burden it placed upon our souls. *At some point in a person's life, either through crisis or after embracing a strong commitment, a healing choice arises to be made.* Healing bodywork utilizes this incentive to break through to unresolved anger, grief, fear, and betrayal that yearn for safe release so that freedom can be achieved.

If we choose to heal we call the process of healing a *breakthrough*; if the need to heal demands our cooperation, and we resist the healing process, we call the inevitable healing a *breakdown*. When we become aware of our sensations, through meditation, and listen to them for guidance, we find our lives easier, more joyous and precious—even when the process is painful.

Sit now and allow your mind and body to rest.

We are the "white Space" on the artist's canvas; and we are the artist reflecting upon the canvas; and we are the experience of the reflection itself...Hmmm

Accept whatever arises with grace and love yourself as you are.

As a person walks into my treatment room, I notice how he moves his legs, how he holds his shoulders and whether his breath is rapid and shallow or deep and relaxed. After an interview and the person is lying on his back, usually unclothed under a blanket, I will hold his hand and feel pulses or sense the energetic-sensation-field, the energetic signature that he has created for himself.

Unlike talk therapy, the bodywork I do is not necessarily concerned with biographical story as a primary focus. I appreciate, from my work, that one's biography is concurrently biological; my hands read a version of this story which is a less linear biographical take on *what* happened and *how* it happened. My intent is to understand and effectively transform the client's *energetic field*. Changing the feel of static electricity to the harmonic experience of a major or minor piano chord is somewhat analogous. By cultivating awareness in the energy field of a person's body, a meta-story surfaces along with insight about how defense structures were originally created to cope with that *story*.

Perceived functionally, the leg muscles, for example, can be seen as the forces which govern either the reaction of running away (flight) from an undesirable situation or the proactive moving toward an attractive goal or the static tension of "holding onto ground." As I touch this leg I tune into the tension, the temperature, the moisture and the resistance to pressure that exists in the muscles of this leg.

There is no judgment as I take in all this information because it is done from the perspective of a *fair witness*. In observing a client at this impersonal yet intimate level, it is sometimes possible for me to energetically infuse my awareness within their energetic field for a brief period of time. Much insight arises out of this merging. This is an intuitive skill that has taken me many years to develop.

The process I use is an active one of stroking to discover *charge* in a muscle and then probing that charge gently to discover its quality of resistance. I then hold that point, sometimes with another point on the body, and remain still for a period of time. In this stillness an energetic story begins to unfold that is both mysterious and on some level, radically obvious— like finding, in children's books, the hidden picture within a camouflage. Depending upon how receptive or distracted my client is with verbal input, our session may involve talking. Usually, I keep this to a minimum and encourage a natural breath to be the predominant focus. At times I may ask my client to breathe in a particular way to assist what I am doing.

****

Jim was in my bodywork course and volunteered to be the model for a demonstration on how to massage the pelvic and leg segment of the body. After demonstrating the movement sequences on Jim I noticed that his body had stiffened and he was breathing rapidly. Within a short time, Jim's mouth puckered up and his hands became rigid with his thumbs stiff but tucked into his palm. These physical symptoms are referred to as *tetany*[1] and they indicate that a major release of energy is underway. Energy being released can be a form of karmic resolution. Karma, in this sense, can be viewed as the unresolved intensities within a person's energetic field. These intensities, as we've explored, can be experienced as sensations of inner heaviness, heat, electric itch and others.

The body is a conduit for balancing out karmic propensities, as Jim's experience reveals. Jim began to get very anxious. I asked him if he was with us in the room. "Not really, I'm somewhere else; I'm scared. I feel small. I'm really pissed but I'm much more scared." I reminded Jim that he was safe with all of us here and that he was experiencing some unconscious *cellular memory* of a frightening time. I explained that something that was being held in his leg was leaving him and that when it left he would feel much better than he has for a long time.

Suddenly, Jim's legs stiffened as if to run away but couldn't and he began to shake all over, squirming as if to get away from something. It took four of us to contain Jim from falling off the massage table. "Oh my God! Oh no!" Jim shouted, "It smells so bad, what is that smell?"

During the next half hour, Jim recalled the whole forgotten scene of a childhood incident. At about age eight, Jim's mother and he were in a taxi on their way to visit an uncle. On the way they stopped at a hospital presumably to visit a friend of Jim's mother. Once inside the hospital Jim was taken away to have his appendix removed. He was totally shocked. He tried to run away. His legs were energized to flee, like in a dream where he couldn't move his body but tried, nonetheless to get away. His legs held this frozen history of terror, outrage and betrayal. The memory complex of these negative emotions was muted by what turned out to be ether.

Jim was put under by ether. After coming out of the operation he was met by a smiling mother, ice cream and the convenience of a short-term memory which saved him from totally shutting down to his mother for the remainder of his childhood.

The unfolding of this story was exhilarating for the whole group. My students were all amazed, but somehow the energetics didn't feel quite complete. I asked everyone to be silent and just gently rest a hand on Jim's body and remain calm. After a while Jim really relaxed and opened his eyes and with lucidity and sincerity said: "Boy, this really explains a lot. I'm thirty-two-years old, I've been in at least half a dozen long-term relationships and about two dozen short ones. *Every time I feel close to a real commitment, I freeze up and run away.* I've been running away from women all my life because I feel, down deep, they just can't be trusted. Oh wow.....all these years I've been carrying this shit, this feeling that every woman is going to set me up, betray and abandon me, and pretend with me." Jim broke into a deep soulful cry and said that he was looking forward to getting to know both himself and women with his heart more trusting.

Jim healed something deep inside from his work during this session. His body's wisdom sensed that he could handle the presentation of this charged cellular memory, and it went into a release mode. Riding atop the energetic wave of release was a package of specific psychological content — betrayal, rage, and fear. In my work I seek out, with my hands, an energetic field of charge and then invite the mystery to express itself. My intent is to understand and effectively transform the client's energetic field. After expression there is a relaxation cycle that is ripe for awareness and reflection. Much healing occurs during this time of heightened awareness and physical discharge.

Over the many years of practicing bodywork, I have been amazed at how much fragmentation, abuse and pain exist in the lives of "ordinary" people. These unhealed wounds that people carry get passed on through negative relationships which become a stage to act-out further abuses...ad infinitum. So to stop this cycle of reactivity, we must return to our original wounds and do the necessary healing work.

The Body In You

Beyond the world of fight, flight, and freeze there is another world called FLOW. It is not without tension, pain or risk. The difference is in consciousness. Rather than reacting to the conflict of body against mind or mind against body, Flow unites all superficial dichotomies into a seamless web of intelligence, an intelligence that contains and expresses every intuitive flash and hormonal secretion within our minds and bodies. *Flow is, indeed, the state that erases any distinction between mind and body. Flow creates bodymind through its waves of energetic trust. Flow originates and returns us to that which is our source.*

Many spiritual traditions inform us that there is inherent pain and suffering in the very nature of the human condition here in the physical plane. Misery arises out of our reactivity to this pain. *If we can learn to respond to painful experience, rather than react to it, we could just have our suffering and avoid our misery.* Healing bodywork has the capacity to directly reframe the personal world of sensation, emotion, thought and memory. This reframing of awareness helps us learn to become responsive, rather than reactive, and therefore flow with life, even when there is pain.

If there is anything that can be done to transform our culture's perception of the body, it is through the reframing of awareness itself. A classic reframe is the exchange between the Sufi teacher, Nisargadatta, and his student who asks: "How can I be free when I feel trapped inside this body?" Nisargadatta replies: "You are not in your body, the body is in you." This transformation of perception is, in fact, one of the goals that spiritual practice is designed to accomplish. And, coincidentally, it is one of the goals that healing bodywork can accomplish as well. Something amazing happens when we make this shift in perception; we see the healing in the core of the wound. With reactive perception, all I want to do is numb out, run away or lash out. With transformed perception I see the creative possibility of learning something from every experience. If I merge with what is happening, I can respond to the overall situation in a way that is harmonious.

I once walked into a stinging nettle plant in a wilderness area. My skin blistered and itched tremendously. A passing hiker noticed my distress and showed me how to slit and open the stalk of the nettle plant and apply the moist inner pulp, as an antidote, to the blister. I felt instant relief. With this faith that a solution lies in the heart of each problem, that a healing lies at the core of each wound, and that a resolution waits in the center of each conflict, I now go directly into the heart of every matter. And when I patiently sustain contact with my client, with this faith, I silently ask, "Is it time?"

You cannot cause a rose to bloom, or a pimple to pop any faster than the organic process will allow. Bringing unveiled awareness into the unhealed wounds of our life does not magically transform everything. It only sets the stage. The stage was set and Jim was ready to work through the cellular memory of his abandonment in the hospital by his mother. Sometimes I must wait until a person's body is ready to reveal a past life cellular memory that is ripe for transformation.

Jean came to me as a student and then as a client. She moved to the coast after a year long recuperation from the unintended consequences of a sloppy medical procedure done to her fifth lumbar disc. After our work she could move freely without pain medication. Jean had a new lease on life. She bonded with my family; we had fun together. This happened naturally over a period of three years. During this time, I got to see her modus operandi up close but could never intuit or discover the source of her shakiness.

Jean's issues were fear-based. Jean had raised her daughter alone, was an extremely competent professional person with the best of friends, but the people she chose for intimacies were either not available emotionally to really meet her or were casual sexual partners. Getting really close was always felt as dangerous, so Jean would sabotage a potentially good thing if it meant that she might actually get the "good life" she claimed to want.

Jean's cellular identity was geared to escapism and intensity. She could party with alcohol or other substances and go into incredibly lucid, often deeply spiritual, places, but she loved the body. Her touch, however, had a high frequency shakiness to it. This vibration was core to Jean's cellular identity. I frequently asked myself, "Why can't she just relax?"

Jean was an adrenaline junkie. If she ever stopped her motor long enough, I figured, she would have to deal with this high revved unconscious flight that always seemed more intense than her childhood history suggested.

What was she trying to get away from?

One evening I found her passed out from drinking at her home when she was expected at our home for dinner. The next day my anger softened to concern leaving me wondering what kind of unhealed wound prevents someone from letting in the "good life." For Jean, relationships, financial security and long-worked for goals were all coalescing in very positive ways. It was like we were all at Jean's wedding to her "good life," when suddenly she bolts from the altar and says, "No Thank You....I'm already married to my wound."

The next day I gave her a session in which this issue of commitment to her life came up. She decided to once again participate in a five-day course she had done previously with our school called, "Healing the Wound of the Practitioner." In retrospect, I can see that the big healing Jean needed could only happen, for her, within the context of close personal friendship, because intimacy and being cared for were the big, scary charges that ran her life.

For two days, other students were models while we practiced our work with one another. Previous to the morning demonstration when Jean would be the model, a heavy rainstorm hit the coast and pounded the roof of the cottage where Jean had been sleeping. She had worked out strenuously with weights prior to arriving, so on top of being tired from her sleepless night, she was muscularly spent from her work out. The stage was set for a session that would rip away her veil.

Jean looked somewhat altered. Her moist eyes darted back and forth as she combed her hair back with her hand explaining to me, our class and the video-camera, that she had been dreaming about being on a boat during the past several nights and that she wanted to forego the interview and immediately get on the massage table and allow the mystery to unfold. On the table, and in less than three minutes, between short and fast breaths she began:

"I'm on a boat......all last night these memories came up." *Are you alone?* I'm with my wife, my son...and my two daughters. We are way out to sea...we can't see any land. We're in the North Atlantic Ocean; it's the late 1800's...I don't know if we're English or from New England...it doesn't matter....the boat has been damaged, we're all five holding on."

"Oh my God...I can't believe this is happening....Oh No!!" *What's going on?* It's SHARKS!....they're coming from underneath...Oh my God."

Jean's body is squirming all over the table. I am all over and around her wriggling body. She is definitely re-experiencing, on a cellular level, this shark attack. All the other students are totally with Jean. She can see them in the mirror and feels their support helping her to stay in the reality of this experiential recall. It is so intense that she attempts to return herself to the relative calm of her current life but is unable to find any solid ground. She is in water and all of us are supporting her in this process.

The boat has deteriorated...Jean and her family have been swimming to the point of exhaustion. Jean's legs have been kicking pillows off the massage table as if they were sharks, then her legs would frantically paddle and thrust to get away.

"Where is your wife?" I asked,*"Where are your children? "*

"I've drowned them, only my son is left...he's sixteen, he's brave, he's so brave. We love each other so much...we all loved each other so much. I can't believe that this is happening....It was just a weekend holiday..... These GOD DAMNED SHARKS! Come on and get me, you FUCK-ERS!!"

Jean was completely hysterical and thrashing all over; and then suddenly, she became very quiet and said softly: "This explains everything. All my life I've been in terror of being attacked from beyond where I can see and totally afraid to love, especially to commit to love, for fear that I would lose the people I love to tragedy. Each time I get really close I run away so that disaster won't happen to me and others."

Jean reflected through gobs of tears and mucous how these unconscious memories have run her life forming her basic attitudes into a posture of terrorized defiance — a shouting out to God almighty, "Oh what the fuck — who cares anyway!"

Jean started crying tears she had never shed. She was in present time reflecting with me and also, like in a split screen movie, still in the water with her defiance and terror. Another wave of shaking erupted and then a very emotional speech to the darkness of her despair that I will never forget for as long as I live.

"God where are you? This is so painful. There is no negotiating with these forces. There is no mercy. There is no hope. There is just my few moments of insanity left before I am destroyed by this....but first I must drown my son before these sharks tear him apart while he is still alive."

Jean is back into struggling against her son's body's instinctual need to surface for air. It is taking her every ounce of strength. I am wrapped around her lanky body, giving her a strong and elastic envelope to struggle against. Finally, after drowning her son, Jean is alone, crying over the loss of her family. Her legs are doing their shaky swim, half in the air, half on the table.

"All I want to do is get out of here....just give me anything....." She's talking to me, to God, to herself...and then reflects: "All I want to do is numb out. I see that's what I've made a habit out of in this life whenever close-ness gets too real, I don't want the pain. I was a doctor in that life, I had it all, I had a beautiful family," and here she wails again for a long time, and then continues, "We all loved each other so much...and at the end, we looked into each other's eyes and we knew there was nothing left to say... there was no blame...there was only love and surrender."

Everything got very quiet. I just nurtured her body. There was no more shakiness. Jean finally looked relaxed in a way I had never seen. I encouraged Jean to breathe easily and travel through her body while in this relaxed *and* aware state of mind. She found it easy to travel in this way and could actually *see-feel-sense* the physio-emotional patterns. The old charges of running and fighting were now spent and dormant. Though this micro-traveling through the body to encounter cellular charge, *and unhook from it,* may sound fanciful to most people, it is precisely what actually happens in the clearing process of many advanced forms of meditation.

How do we do this unhooking?

Jean found the analogy of the "delete" button on the computer keyboard an effective metaphor for the re-programming of her own nervous system. I know of many valid approaches to unhooking from cellular memory. Intent is one of the strongest interventions I know in release work. One could argue that drugs, herbs, homeopathic remedies, mantras, affirmations, crystals and needles re-enforce healing work as secondary forces or serve as placebos in the healing process. Common to healing traditions in all cultures is the exchange of some "prescription" between healer and patient/client. I told Jean that she could now visualize herself opening to the "good life" she deserved, that a healthy and relaxed cellular identity was being formed around her as she allowed herself to receive the love we all felt for her. Just as the old saying goes, "When the student is ready, the teacher appears," healing happens when one is ready for it.

Jean's unhealed wound became a fertile wound because her body's "dynamic tension" had reached the point of ripeness. Also true is that her ripeness accelerated her dynamic tension enough to generate a healing crisis. Karmically, Jean had exhausted the false benefits of maintaining her unhealed wounds. These false benefits occupy opposing walls between which an individual runs back and forth. On one wall is the adrenaline we get from our reactions to the wound as we bang up against it. On the other wall is the relationship we get with our spiritual depths as we lean against the wall in spiritual exhaustion and feel supported long enough to catch our breaths.

In a perverse way, a part of us gets energy and solace by reacting to the unhealed wound. If we heal, this part of us cannot exist any more. This threat of annihilation drives the desperate, wound-licking part of us to sabotage our best intentions. My job is to help reveal the nature of these wounds to the client's consciousness and let the natural laws of karma work unimpeded by self-sabotage. I cannot do this until there is a degree of spiritual fatigue. My work is to meet the saboteur and assuage its fears while simultaneously bringing to awareness the 'unconscious karmic forces', whatever their origin. When awareness meets these karmic forces, as happened in Jean's body on the table, a re-configuring of energetic patterns can result.

Never knowing why she was acting self-destructively, Jean's saboteur was having a field day running her life, while Jean's soul was, in part, still swimming in a sea of misery. In the "past life" of fighting for her life against overwhelming and terrifying circumstances, Jean fragmented out of necessity. At a core level, Jean's intense survival episode never resolved itself because she fragmented out of her experience before her physical death. Upon reading the rough draft of this story, Jean commented how she has tolerated people gnawing at her, feeling that there was no choice but to inevitably give in.

In this life she could never relax because she carried the seeds of her past fight for life. Because this dynamic usually operates below the conscious level, we keep looking for explanations for our life experience within the linear story of post-natal biography. In this way we miss the hidden door into the ongoing evolution of the life of our soul.

Within this context, the concept of "past life" is too linear. Soul-life, in my opinion, co-exists (simultaneously) in different bodies as karma plays out its propensities until there is resolution. Resolution means retrieving all our fragments. Once retrieved, resolution involves the placement of, and the gluing down of these fragments into the template of spiritual logos. And the glue is love in all its forms.

****

Upon returning home from doing bodywork in Hollywood with "the sophisticated people," I went to a local church where I was scheduled to deliver a talk on stillness and healing. Arriving into the sanctuary with jet lag and diesel fumes in my ears, I led the small group in a body-based meditation and discussion. It was a sweet experience and led me again to appreciate the rural community I live in and the simplicity of the work I do.

I asked everyone to breathe into their bodies and just notice any sensations, especially the thick, heavy and dense ones, or the cool, shaky and electric ones, or the hot tingly edge kinds. We meditated briefly and then I told them that the body stored unresolved emotional material for us until we were ready to fully digest the experiences. We discussed how grief, fear and anger were the basic emotions that those sensations referred to, respectively. I then shared with the group that the digestion of these emotional experiences involved the cultivation of detachment, faith and forgiveness, also respectively. With that, a lively discussion ensued in which we shared our experiences of the meditation.

Two women spoke of "stuff" in their shoulders; one woman who had never had children felt her left shoulder, on top, carrying the heavy load of her incomplete feelings about womanhood and the felt judgment about that, as if her ancestors were blaming her for not carrying their genes into the future. The other woman had these hot tingly feelings in the front right shoulder and, together, we explored, how the right arm was about manifesting our work in the world and the hot tingly sensations could be seen as her frustrations. This all made sense to her. Then a man quietly said that he had volunteered at a rest home for the elderly, playing music for them with his guitar, but that he had to stop because he felt physically ill every time he left. I told him that he was probably taking on their symptoms by leaving his own energy-field wide open. This often happens with new healing arts practitioners who have yet to learn about opening and closing the various doors in their body, and "grounding" themselves when they encounter other people, especially those in pain. It is so natural for us, when we are caring to take on the pain of others; but unless we know how to channel it, we usually burn out in our work with others and often do a disservice to ourselves.

I shared with this man how to close his second *chakra,* the energy center between the pubic bone and the solar plexus. By closing down here, a person can feel with another without feeling for them. A number of other themes were discussed and then we went into a longer meditation. I rang the bell and we opened our eyes; we then all sent loving energy to the rest of the community and said "good night." As I was walking to my car, an elderly woman came up to me with moist eyes and words of gratitude. She touched my arm to make her point and said: "you know, ever since I was twenty I've been talking to God; it's been over fifty years, I reckon, and tonight's the first time I've listened. I'm going to do more listening in my prayers now."

I drove home smiling about her revelation with two thoughts. One was how simple it all is and the other was about the murder in Los Angeles and the healing that took place.

About a year and a half ago, a woman came into my Los Angeles studio with a major problem. Her boyfriend was shot and killed in a drive-by shooting. She was in the passenger seat and could not see the fast moving incident as it transpired. All she remembers was hearing, "Hey Mister" and then the one gunshot. The next thing she knew, her lover and best friend fell back into the car dead, his head bleeding all over her lap.

Eve was incredibly beautiful; knockdown gorgeous in the Hollywood sense. She had a presence that was striking; but for all the visual charisma there was one glaring contradiction: she wasn't in her body. When I mentioned this to her, she readily agreed and I told her, after hearing of the murder that I thought I could help her. That was the good news. The bad news was that we would have to revisit the scene of the murder in slow, drag motion and stop at the cellular break-point where she left her body.

By the time Eve came to see me, she had been through a number of therapeutic interventions, all of them unsuccessful. She had no appetite, was deeply depressed, resigned and suicidal. Eve could not stop thinking and dreaming of her lost love, David. Eve's current boyfriend, Jason, had made this appointment for her with the hope that she could complete her grieving for David and show up for him.

Getting Eve back on earth in her body was my primary goal. The grief could only happen once she was embodied, and that would transpire organically in time. Apparently it took too long. After going together to a therapist, Jason and Eve decided to split up as friends and move on with their lives. They got back to their home and started packing up their respective stuff and, somewhere in the process, made love.

When Eve discovered she was pregnant, she told Jason, thinking it would probably lead to an abortion. When they met to discuss the whole situation, they both came to realize that there was something here that was *meant to be*. They saw Eve's pregnancy as their mysterious bonding. All of their earlier struggles dissipated and they moved forward in their lives with joy and anticipation. All was well in the kingdom until, as Eve's pregnancy continued, a shadow fell over her heart. She couldn't fall deeper into the joyous anticipation because, if she felt any deeper, she'd access her unresolved grief about David, that deep longing she had hidden away in her attempt to move on with her life.

When I met with them both in Los Angeles, all of their "stuff" was up. Little things turned into arguments. Jason was feeling very alienated in ways that went beyond the textbook stuff couples experience during pregnancy. Eve was afraid to really bond with him because, on some level, she was afraid that if she really gave herself to Jason, he would leave her just as her father had, and all the other men, and especially David. So Eve hunkered down into her remote inner cave while her body, now eight months ripe with destiny, heaved with the need for resolution. She laid on a bed in the massage room while I deeply massaged Jason's body and released blockages one by one.

All the pressure Jason was under trying to stay calm while all his instincts screamed to be heard, finally broke his heart wide open. Jason pleaded with Eve to show up for herself, for him and for their little boy, Scott. (They had done amniocentesis and had already named their child Scott.) Jason so wanted, so needed and so deserved to be loved by Eve that he cried from his guts "PLEASE LET ME LOVE YOU, let me share this journey with you. I want to be a good father; I will never abandon you or Scott." I brought Eve to the end of the table and showed her how to hold Jason's feet, as his body writhed in deep emotional agony. Tears streamed down Eve's face as the session ended in silence leaving us all tired and without much to say.

The next day Eve came for her private session. We had all come to understand that Eve needed to embrace the realities on the ground here and that the time was now. Jason had told her he thought that perhaps Scott's spirit was David coming back to be with her. So, in essence, Jason had given Eve his blessing to see *their* child as her lost love re-incarnated. Eve felt this to be true but was reluctant to fully accept it as TRUTH.

What do we need to make our myths real?

If I could read tea leaves or coffee grinds, or find a cosmic DNA lab test to administer, or perform a double blind psychic identity match— similar to the way the Tibetans recognize one of their re-incarnated lamas—then I could categorically tell Eve that Scott was David coming back to her. I lacked the authority or confidence to project that assumption as TRUTH. So I told Eve that if this belief allowed her to relax and feel free and loving toward Jason and Scott and their future life together, then this belief serves a valuable purpose and it is worth maintaining, at least for the present moment.

Eve's entire countenance softened. Eve was propped up by a half dozen pillows on the massage table to ease her low back and accommodate her huge belly. I worked the rib cage muscles upward and out with each exhale and also the low abdominal muscles at their attachments on the pelvis and pubic bone. Eve's whole abdominal cavity opened and became more alive, as her breath deepened. We both felt the baby repositioning himself into her expanding womb. It was beautiful. Light emanated from her face and after a few minutes, Eve opened her eyes and said "I can do this."

Eve lay there on the massage table, relaxed and glowing. I sat on a chair and together we reflected about her life and death saga with David, Jason, and now Scott. We explored how in every mother-son relationship, as in every father-daughter relationship as well, there are elemental yin-yang, *oedipal* and *electra* bonding forces of transference at work. I felt it imperative for Eve to see Scott as an individual, independent of her romantic and idealized relationship with David. She nodded in agreement. In this discussion we came to the mystery of life summed up simply as *Don't know*. We don't know...and that's okay.

How do we know what happens after death? Granted, we've heard enough about near-death experiences where people, after traveling through a tunnel, find a white light, are met by a dear friend or relative who has died before them and then, after re-considering their existence, they return to their death bed with amazing tales and a sweet book contract. The bottom line here is that this reality stuff remains a mystery and all the religious vernacular is dogmatic hearsay and not very interesting.

The mystery, on the other hand, is very interesting! And this is where Eve and I arrived at in our session. She embraced the reality that Scott was not David, that their souls had some connection with one another through both of their relationships with her, with the mystery and possibly with Jason too. We then discussed how her mothering of Scott would be an exercise in mindfulness in that she would be, through her sensitivity and awareness, nourishing, supportive and respectful of all the appropriate boundaries including the psychic dimensions of her very thoughts. My own thoughts on this subject took me into wondering whether Jason was sabotaging his own relationship with Eve by throwing out to Eve the possibility that Scott was David's soul re-incarnated. It all felt like a child chasing back waves on the seashore.

For Eve, transforming her perspective on Jason, David and Scott had to happen. Believing Scott and David to be of the same soul allowed Eve to stop grasping for a ghost. Now she could embody her life and carry her baby into this world. When Jason entered the work room toward the end of Eve's session, Eve looked at him with such love. It was as if a huge weather system had cleared, leaving a blue, blue sky. I showed Jason some pressure points to hold to ease Eve's cramps. Together we massaged Eve and then I left the room to give them some privacy. When I returned, they asked me to perform their wedding.

****

Footnotes:

1. Tetany: Classical medicine explains this phenomena of the stiffening of the fingers and arms as the "over-oxygenation with lowering of the alveolar carbon dioxide resulting in alkalosis and diminution of ionized calcium...it is looked upon as contraction against the movement of energy which is beyond the individual's tolerance." from *Man In The Trap,* by Elsworth Baker, M.D., (Avon Books copyright 1967). This state is not a casual massage experience and it is not recommended for exploration by persons unacquainted with the experience.

Dragon's Brew

Photo Tamyra Thomas

If a man wants to become a hero, the serpent must first become a dragon:

otherwise he will lack his proper enemy.

—Friedrich Nietzsche, *Human, All Too Human*

Through my work, I attempt to bring about wholeness for an individual by seeing into his true essence or soul. I look at the client's posture, his skin color, breathing rate, the quality of eye contact, and the pulses around his temples and neck. I remain aware of his energy field in general. I then look for what is missing in the picture or what is distorted about it. Is there soul loss? Perhaps there is a blank spot around his heart, or a reddish-orange haze over his sexual center or a feeling of static charge around his head or sweaty feet. It could be anything that signals that some distortion to wholeness exists.

I've always been amazed how relatively minor diseases become fatal for some people whereas, for others, serious life threatening ordeals can be transformed, leaving those people vital and empowered. Most people involved in their own healing process discover what has been called *cellular healing*; it refers to cellular resonance to our INTENTION to heal. My basic approach is to directly activate my client's soul capacity to self-heal. My intervention is not the healing; it is only a catalyst, clarifying and directing the intention to heal in my client.

I remember that day in a beginning massage class when one of our students was practicing a move on Kathy's scapula. She must have hit a loaded area because Kathy was crying by the time I came over to her table. Her lips were moving as if she was trying to say something, but no sound came out. When she finally could speak, she told us that the sensation-experience was exactly the way she had felt at age thirteen, when she could not speak up for herself right after she and her mother had moved into a new home. Kathy's mother remarried a very abusive alcoholic and Kathy gained two step-sisters and one step-brother who resented her and teased her. Because her mom was very co-dependent, Kathy felt unprotected. When her breasts developed, her shoulders rounded forward to hide from the world and from the ridicule she constantly endured. Kathy's mom thought a back brace would be necessary; this caused further humiliation. Kathy, in her attempt to push her shoulders back out to convey an aura of normalcy, developed huge knots in her shoulder blades, especially on her left side. I worked these knots until they softened. And with the softening, her breath deepened, her eyes cleared and something else, something very beautiful happened.

Kathy writes about it. "After Fred worked on my back and I could catch my breath and talk, he made me repeat a positive affirmation: 'I am a woman and I deserve dignity.' After repeating this and understanding it I went to the shower and sauna and started my period. My body was not going to forget my womanhood. Once my body released that cellular memory of my shaming and sense of defeat, I felt my spirit lift and to this day I walk with pride and settle for nothing less than respect. This freedom I've achieved could not be realized unless all three aspects of my being—body, mind and spirit—were addressed."

There are all kinds of blockages, implosions and explosions of soul. If we just get massaged, or just talk about our sad story or meditate away the pain of it all, nothing really transformational happens. The zealous materialism of our medical model and the attendant relationships between insurance companies and drug manufacturers all conspire to keep us wounded and addicted to the secular rituals of wound licking, symptom management and politically correct co-payments. So when we talk of real healing, we're looking at an individual decision to do *whatever it takes* to become responsible for her own life.

****

Linda had read Bob Taylor's book on incest and wanted to do some healing work with me. Preceding our first appointment, I had been examining the view point that, in varying degrees of subtlety, most men view women as objects to be controlled. The myth that rapists were always social deviants was quickly being eroded by news headlines of date rape. The other myth that was being exposed in op-ed pieces throughout the media was the myth that it is uncontrollable sexual urges that drive men to rape. "The facts are that it is the control over the woman that turns on the rapist."[1] I wondered if wires were crossed in the hypothalamus or if sexual feelings, and the vulnerability that the sexual encounter could generate, made many men rebel against their own vulnerability and react with aggression, instead of relate with sensual and respectful passion.

I was deeply in the midst of my own self examination. In therapy, I was reviewing my childhood years and combing my dreams and fantasies, all the time building what I believed would be a healthier relationship between my inner male and my inner female. I had come to embrace my own imperfections, forgiving my less skillful moments and graciously giving and receiving forgiveness for boundaries crossed. Linda walked into my San Francisco-Tiburon office innocently enough. We began our preliminary work with my teaching her how to feel into her breath and stay in her body when feelings came up. As I worked I became aware that something mysterious was surfacing and that all of my self work would be summoned and tested, and at moments be barely adequate to contain what was to be released.

A month later I requested a write up from Linda as a documentation of this journey. She writes:

"I'll never forget the day I discovered Jackie—June 28, 1992, the day of the Gay Pride Parade here in San Francisco. I had gone to the parade with my friend Martha, another incest survivor and a multiple (personality). After the actual parade was over, we made our way to the Civic Center to enjoy the festivities there. Crowds thronged the Center, and we held hands most of the time to keep from being separated as we jostled our way through. At one point a man bumped into me, rudely, knocking me out of the way. I turned on him with murderous rage. He slipped away into the crowd before I had a chance to throw a few obscenities his way. Later, when we were trying to get home, a man on the subway refused to move to let more people onto the train. Again I felt the murderous rage. Only this time I confronted my victim, firing a few four-letter epithets at him as the train pulled away. I felt out of control. The better part of me knew that picking fights with strangers could land me in trouble. I couldn't help myself. Martha and I talked briefly about my behavior; it made her uncomfortable. She sensed my rage and told me that it seemed almost vengeful rage to her. She said she could feel it."

"I could feel it, too: free-floating, nameless, primal. It had stalked me now for days. When I got home, I decided to try and write about it, to see if that would shake it. I became willing to go wherever the rage would take me in the writing. I had to. I wanted to be free. Anger and shame and despair came out onto the paper at first—the usual—but then I went into *memory*. I cannot describe to someone who hasn't gone through this process what the place of Memory feels like. Memories are a recognition and a horror all at once. What they reveal, no matter how unbelievable, comes in such devastating fashion that it must be believed. Memories both destroy and restore. They give back the past. They take away dreams."

Linda knew that sexual abuse had happened to *her* and that her father had done it. For a long time she knew no more than that. Later more memories came. She learned that he had molested her in the bathroom, that he had forced his penis into her face, and that maybe he had a knife in his hand and that he breathed alcohol into her face. Linda knew that much. From Jackie, she learned much more. As Linda wrote about her rage, the words poured out:

"No longer was I sitting at a desk in an apartment in San Francisco. I was back in the bathroom. I was two-and-a-half years old. Every detail came clear. In the place of Memory, horror overwhelmed me. Father came closer. I smelled him, fought him, hated him, in that memory. I was a little child fighting a monster. My legs shook so much I could barely stand. I knew he was going to kill me. I couldn't stand up. The words poured out faster than I could write them. I switched to the typewriter, and they tumbled out of their own accord, flung onto the page in a fit of white-hot rage. That's when Jackie came".

Linda had never known that another person was present when her father molested her; but she could not have survived the experience alone. She needed help. Linda split off from her body and found safety on the ceiling, next to the naked light bulb; only it wasn't Linda anymore on that ceiling. That person on the ceiling—a boy—was someone else. His name, she found out much later, was Jackie. He had enough detachment to record the experience. He played it back for Linda that night at the typewriter, furiously pounding out the words that hardly made sense.

Jackie saw Linda's father force her into the corner, next to the bathtub, and pull her back and slam her into the wall when she tried to crawl into the bathtub to get away from him. He saw Linda's father thrust a kitchen butter knife once into her vagina with a look of triumph on his face. He saw Linda's father shove his penis down her throat and then rape her three-year-old body with it.

"Jackie saved my life that night," Linda writes in her journal. "When my legs buckled under me and I could not get up out of my own mess, Jackie was strong for me. He was pure rage. Once he had told the details—while I howled and wept and shook in disbelief—he had only one thing to say: 'We'll make him pay. We're going to get him. He's going to pay. If we have to wait forever, he will pay. We know what to do. We will wait. We are hate. He will pay.'"

Jackie had plans. They were detailed, concrete, and superbly calculated for maximum revenge. Killing Linda's father wouldn't suffice. Jackie wanted to torture him, make him beg, make him suffer, to place his life in danger until he crawled and slobbered and pleaded—like he made Linda do. Nothing less would do.

Linda considered the possibility of carrying out such a plan. She needed very few things really: a gun, a bus ticket to Sacramento, a dull but serviceable knife, a moonlit night. She only lacked sufficient recklessness, which a few beers would easily provide; but Linda hadn't had a drink in over nine years, and staying clean and sober had been the highest priority in her life. She reflects: "My AA friends pointed out that my scheme would land me in prison, and that, again, I would pay the price for what my father did."

Jackie didn't get his revenge, but he stayed with Linda. Every time Linda saw the innocent eyes of a child, Jackie would murmur his hate: "How can she be so free?" Why does she get to have that? Let's rape her! Let's make her pay!" Linda distanced herself from children as much as she could, ashamed and afraid. Linda accepted that she would never have children; she was unfit. Linda ground her jaw in her sleep every night, suffered under an avalanche of shame and self-loathing, wallowed in self-pity and self-recrimination for carrying around such hatred, such murderous rage. Linda could not wreak revenge on her father, or on other children, so Linda took it out on herself. This was about the time Linda began to do bodywork with me. She told me all the facts just recorded plus the fact that there had been a younger sister involved in the situation who was no older than a year-and-a-half. In our first session, our major task was to build a trusting, working relationship, especially as a tactile phenomena. To reframe Linda's sensory cues to a man's touch is a huge undertaking by itself. It can often take years. But all too frequently all the good work fails to neutralize the power of the wound because the personality has become so identified with its armament, that to heal means to die. Although the death is metaphorical, the fear that there will be nothing to replace it can cause a flight from healing and catalyze yet another cycle of reactive surviving.

Prior to our work, Linda did just that. She would choose abusive men who treated her poorly. She and her partners would often seduce younger men and women to engage in sex that was demeaning. I listened to her history and wondered if there was really even a natural pleasure space in her brain circuitry. I asked Linda if she were orgasmic. She said that she could bring herself to orgasm but not experience release with a partner. She always felt disgusted with the temporary relief, and the whole process was effortful, filled with shame. When I asked if she employed any mental imagery to facilitate her arousal, she calmly said that one of her mental aides to achieving orgasm while masturbating was to imagine herself "taking a shit" simultaneously.

When I heard this, I immediately felt such sympathetic resonance to that little girl who had probably mastered toilet training so close to the time of her "bathroom war" scene, (as I came to think of it). During this first session, I also worked on Linda's jaw because she had a serious condition developing there from all the effort it took to keep Jackie under control. I found myself, during one of the more poignant physical releases, remembering Linda's sister, and asked: "So how's the family?" Linda and I both cracked up. "Oh, they're all fucked up. Terry, my sister, is on constant medication, lives with my mother and brother. She mutilates herself with cigarettes and sharp objects and is a mental out-patient and has spent periods of time hospitalized. She is not ready to receive the information I have recalled; I want to speak with her therapist or at least give some documentation to a file for her to have if something were to happen to me."

In the month between our first and second sessions, I was haunted by the energetics of Linda's story. Front page news was about concentration camps, mass rape and ethnic cleansing in Bosnia-Herzegovina. I felt enraged and realized how easy it would be to fixate there. I knew Linda would need to re-visit her original wound on a cellular memory level, with my support and with whatever internal support she had available to make this journey. I did not know of Jackie at this point.

In our second session I asked Linda if I could talk to the "voice of rage" in her. Immediately, a fully developed, very articulate and dead serious personality met me with eyes like I had never before seen this close up, except perhaps in a movie theater. Jackie explained to me that Linda kept only the bodily feelings of that fateful night her Father raped her but that he, Jackie, had assured her psychic (and maybe physical) survival by fragmenting off of Linda to keep the memories until Linda was powerful enough for him to reassociate with her.

Linda writes: "Jackie told Fred everything; my urge to harm children, my abortions, my demand for revenge, everything dark and evil. I writhed and stiffened on Fred's table under the power of the rage. I felt like an animal. The rage threatened to unleash itself. I wanted it gone. It was Jackie's rage, and he had a right to it, but it was killing me. Fred feared it, also. He pulled me back to myself. He told me the anger could be useful, that I could be motivated by joy and that joy came from passion and that passion came from will and that will came from anger. I could see that anger, properly harnessed, could become a powerful motivating force, but it must first be separated from the murderous rage. We accomplished this. Only time will tell the results."

I had unleashed a killer and Linda could clearly see her relationship with Jackie within the heightened awareness that we had inducted into our work space. Several times, it appeared that the walls of my work room shrank and expanded as Jackie's energy undulated through Linda's body; all the while I maintained contact with the body that was both of theirs to share. Linda reflects upon her meeting with Jackie and the dialogue I facilitated between the two of them: "I talked to Jackie, directly, and in doing so discovered our bond. We had made a pact. Jackie promised to protect me and strengthen me and keep me going. He also promised that when the time was ripe we would have our revenge. He would be my energy. I would be his brain. Together we survived. I realized that Jackie was steadfast, loyal, faithful. He never forgot our promise. He never forgot to wait for a chance for revenge. He waited almost thirty years. He would have waited thirty lifetimes. I loved him for that. I loved and honored and respected him for never giving up, for always being there for me, for giving me the strength to go on when I would have fallen by the wayside, even if the strength he gave me was only hate. It was all he had, but he gave it to me freely. He never let the anger go. He never forgot, even though I did."

The armament and reactivity which characterized Linda's relationship with Jackie was being revisited, big time, right before all of our eyes at such a rapid pace, I could hardly track the energetics and content fast enough. It was as if we had "poured water and stirred" and out of the ingredients came this sudden monstrous force that breathed fires of urgency out its nostrils—a real dragon. Our work space became transformed into a karmic "holding cell." We had accomplished something very significant but also quite tenuous and explosive. We revisited the tension space of the unhealed wound and found here some fresh opportunities along with Jackie who was the total personification of primal rage.

Linda was always relatively powerless...until now. As a child her rage had gone underground and secondary characteristics formed within her personality to insulate her profound vulnerability. All of the examples of psychological defense were visited by Linda as she grew up; she was quite numb in crucial places in her life. The incest scenes continued in other forms throughout her childhood. Linda used alcohol and other substances to keep her memories blurred and her emotions sufficiently muted so that she would not explode and hurt others or herself. She did not want to divulge to herself, or the world, the terrible truth that festered just below her conscious mind.

Now, on my work table, after years of sobriety and therapy and meditation, Linda's *kairos* moment (destiny point in Greek) had arrived. Face to face with her inner protector and completely vulnerable to all that she was feeling, a cloud of intimate truth had descended. "I sobbed as I spoke to him," Linda remembers, "for I realized he had always been with me. He never failed me. Everyone around me had failed me, because of their own inadequacies, or later because I never gave them a chance, but Jackie hung on. He wanted his revenge. We had made a deal, a very important, life saving deal. Now, just as the time came ripe and I had the strength and energy and physical resources to carry out my revenge, I had to renege. I couldn't let Jackie have his revenge. Yet until he did have it, he couldn't leave me alone. Our deal bound him."

Jackie was a disowned self in Linda's life for over thirty years. Linda had created many primary selves which functioned variously to satisfy her requirements in her life, but she was much too integrated to be viewed as a multiple personality. She could be a successful student or a reliable worker but when it came to personal relationships, which depend on our abilities to step out of roles and just be, Linda found that she had a great many defense mechanisms that operated to keep her disowned energies submerged and other people at a safe distance.

Linda couldn't relax. If her defenses softened, if she relaxed her boundaries in relationship, her true psychic terrain would be suddenly revealed in stark relief like the rocky seashore at low tide. Then everything Linda had been running from, or hiding from, or reacting to all of her life would explode and leave messy fragments everywhere between heaven and hell.

This does happen to some people, and each of the fragments, in a clinical sense, can be thought of as psychic aspects of a multiple personality. Jackie was one of the homeless personality forces wandering in Linda's psyche. I realized that Jackie could "come home" into Linda's life and help her if the two of them could renegotiate their "deal." My job was to broker this *deal*.

Linda cried out: "Jackie never wanted to hurt me, he wanted to help and protect me." Linda writes: "Jackie was utterly, single-mindedly devoted. He lived to help me survive, and I had to persuade him with that motivation in mind. Our mutual survival was at stake. I told him that we had to make a new deal, a deal cut not in the darkness of desperation but sealed willingly in the light, for the sake of the light. A new deal. A light deal. Jackie only wanted to help. I asked him to promise not to hurt my father. I asked him to promise not to hurt any children. He agreed. He didn't want to hurt anybody. He only wanted to keep his end of the bargain. Now I needed him to help me combat my shame. I needed his strength and power."

As I write about Linda's journey into the transformational healing zone, my eyes are puffy with unshed tears. I feel so much of the power behind the mystery that Buddha called suffering, and I feel so much awe and humility in the face of God's redemption. I do this work alone; sometimes it has been lonely. But there are times when I feel the truth of Christ's words to his disciples when they asked Jesus anxiously: "What shall we do when you are gone?" and Jesus replied "When two or more are gathered in my name, I am present." In healing work we always co-create with universal intelligence to make a bridge between that which is wounded and the source of universal intelligence that is always utterly whole. That afternoon, in my work studio, I did not feel alone.

Linda, in her own way, had decided to fully heal, to fully forgive her father, in time, and to fully embrace the light. She spoke to Jackie as a loving parent in ways she was never shown. Linda recalls: "I told him we would be a lioness—strong, powerful, beautiful, not menacing, but not a victim. We could do it together. I told him that if we followed through on our original deal that we were just like Father. We were working in the dark, just as he did. We had given him enough. Now we needed to give to ourselves, to make something new out of the violation we had suffered."

"I wish I could repeat everything I said to Jackie, because they were some of the sincerest words I have ever spoken," Linda writes in her journal. "Only fragments come back now, and the beauty of the moment eludes me. I wish so much to preserve it. I want so much for it to be true, for Jackie and me to be friends, to recover this lost part of myself."

At the end of this two-hour session, I knew Linda had, with the help of grace and her own inner guidance, tapped into her own divine birth right and reclaimed it for herself, finally and completely. To reinforce her new found freedom and awareness I insisted that she go home, take a hot bath and write about our work together this day. No words can lay claim to the power that came through the cosmos during our session.

Reflection in healing work is essential if we are to build functional lives on the ashes of our wounded stories. "Where was your mother in all this?" I asked Linda.

Where was my mother?

Linda wrote about this much after our intitial work:

"How could something like this happen and she not know? I have turned this question over in my mind for years. Obviously my father was much given to violence. He beat my mother frequently—once when she was eight months pregnant and I know of at least one occasion where he knocked her unconscious. My mother admits this much. Under such circumstances, how could she possibly protect me? She, too, was a victim.

It would be so simple if my mother and I could sit down together and frankly discuss the rape, comparing details, filling in the gaps for each other. Her denial prevents such a conversation. I am sure my mother knew something had happened. How much she actually knew, I may never discover. For with the truth comes the admission that she did not protect, was not, by her lights, a good mother. So, she denies the incest—vehemently, passionately, desperately. She needs her denial in order to survive, just as I need the truth to heal.

I cannot gain my psychic integrity at the expense of hers, and I know I may never know what role she played. What I do know is that she fixed my meals, sewed my clothes, taught me the names of colors and how to count to 100. Another woman might have left, drank herself into oblivion, or abused me herself. I have heard such stories. For what my mother could do, I am grateful. We survived separately, yet together.

I told Linda, at the start of our work, we would be revisiting her most wounded place but that she would not be alone this time. After she left, I changed the sheets, lit some sage in the room and had a glass of water. My next client arrived and situated himself on the work table. I entered the room and found a peace and spiritual calm that has never left me since that day.

When we face our shadows directly we bring light into our lives. When we react in fear, we add more darkness and the shadow grows more ominous. Who lives in the shadow, anyway, but those parts of ourselves which are afraid to come out. These inner selves, or sub-personalities of our identities, hunger for unity with our larger selves just as we hunger for the unity of being integrated within our soul and within the universal oneness in which our souls abide.

In her reflection, after three more sessions, Linda writes: "So much of the work involves recovering the lost pieces. Who can mend the shattered vase without picking up every last one of the shards and fitting them back together? My personality had always been a makeshift one: fragments of other people's expectations bound haphazardly together with the glue of rage and defiance. I was driven by the pure will to survive, even if I had to survive only as a fragment, as a shattered vase. I had never had a chance to be me. There was too much to hide. I had to hide Jackie, and the rape, and the shame, and the playfulness (lest we be caught off guard). Now maybe I could become new, could let the glue of defiance fall away to reveal the forgotten parts of myself that had never breathed the living air nor seen the light of day. Maybe, with a lot of help, I could reassemble those parts into the human being God made, a human being who did not have to hide, or apologize, or shrink away from others in shame. To be what God made, not what my father made. To be free."

From the moment Linda grasped how her anger, once separated from her rage (Jackie), could be useful to her building of that new life, she entered a transformational process. Her insights became a passport out of reactivity. She no longer identifies herself as a victim or even as a survivor but increasingly sees herself as a full person growing into greater health and empowerment.

Prior to her work with me, and continuing through our work together, Linda regularly saw a psychotherapist who had the compassion and skillful means to assist her in many ways. Whenever I work closely with someone engaged in depth healing, I make sure that they are actively supported by a professional psychologist or psychiatrist. Linda came to work with me only seven times in five years. She did not originally discover her story with me but came to my table to process it. She came to release or transform her bodily memories or to access a part of herself that was without a voice but was, nevertheless, embodied.

In this work I do at the edge, I do not have the luxury of some typical buffers common to psychotherapy. Touching the flesh of another human being who is engaged in the active release of deep and complex psycho-emotive states of consciousness is close, challenging work. What is most challenging is the need to balance objectivity with what is happening with the client, in real time, with what comes up for you, as the practitioner, while you are doing the work. Relationship with this energetic presentation engages many human qualities such as humor, loving advocacy and passion—to name a few. This natural engagement with a client's process should not be confused with, what psychologists call, "counter-transference"—the therapist's projections back onto the client.

I generally work in some relationship with my client's psychologist, even if it only involves knowing that my client is working with someone professionally in this way; this alleviates any concerns. In bodywork, the actual work teaches a practitioner how to ground and energetically discern what is his energy and what is his client's energy or he quickly burns out. It's similar to how an apprentice in the electrician trade learns about his field by getting shocked. When ground and discernment are present, a unique visceral resonance with the client's body is achieved and much deep healing work transpires. This is what happened with Linda and me. Her organic expression of primal and profound rage, grief, joy and empathy set in motion a transformation of her heart and also affected me and my view of healing.

Linda's journey and process has helped me to relinquish the relatively minor abuses that have characterized parts of my life and to forgive others and to forgive myself and to be open to receive forgiveness from others, regardless of whether or not any communication has occurred. I am astounded, sometimes, when I see some people hold onto abuses in their lives because it feels so good to punish ex-spouses, parents and acquaintances with their unforgiving attitude. We do more harm to ourselves by not forgiving another than we ever do to that perpetrator in our lives by withholding our forgiveness.

Vietnamese Zen Master Thich Nhat Hahn, who lost his entire family during the Vietnam war, brings the spirit of compassion and renewal and transformation to his teachings. He writes: "When the sun rises in the sky, it projects its light on the vegetation. That is all the sun needs to do to help. The green color that is seen in the vegetation is the work of the sun.

The sun does the work of transformation. Imagine a flower in the early morning—a tulip or a lotus. The sun shines on the flower. It is not satisfied with going around the flower. It makes every effort to penetrate it. The sunshine penetrates the flower, either in the form of particles or in the form of waves. The flower may still resist and stay closed for a while. But if the sun persists in shining for two or three hours, a transformation will occur. The flower will have to open itself to show its heart to the sun."

"Our anger is a kind of flower," he continues "and our mindfulness is the sun continuing to shine upon it. Do not be impatient. The very first moment you shine your awareness on it, there is already some transformation within your anger."

Thich Nhat Hahn asks us not to dwell on our suffering but *to look deeply into it and, in so doing, we will come to know what to do and what not to do to transform our heart and change our present situation.* He says: "My brothers and sisters and their babies who died during the war in Vietnam have now been reborn into flowers. We have to harvest these flowers. When we learn from our own suffering, then all the flowers will be smiling at us."[2]

****

Footnotes

1 Putting an end to rape, men's violence by Tomas Hakanson, Press Democrat Editorial Santa Rosa, CA 2/10/93

2 Transforming Our Suffering by Thich Nhat Hanh, Parabola, The Magazine of Myth and Tradition, February 1993

Zen Gardens

Many years ago, I took it upon myself to build a Japanese garden. I researched the traditions and applications and let the land speak to me. Lately, I've had little time to work on the stream bed leading to the tea house site, so I've contented myself with raking the leaves and sitting by the ponds. Whenever I am in this garden, reflections play with me in delightful and mysterious ways—sunlight shines through the Manzanita branches and leaves cast shadows upon the water in which multi-colored koi swim lazily in the late afternoon. The koi break the platinum surface of the water, sending undulating thrusts of mirrored sunlight back through the same manzanita, causing shimmering shadows onto the statue of Kwan Yin, the goddess of healing, mercy and compassion in Buddhist cosmology.

Kwan Yin is frequently used in artistic renderings of the oriental healing arts. My students and clients frequent this zen garden to be quiet and alone with her or to share an intimate conversation with another person in her presence. The statue of Kwan Yin is poised under a muscular and twisted, wind swept manzanita tree. I am convinced that if the Japanese had manzanita, they would have never elevated the bonsai to its mythic proportion. In Zen gardens, the "wind swept" appearance is appreciated because it expresses the elegant simplicity of character and artistry that nature sculpts. And, for me, nowhere is this artistry more evident than in the curves of the manzanita that embrace Kwan Yin. I also see this same artistry at work in human bodies, all sculpted by the forces of each individual life.

Year into years, I need to wash the gravel filtration bed in this koi pond. It's a big messy project; no one can do it for me because of the idiosyncrasies I have installed into the project, (not by design, mind you). Recently, I found myself knee deep in years of mellowing fish shit, with hoses, pumps, and dozens of freaked out koi. Alone, I go about my business, pumping the mess out onto a hillside that is grateful to receive such good nourishment.

I contributed to this hillside years ago when I gave it plenty of my own "waste" while digging this mountain's rocky stubbornness, laced with these enigmatic manzanita roots. I was younger then and much angrier—still reacting to that itchy egoic grain of sand. All that old garbage I had been carrying must have had dreams of becoming fertile compost one day.

While cleaning the gravel, I began to appreciate just how much human suffering, mine and others, I've composted in my practice. Like the dry, stubborn and rocky hillside, feeling gratitude for the underwater fecundity cast upon it, I too felt grateful for all the rich opportunities that have been thrust upon me in my work.

Cleaning this pond reminds me, dear reader, of our original sitting down together—when you first began this book and I first began to write it. Throughout this sharing, I realize, I've always been in this water-garden with you—with all these shadows and ripples—reflecting upon the variations of the aphorism: "when life gives you lemons, make lemonade." It allows "what is" to be real, and it is optimistic about the possibilities for happiness.

Without the lemons, there is no lemonade; without suffering there is no capacity to realize compassion. Compassion is the flower that grows in the rocky hillsides of our suffering; it allows us to meet life with strength and joy. Compassion also allows us to meet another human being in the dimensions that lie between what is happening and what is being learned on a soul level, especially when there's a mess to address.

Tom came to see me for lower back problems, a calcified neck and a mental attitude which included suicidal pre-dispositions; he was also on Lithium, a mood elevating drug. He could not access any of his depressive feelings that ordinarily governed his life when the drug was operative. Tom had been in all kinds of therapy and was especially sharp at following my mind as I worked with him. He was one of those really tough cookies that therapists work with to better hone their skills. Tom had never really explored healing bodywork, done breathing exercises, or hung out in feeling states in silence for extended periods of time. He makes his living as a heavy equipment operator. In 1961 and 1962, Tom was in Laos and Cambodia killing people as a counter-insurgency paratrooper before the Vietnam War heated up. This was the secret war we are only hearing about now. Tom is a big man who occupies the entire massage table with his six foot two inch frame. He had a desire to heal, but so much habit to overcome, and a body that was like a rusted Sherman Tank.

From his journal he writes: "It is difficult to talk about suicidal depression when I am not in it. When depressed I am so identified with the despair and wanting out that no other reality is available. In present time that reality is only a fuzzy memory. The memory is not unlike losing one's personality in deep Samadhi, (a rarefied meditative state), and then returning to personal consciousness knowing significant experiences took place, but remembering only a few lights and vague images. Very few of my early memories are conscious for me. Kneeling for long periods in Catholic mass, and school, with my back and knees aching, is a predominant memory. It was painful. Coming home from grammar school, lying on my bed, I would think 'why bother changing into play clothes, there is nothing to look forward to.'"

Tom's body stiffened year by year along with his feelings. He would fall over backwards if he tried to sit with crossed legs. By his late teens he could not touch his toes with his knees straight and his mental attitude was equally constricted. His body felt like a prison he was sentenced to for life. His incarceration and depression were two sides of the same coin.

There were, however, irregular periods in which Tom's symptoms and dark moods abated. This gave him just enough relief and a glimpse into another way of being that, when his psychic weather changed again, he would usually feel even more angry and bitter because of the tease.

In one of these extended periods of freedom, Tom was working full time as a fireman and seeing a psychiatrist four days a week. He owned and operated a janitorial service with several employees while completing a full course load of Zoology, Anthropology, Trigonometry, English and Botany in college. And he bought and managed four resort properties and courted a girl and got married. This lasted six months and then he crashed. Tom writes, "I quit the fire department, school, the janitorial service, and lay in bed for several weeks, fearing I was going bankrupt while my new wife ran the resorts."

"After another thirty years of this kind of cycle, my periods of depression got longer, my body more bloated and my joints stiffer than ever. I was unwilling to start a project of more than a few days duration for fear I could not complete it. I was driving my fifth wife crazy and it was November again, the month of my birth and the fading light of the sun. My emotions began to dip dangerously low, and then I found Fred."

"Working with Fred is not Samadhi. Through my Lithium induced haze, Fred would rub and probe my body parts. Amazingly, they would show signs of life, as the exo-armor started to give way to tingling and some relief from chronic pain. With all his weight and might Fred would gouge, elbow, jump, walk on and torque my limbs and trunk to get at some real, or imagined, flow in the blockage. With all this he never went beyond my acceptance or my tolerance level. Sometimes he was gentle and just vibed me."

I had to go to some physical extremes to get Tom's body to respond. To do this requires a great deal of focus and skill, but I'm careful not to do the physical work with an agenda for a specific mental or emotional response from my client. I just allow the body to present itself organically, moment to moment. Tom sensed this non-agenda and began to trust his experience. But when I asked him to access his anger, he said that he couldn't, although his anger would explode inappropriately in his life, which was the expressed motivation for coming to see me in the first place. The Lithium prevented him from feeling his feelings in a real way; I told him that I couldn't do transformational work with him if he wasn't here to do the work and that he needed to check with his psychiatrist about dropping his prescription medicine.

Tom wrote his impressions of our work together, as do most of my clients,

as part of the healing protocol we do. "I took to this stuff like a Cape Buf-
falo that wants to be tamed but has eons of genetics and karma saying 'the
cyclical suffering is safer'. I am intuitive more than analytical. I knew this
work was positively changing me. Knowing the shrinks say you must take
lithium for the rest of your life to avoid a life ending depression, I stopped
taking the meds in the hope of being able to learn to be with the sensations
in my body and the feelings it had stored."

By our fourth session, Tom quit his Lithium, announcing that he had not
felt so limber since he was ten years of age; he also wanted to talk about
his sexuality with his wife. Over the next three sessions, I worked his body
in the low back, legs, groin and belly. A great deal of early life history
became unveiled, especially his shame and fear of being vulnerable with
women. Tom, I learned, was slapped across the face as a small boy very
hard and often by his mother. Now things were getting very interesting.

In progressive sessions, when we opened his body, his face grew sadder
and sadder. I thought how silly his Lithium grin used to look compared
to the real life sad face which was showing itself now. I told Tom that I
needed his commitment to stay with the process when feelings came up
for him, from now on.

As the layers of armament began to peel away, both of us got to meet,
unexpectedly, an overwhelmed little boy. Like a deer caught in the head-
lights, little Tommy was stuck in *frozen flight*. Working with Tom's breath
and massaging his belly elicited deep moans and feelings of profound
magnitude. Tom shut down to these powerful forces, but he did not want
to stop our work. Tom stopped the breathing exercises in one session, just
as he was accessing some powerful memory. I felt certain that he was
beaten quite severely by his mother, at about the time he was last feeling
this intensity. No wonder he chose not to feel the "tension space" as potentially creative.

Tom could not go on further until he had integrated what he had learned.
He was accessing his power in our work, but that had gotten him into
trouble as a boy, with his mother. He was also accessing his vulnerability,
and that made him feel he might lose control and be taken advantage of by
his wife. He did not want to put on more armament because he knew that
would not provide him with any more security. He also did not want to
take off any more armament because that would make him too vulnerable
to the old feelings of suicide and depression.

This is a delicate time for anyone in a transformational period in his life.
Tom could not move forward or backward. Nor did he want to go up

above his experience, through transcendent meditation or with drugs. Tom was experiencing his "existential tension" for the first time while being supported. He stood at the precipice of a new life feeling both terrified and in awe of the fact that he could actually choose the kind of life he wanted.

Tom's fearful personality wanted to remain in "The Reactivity State" and explore himself there. I spoke to this part of Tom and told "him" that it is very hard to explore yourself there, because the whole point of living in the reactive zone is to escape the discomfort of the universal tension. I told him that The Flow State experience is not always pleasant but that "going with the flow" is real and that it is the only place where real healing and real loving can happen.

The realization that we have choice makes us responsible, and Tom wanted to be responsible for his life more than anything. It's not easy, however, to make this transition from reacting to responding without support and without a vision of an authentic and congruent way of life.

For many of us, the childhood bonding patterns with our parents, and our observations of how our parents treated each other, have so distorted our perceptions of relationship that we go into automatic pilot in intimate relationships. My work with Tom was about supporting him unconditionally in exploring a new vision of his life where he could show up and be vulnerable and be loved. Old childhood memories of shaming from his mother surfaced right alongside war memories of jungle parachute drops through clouds of bullets. Tom went with the deeper breathing with less and less resistance, and his body loosened up as a result.

By relaxing his armament, Tom gained energy to use for his family life; and Little Tommy had a second chance to have a happy childhood. Tom exercised occasionally and learned to pace himself more moderately. In his journal, Tom summarizes his transformational journey with this entry:

"I have had a couple of long bouts with depression in the last several months. There is a more 'let it be, this too shall pass' quality to all my mood swings. They don't *have me*; I observe them. The flip side to the constant threat of self-destruction was always the apparent fight for survival when I was not depressed. Now I live with the certainty that the major threats to my life are inner and that living with my own natural rhythms makes the world a safer place to be in."

"Living more in the present, I respond to my three-year-old's antics with joy in my heart. My wife is relaxed, knowing I am here for the long haul; we are planning and working together for our family. As I write this, gratitude is swirling through me, for in a sense I am being born anew each time I disengage from past reactivity, forgive myself and go on with my day."

****

In my practice I help people transform their catastrophes into a deeper understanding about life. If they're lucky, wisdom is gained in the process, and they can dance on the graves of their sad old movies just as Lao Tzu invites us to do. We must stop our resistance to suffering if we're ever to get this dance right. When we stop resisting, an alchemy begins. Like a trim tab on the rudder of a huge ocean liner, a subtle energetic shift in awareness leverages the complete revolution of the human mind. *What is this powerful awareness that turns a human mind away from resisting and reacting toward allowing and accepting? What aspect of consciousness transforms our pain from curses into blessings?*

It is Grace.

It is Grace in the beginning and Grace in the end. And without Grace we are, as Aldous Huxley stated, utterly helpless. Some Christians might believe I am describing a version of being "born again". But the experience is beyond the religious vernacular. If it were as simple as accepting Christ as savior or Buddha as refuge then we could just take our vows, surrender our lives to the order and never look deeper into the mystery, because others before us have already done that and packaged the mystery into neat and tidy paradigms. How convenient. How disappointing.

The mystery is the mystery is the mystery. One of the things I appreciate about the Jewish cosmology is that it leaves open the individual's relationship to the divine. The basic bias is that there are ways to live a life on earth, but as far as your relationship with the realms beyond this world, "You figure it out." It is this freedom to explore the mystery, of course, that accounts for the ten thousand and one interpretations and explanations of why, if you have ten Jews discussing something, you'll get eleven opinions.

Until we surrender to the mystery without any convenient buffer, we separate ourselves from direct participation with our lives, as Krishnamurti so often observed. We can die with all the support of loving family, friends and community and still not feel engaged with the essence of existence itself.

There is a flow that transcends the world of appearances and up until now, only mystics have described it. What I love about touching flesh with reverence for the mystery is that I feel my own merging with the oceanic while remaining still a single droplet. I can feel the singularity of my experience simultaneous to the experience of another droplet of conscious-ness. And that which is oceanic in me recognizes that which is oceanic in another human being; and, for a time, duality ceases; there is no loneli-ness, for everything is resonant with Grace.

****

Zoe has been a client and friend of mine for many years, and we have explored spiritual realms together. There is a lot of fun in Zoe, and things in her life went along just fine, until....she called me, one night, with the news that she was pregnant and very confused. She shares her story: "I wish I could be sure that the telling of this story is truthful. That the expe-rience will invoke wisdom and relieve suffering for somebody, somewhere maybe. So I will stay here, in my heart, and tell you the story, just as it happened.

"Waking up in the morning I knew the feeling. Three beautiful children have been born to us over the last four years, and the familiar taste and feel of morning sickness was easily recognizable. How can I do justice to the overwhelming sea of sadness and confusion that enveloped me. We had not planned for this child and we did not want this child. Or so we thought.

"Certainly others have had more reason to feel stressed—financial prob-lems, marital or physical problems, or even twins! None of these realities tormented my world. Yet I felt crowded out emotionally, and couldn't imagine adding a fourth child to an already full life. Perhaps I could imag-ine it, and I knew I didn't want it.

"Abortion. A nightmarish experience no matter how professionally it is handled. As in many of the most personal and profound experiences life provides, such as birth and death, the truth of the experience is never clearly discussed. Sometimes simply not discussed. Abortion is a very ac-cessible solution, often described as 'relatively painless'. The truth of it is never clearly expressed as the voluntary sucking of a child out of your womb. No one had ever explained the experience to me in these graphic terms. Perhaps if they had I could have anticipated the sadness to follow. It was a true death in the family. The death of a spirit child, very much alive inside of me.

"Certainly this can be disputed. Some would say the embryo is only a con-figuration of cells at that point. If I hadn't been sure before the abortion, (I was one month pregnant), I felt an absolute sureness afterwards; the being exists! It is no group of *selfless* cells. The spark is alive. And I had killed my own child.

"In realizing this after the fact I felt ashamed. Ashamed to have made a decision about existing spirit with so little understanding of the preciousness of life. My head had been in the clouds, and now I saw the black earth of life. How uninformed I was on the value of every moment.

"One can only reflect until the experience can be placed, and then the graveyard of the past must be left behind. My reflection up until meeting with Fred was tortuous and full of self blame. Through bodywork and conscious guided reflection, I was able to meet the being, (my baby), and send my deepest love to the one that died to teach me the value of life. Equally important, I was able to forgive myself.

"The loss, like every loss, is a gain. Moments stand still for me now, when I am mindful. I see my children, and am not so often overwhelmed by the abundance of need, but rather feel an abundance of love. While I shall never be able to reflect on my action as having been a "good decision," a deepening from within allows me to appreciate and cherish the being whose sole [soul] purpose was to come teach me the preciousness of this which we all share."

Life and death pull us into the mystery. If we don't resist, a humility delivers to us the consciousness of gratitude, Grace's child. Zoe's story illustrates how gratitude allows the soul its passport into our wounded territory and sets the stage for a spiritual alchemy to ensue. Prior to her abortion, Zoe had a profound spiritual initiation in India. The abortion experience, as painful as it was, grounded Zoe's beautifully expansive heart and mind in ways that could not have occurred without this suffering. She titled her reflection: *White Cloud/Black Earth*.

****

There is an old saying about love, "Love me or hate me, but please... don't ignore me."

It would be easier to heal the human problem of alienation if it only took an authentic spiritual practice, and that alone. The reality is that we live in physical bodies that also have needs. Many human beings never received loving touch in their infancy, and most people have not received enough.

All the transcendence in the world looks like more escapism to someone who only needs to be held and affirmed that they are really HERE! We need loving touch because it is the glue that holds our lives together. Loving physical contact in the mother child relationship at birth is called bonding. The lack of bonding can produce feelings of extreme anxiety as many scientific studies have shown with primates who were deprived of tactile contact. Sense deprivation leads to "failure to thrive" and in healing work we see this as sorrow. This is the suffering that arises from some death, an abuse, combat stress, an abortion, an illness, or from any number of other traumas.

Though much healing goes on in ashrams, resulting from the universal love that is generated through meditation, many wounded people leave their spiritual retreats still wounded—and even disoriented. Bliss does not assuage the alienation that characterizes much of our sensate temporal life.

In fact, it has recently been observed by many cutting edge philosopher healers that most healing approaches take patients to the far shore, but don't escort them off the boat. I believe that the same can be said for many spiritual approaches as well. All healing work will be limited if the body is not included.

I came to understand how important the ordinary life of the five senses was when a client, M, was referred to work with me by a psychologist who was wise enough to know that talk therapy could not contact the source of her despair. Though M had experienced much blissful union with the divine in her spiritual practice, something always remained unhealed.

Through my work with M, I came to appreciate the profound simplicity of human bonding and how skilled loving touch can cut right through all of a person's denial, repression, and transcendence and take a person right to her very edge.

M met me when she was on the edge, the edge between her old life (as a driven professional) and the new one she was born to live, (as a healer). M had taken herself to the very edge of her metaphorical cliff but was frozen there, still needing to jump off to reach her new ground. She was poised but did not have confidence in her new wings. She was out of her cocoon but weighted down by ancient cellular memories.

"I wouldn't go over the edge on my own", M writes, "because I thought it would kill me if I jumped alone. I didn't fully understand why, but I knew that in order to move into the life I came here to live, I would need someone with me in a way I had never experienced before, and I had known this literally as far back as I can remember.

"When I met Fred I had done so much deep inner work and solo surviving that I had come to love taking care of myself. I can't stand 'fixers'; I was beyond the needy and clinging stages, and I was asking for help at a level most people don't know about, a level I barely knew how to verbalize. The depth of my journey and search for help seemed to frighten people, so I still had no trust, even after fifteen years of intelligent, caring, intensive therapy that had taught me a great deal about myself and my journey.

This was a successful therapy, even by my own strict standards. I came to the surface of my black pit in this therapy, having done a tremendous amount of healing and growing. The message I got was 'You're OK now", but I knew I wasn't OK yet. I was still living outside my own life, discon-nected from my own energy source. The message I got was 'You're not alone (even though you think you are)', but I knew at one level I was still profoundly alone; I wasn't bonded."

Over the course of our sessions, I saw and understood that M needed to bond with a friendly universe before she could leap into her new life. In one pivotal session, we began to clear the way for M. I had been watching her intently throughout this particular session, which was an emotional one without much insight or resolution of feelings for M. I was very frustrated because she was unable to give me any verbal cues as to where her con-sciousness was focused. As I have learned to do in situations where I don't know what is happening, I quietly dropped all thought and merged with M's energy field. I breathed at the pace she was breathing for a little while.

When I opened my eyes I saw this totally confused and fearful newborn infant living in M's adult body. It was so clear; and I spontaneously began to massage her in the way I learned to massage infants when my son Seth, was born.[1]

"Fred touched me in a way I've never been touched before", M reflects, "then he quietly got on the table with me and stroked the whole front of my torso with long, reassuring moves.

It wasn't medical touch and it wasn't sexual touch. It wasn't even mas-sage. Perhaps it was the way you would caress a baby. I had never experi-enced it before but I knew immediately *that touch* was what I needed. In that instant I was seen and met at my roots. In that instant I began to bond.

"I was awed and in tears of relief and in another plane of consciousness all at once. Fred's contact with me was very clear. There was no question of violating boundaries, or of improprieties because we both knew what I was in need of and we both had sufficient grounding. So I didn't bond to

Fred. I began to bond to life. Finally I could trust that someone was capable of meeting me because Fred did. He met me openly and willingly where no one had been willing to come before, at an infant level where I had never been touched. And he came without ulterior motives, fears, or demands; he came as he should, simply to be there for someone making this passage.

"Practitioners need to understand this. People *need* this level of touch to join the human race, and it is possible to learn to give it without being caught in the web of transference and counter-transference. This need has to be recognized, accepted, and in some way openly loved by the practitioner. This need is part of the modern human condition and must be met."

Working with M at this level was very rewarding and challenging. Perhaps this level of work between people cannot truly occur until mid-life, when our imperfections have been wrestled with enough, and we no longer are trying to prove something to ourselves or trying to tuck other people's discomfort into tidy and convenient boxes. When I saw this scared little baby in M, my inner parent instinctively knew what needed to happen, and the natural unfoldment was very human and very simple.

For so long M's needs were bypassed by competent professionals who, with good intentions, would say the customary, "Well you should have gotten over that by now. You have yourself, you know. You can hold *you*." To all those who have ever offered such words to the unbonded, M would say: "We already know this more deeply than anyone. We're all we've ever had, and if it weren't for our own selves, many of us would have died as infants. We wouldn't be alive on your tables today courageously asking to be met on this very deep level. We're not asking to be bonded to you; we're asking for help in bonding to the universe so we can meet our lives."

This work of meeting another human being at this intimate level is also, ironically, impersonal; for the journey—through the body's need for loving containment—goes directly into the universal need for inclusion within the mystery. This kind of healing work somewhat mitigates the issues of transference because there is a "selflessness," (*annata*), that permeates the exchange. If "no one" is present *doing* the healing work, the work of healing happens for the individual because the practitioner is "empty" of the egoic trappings that characterize the conventional therapeutic relationship.

Here is the background on M. She is the third child of three, the only female child of a woman who didn't want children, and most of all, didn't want a female child. When she was born, her mother had a cold and was told by her doctors to leave M in the hospital until she was well again. The result of her following this advice was that M had no physical contact with her mother for the first few weeks of her life, and very little for the rest of her childhood and early adulthood. M was rarely spoken to or touched.

She was born with a cyst on her shoulder, about the size of a plum. This was removed when she was six months old, leaving a scar at the base of her neck that is over two inches long. M has had memories of her feet and hands tied down so that she wouldn't rip her bandages. She had memories of the male doctors poking at the cyst. She remembers being tied to the bed and trying to squirm away and literally "back out" of the bed. This squirming movement, a real cellular memory, spontaneously occurred in one of our sessions when I worked near the scar on her neck and it cued me to the primacy of the event. Later I found out that M's mother did not visit her at the hospital at all.

The memories of her "escape movements" afforded M an explanation for the flattening of her energy field at her back, the rotated left sacral-iliac joint and the scoliosis of her upper spine. M had a flashback, in one of our sessions, to the surgeon cutting her neck. In the moment of the memory, she realized that the anesthesia had not yet taken hold or it hadn't been used; this helped to explain M's hypersensitivity to doctor's needles, blood tests, and physical pain in general. In cranio-sacral therapy sessions, M has had memories of her birth that include a recollection of being dropped on her head. These cellular memories exist at unconscious levels and form the matrix of our perception, even though they may remain unconscious.

M's childhood was characterized by fear and non-support. She basically raised herself with her father as silent mentor. She was always insecure. M was not beaten or sexually molested but she was emotionally abused by her mother. The old saying about love, "Love me or hate me, but please... don't ignore me," truly applies in this case and describes a kind of wound I call existential ambiguity (To be or not to be, I'm not sure). Don't ignore me; because if you don't see me, I'm not sure I'm here. M's mom would alternate in her behavior between neglect and dumping. M remembers "I never knew when I'd get "hit" emotionally. I never knew if I would have a place to be the next day because the lack of contact and support was so complete that I felt myself constantly at risk. I was afraid in my home, with my family.

"I put my real self away, piece by piece, to protect, until I could come out. My intelligence was the only part of me that received substantial recognition, so I moved into my head. I was told so often that I was too small or weak to do physical things that I didn't discover my considerable physical strength for twenty-five years."

Through great discipline, will, and aspiration, M brushed up against her magnificence and sweet brilliance often enough to survive quite well (thank you very much), but she could not sustain this contact with her flow state. She writes: "A large part of the reason I hadn't been able to feel fulfilled by life, to be in my own state of flow (which for me is being in my energy body), is that I had ceased to believe that anyone would ever be there. This is not about dependency; this is about being part of the whole. Every human being needs to learn to find his own center and ground, *and* every human being needs to have some contact, something coming in, to feel a part of the universe and to continue to be able to care for and heal himself."

Working with M, I saw myself, my own loneliness as spiritual teacher, with my own unique and different twists. I felt her pain and knew that it was no longer just psychological, historical or even karmic at this point in her development. Her pain was like a heavy psychic weight, not unlike a dead fetus being carried to term.

M arrived at one session with tears of despair crying, "I can't do anymore." M could not go on feeling separate. She had proven a million times over that she could take care of herself, but she couldn't find her connection to life without bonding. She writes, "People need positive bonding. We need it to come into our ability to connect so we can return to the flow of our lives, to be in our energy, and to be one with the universe. If we remain outside the universe unbonded, never becoming part of the whole, I believe we die -- perhaps not always in body, but certainly in spirit, and then our gifts are never given."

This separation from the whole is what spiritual light assuages. Light cures the separation, but there is a difference between a cure and a healing. Unless there is loving bonding with other human beings, we will continue to suffer our separation in the deepest of places and rely on spirit to endlessly dress the wound that requires only the presence of loving touch to fully heal. We need each other.

M had been frustrated, in her fifteen years of therapeutic exploration, by the fact that so few people are equipped with smarts and heart to work through the limitations of language. Actually, most damage to a wounded person occuring before the age of two is filled with psychic anxiety and is, by its inherent nature, non-verbal. Healing is different than therapy in many ways, and it transcends many of the common boundary

WOUNDS INTO BLESSINGS

and identification issues with which most therapists and patients struggle. In significant ways, a merging occurs between the practitioner and patient. In mature practitioners, this merging is both intimate and impersonal. There are times, however, when distinctions get blurred and then all we have is self-discipline and grounding.

This work of meeting people at the edge is definitely not for every massage therapist or psychologist. Healing at core levels involves deep trust, deep integrity, and deep faith. This is not arrived at casually. In every learning about trust and faith, there is always a history of some trial and error, some betrayal, some missed opportunity. This is life. From great suffering, learning opportunities arise, teaching us the important lessons we often could not know otherwise.

M's suffering may not appear as great as Bob's or Esther's, but what difference does it really make. Suffering is suffering and comparisons are futile. For M, her woundedness, in large measure, was not so much about what was done to her but rather what didn't happen, what was lacking. This lack of connection is a wound and is at the root of human alienation; it is the foundation of our *existential ambiguity*.

People really suffer from the pervasive feeling of not really wanting to be here. We are a society that is deeply frightened of intimacy and the body. In these times we need to embrace one another in new ways that are safe and respectful. Healing touch is the means by which bonding unites us to one another, and more importantly, *through* one another to *that which holds us all*.

Albert Einstein, who spent his entire adult life looking for a unified field theory that would explain the wholeness of everything, was quoted on his deathbed as saying: "There is only one question, 'Is the universe friendly?' "

Healing is the work of co-creating with wholeness, or the field of unity, to make this universe friendly. And loving touch is what the Creator has given us to gather and bond together the lost parts of our souls that have been existing outside our very beings, separate from our refuge in unity.

"Bonding happens through touch—of the body, of the soul," M reflects; "both have to be met. Fred met me at my soul through touch, preparing me for my leap off my cliff edge. Then he jumped with me." Time and again I jumped with M until finally she came to feel that we were landing in that friendly universe. More importantly, she came to trust that we would land there again on the next jump. I stayed with M through some very difficult sessions as she attempted to explain feelings and desires for which she had no words. I learned to hang out with a baby that was living on some astral plane, unable and unwilling to enter the zone of "ordinary earth life."

M's trust in me grew the longer I hung out with her in non-judgmental silence. I waited and gently held her and, from time to time, slowly spoke to this astral baby. I told her that she could land here, on Earth, into my arms, and that I would hold her. Like a cosmic bird, exhausted from a transgalactic crossing, M landed on me like a branch, like the olive branch emerging after the "flood" in the story of Noah's ark. The epoch flood, the cosmic catastrophe, was finally over for M. She shook uncontrollably for almost an hour. When she finally stabilized, and found her ability to verbalize, M passionately recounted to me the frustration of her healing journey.

So many kind and caring professionals were unable to meet her, were not strong enough to hold a space for her to experience her feelings for fear that they would negatively affect them. This repetitive experience had left M in despair, despite all the kindness and caring. Much too frequently, M's most basic needs were dismissed by her therapist or healer, leaving much healing work unrealized.

There is great healing and freedom in the experience of feeling our feelings, especially the dark, dangerous and forbidden ones, without fearing that we will die because we have accessed these states of turmoil. Perhaps the practitioners M saw were not clear enough within themselves to avoid taking on their client's issues. Perhaps they were not strong enough to witness real, honest and outraged death-wishes, without being crushed, defensive or apologetic for the tribulations of existence.

To die but not to perish is to be eternal.

Depth healing is scary work and hard to find. Perhaps, in this culture, we have simply not matured enough to hold the big questions gracefully. Many therapists and healers are simply not skilled enough to maintain their ground and resist having their own existential issues triggered when the issues get this deep. Perhaps most therapy and healing work is just aimed at social adjustment to the collective notions of normalcy or at erasing symptoms of anxiety. As Lao Tzu reminds us, "Only ten percent of humanity is truly able to dance with existence."

Most people are asleep, and for good reason. Initial awakenings are touch stones to our suffering. These initial impressions are so potent and primal that most people recoil as soon as they contact their beings at these depths. After the initial shock of awareness subsides, it is very clear that there *is work* to do. Gurdjieff, a spiritual teacher of *the work*, once said that once awake, a person cannot go back to sleep; therefore, one never wants to take on the karma of having awakened a sleeping person. The phrase "ignorance is bliss," alludes to this challenge. When one awakens from his ignorance, he is ready to work and co-create a better world, but if he does not choose to awaken or if he is not ripe to be awakened from without, he will not have the resources to do the work from within nor the ability to fall back to sleep. So, he suffers without the means to transform his suffering.

In contrast, M had already been doing inner "work" for so many years that the issues and feelings she brought to our sessions were multi-dimensional and well informed. She once described to me her vision of our work to-gether as two people having a mental arm wrestling match on the edge of a cliff. In this process, she writes, "We get a feel for each other's energy waves and positioning in the moment; during this time we operate on a level of energetic union where we create something akin to heat seeking missiles that suddenly take off and fire right into the deep places I need to have opened up. We do the work together, which in my mind erases the dangers of transference; Fred doesn't save me, he travels with me. This allows touch at a soul level, and it allows me to receive the contact and support I need to heal my deepest wounds, the ones that exist beyond language.

"In one session this happened while I was trying to express a prever-bal feeling state...I couldn't find words. I didn't know what part of my body needed work, I only knew I was in early pain that was blocking my growth. Fred just kept talking to me. He has a way of using very common-place language in the form of simple, non-threatening, non-academic ques-tions or statements, to reach people. It is such simple communication that one can't help but be touched. It is one of his ways of seeing people; it is one form of the heat seeking missile. He asked, as he changed sides of the table, 'Are you frightened of this major life change you're going through?' I said very slowly, still in control, that I supposed I was. I remember him saying that he would be worried about me if I weren't frightened; I re-member being very silent and feeling myself regress at the speed of light as if an energy vortex was pulling me back in time.

"I remember Fred leaning over at an impossible angle to twist his head and make eye contact with me (another form of heat seeking missile) as I lay on my side. In that moment I began to feel, for the first time in my life, my childhood fear. Experiencing the true quality and extent of the emotional state I literally lived in, day after day from infancy into early adulthood, I became my three year old sub-personality, still valiantly trying to carry me through the terror to some place of safety.

"I was already dissolving into the sobbing of deep release as Fred said that my three year old didn't have to save me again, that my three year old had already taken on more responsibility than she ever should have had to take on, and that she could rest now. I had never felt this fear before, and I had never cried these tears before. These tears, and the feeling experience of the fear, were part of the dangerous air space below my cliff edge that I hadn't wanted to move through.

"It was vital that I allow myself to feel this fear fully. Fred knew this and knew how to hold the space for me to experience all of this. I don't think he cares about knowing what he'll find in a session; I don't think he knew what we were heading for in that moment, but he was willing to accept whatever showed up, without judgment, and he was willing to step off that edge with me."

Over time, I have grown into meeting people at their edges. Perhaps it is a karmic debt or a karmic gift I brought with me into this life. Nevertheless, it is also a skill I have learned, and the learning process has had a suffering of its own for me. In retrospect, I think the issue of infertility in my early twenties, grabbed me and shook me awake. Wrestling with mortality and loneliness was good training. It allowed me to understand where others needed to be met; it helped me practice the wisdom in the saying, "Let go, and give it to God."

Throughout our journey together, we have been cherishing the inner work of human beings. We have stepped into spaces of people's lives where there has been a wounded blockage to the natural flow of the life force energy. We have seen how the healing pathway travels *through* the wound, and not around, under, or above it. Healing takes courage; there are no short cuts, and it requires that we learn how to be vulnerable. For all these reasons and more, people turn away from their healings, but the laws of nature are inexorable and cyclical, and they will bring to us fresh opportunities, in another season, to embrace our healing. "To everything there is a season, and a time to every purpose under the heavens...a time to be born, and a time to die...a time to kill, and a time to heal."[2] These endless opportunities to heal and integrate are the gifts of spirit, from a compassionate universe.

M's story underscores the profound miss that occurs in many primary relationships. Our work together was about her being truly seen. In exploring her huge, indefinable, and highly charged emotions and memories, I struggled to comprehend where she was when she regressed into her terrorized infancy. She could not offer me any verbal cues, maps or guidance. We confronted each other and learned from one another, and developed a language of nuance and vibration, and a true healing transpired.

What is true healing?

True healing is the healing that works. The healing modality is often irrelevant. What matters most is the life-positive connection between the person who is healing and her higher self. As a practitioner, being a conduit for this communication is the primary service I can provide, and this is what I provided for M, nothing less, nothing more. Sometimes, being a screen for the healing person's process to be projected upon is effective. There are countless ways we can support another person's healing; sometimes the sweet simplicity of *just* being present, witnessing and allowing what needs to happen to happen is most appropriate. Midwifing a person's self-birth is one of the noblest adventures I know.

Human beings need each other. We all need bonding, and we need to integrate from the separate stations of conditioned consciousness we inhabit, but seldom find rest within ourselves. Before transformation, the conditioned mind is opposed to the body—we have abandoned our flesh or we have lost ourselves in it. In the transformation, we realize that the universe is here, in our bodies, teaching truth and breathing light.

We are in the midst of an evolutionary phenomena; and, as in all periods of fundamental change, this period will be seen, historically, as the time of mass spiritual transformation and renaissance. Thirty thousand years ago the new humans roamed the same plains as the Neanderthals. The new humans of today are presently awakening to deep and instinctual karmic stimuli that are magnetizing their energies toward joy and service. Their engagement in personal and collective healing work of all kinds will ground the life of transcendence and make possible a heaven on earth.

Years ago, I gave my mother a refrigerator art magnet with these words: "God couldn't be everywhere, so he created mothers." All of my life I felt, within myself, the nurturing qualities of the feminine, but I was denied access to these feelings due to my childhood conditioning. In doing healing work, the feminine became available to me. In a way M's mother could not access her feminine even though she inhabited a woman's body. Today I would rewrite the aphorism to read: "God couldn't be everywhere, so he created healers."

Healers are the "new mothers and fathers" of the next millennium. They will be the co-creators of the twenty-first century and beyond, helping all whom they touch to take personal responsibility for their own evolution, thus setting in motion a transformational wave that will beneficially affect our collective destiny.

****

Awareness Exercise No. 3

Take 20-30 minutes of quiet sitting time. Read slowly.

Your tension will lead you into your wound... and to the healing that will set you free.

Remember the Chinese straw finger catchment? Once your fingers were inserted, and the harder you pulled out or away, the more the apparatus tightened. You actually had to move inward to be released. Appreciate that the tension you feel in your body or heart will only become greater when you try to pull away from it. Therefore, discover now where you feel this tension in your body...by allowing your witness to scan through your body for any sensations or feelings of tension.

Breathe deeply and let your mind quiet down. Smile. Appreciate that everything is okay just the way it is right now. Go deeper now into the part of your body that feels like something is being held there. Just observe whatever is happening.

The body's organs are related to specific muscles and organs and these systems of energy and information are organized through neuro-electric meridians. The ancient Chinese Medical model, *The Law of Five Elements*, tells us that Grief is experienced in the Lungs and in the Large Intestines, which are also related to the feeling of being *stuck*. These are the places of letting go.

Do you need to let go?

Do your lungs feel congested? Do they feel heavy? Are you constipated? Do you run from this heavy congestion, this withholding, by staying angry? Just allow yourself to sense your lungs and colon.

Do your lungs hold onto an old unhealed wound? Do you deserve to take up space, to breathe, to have a life?

Give yourself permission to take in life.

Breathe in this permission into your lungs and colon.

Grief teaches us to say "Good-Bye." In saying "good bye," we have room to say "hello." By exhaling fully, we inhale fully. If we cannot bear closure, we will sometimes linger in agitation and anger. We stop with our anger when we realize that *it's* all over.

Grief can be over the loss of something precious, or familiar; and it can also be over the loss of something we never had or experienced. In midlife, people come to realize that certain dreams they once held dear will not happen in this life. Saying good-bye to these unrealized dreams is an important threshold on life's journey.

Disarmament, taking away the tension, involves a complete re-evaluation of one's personal relationship with all of the buffers that mute tensions and keep suffering conveniently managed. One of the most insidious buffers to the work of personal disarmament is the socializing we do with people who are victims, and with people who hold us in a negative light. Concluding dysfunctional relationships is a powerful and important affirmation to make to oneself on the healing path. Grief is the appropriate feeling to carry this process to a healthy conclusion.

Grief can heal if we allow ourselves to go into it. By having compassion for ourselves, we can finally feel self-less. From this self-less perception we perceive with detachment and can realize that we can now let go. When judgments cease, there is no need for defense.

Allow an outgrown relationship to arise in your mind. Say good-bye and allow your body to let this relationship go. Bless all the memories and remain with the emptiness for some time.

Fear is about reclaiming lost faith. Sometimes we feel the fear of other people, not realizing that it isn't our own fear. The kidneys and bladder monitor and express Fear Energy; the bladder is also about *irritation*. We can be "pissed off" but afraid to express it; this energy which had the heat of anger can cool into ice (Think of steaming water placed in the freezer).

Fear is complex and can degenerate into paranoia or it can be elevated into healthy excitement or even spiritual awe.

Sit for ten minutes...

Allow your awareness to rest gently wherever in your body you feel afraid, scared, confused or alone. If you can sink deeper into the core of this feeling you may encounter a part of you that lives unafraid.

Faith heals fear.

I ask my clients to meditate on a time in their lives when they felt fearless. Sometimes they can go to a memory when they were confident and safe. (In some cases, they may have no memory of a safe and confident time, in which case I invite them to create in their mind a spirit sanctuary where they are safe and confident.) Then, with their spiritual sanctuary safety, they can fast forward to the day they lost that confidence, and from then on, lived with anxiety, nervousness and mental preoccupations.

Take ten minutes and allow a memory to surface from your bodymind when your faith felt vital to you.

Bring that feeling to the sensed time when you lost faith.

Is it time to reclaim your lost faith? What will it take?

Stay with the feeling.

There is no goal to this awareness exercise.

There is only the healing process. I have faith in this process. Do you?

Fear can include shame, judgment and criticism. If we were raised with conditional love, then the fear was that unless we were perfect, or at least measured up, we might not be loved. We had to earn love. Subconsciously we feared that our inadequacy would cause us banishment from the hearts of those on whom we depended.

Allow yourself to just sit quietly now. Love yourself unconditionally. Allow your tension to take you into a deeper place until—like the finger catchment—you can find a calming, in your faith, that can allow things to loosen up.

Anger/Rage is about realizing that it is time to forgive. The Liver and Gallbladder are the organs of Anger/Rage energy; gall bladder is also about *resentment*. Anger is about righteous indignation, about territory transgressed, about boundary being respected. It is healthy and restores dignity. Rage is the fermentation of this healthy instinct. It is highly reactive. It is the shocked over-reaction of many pleasers who have disowned their instinctual truths.

Cultivating love and peace transforms anger. Forgiveness is the healing. We will meet this theme again and again, in our lives, in this book and in every moment we feel overwhelmed by life.

For now, allow your mind and heart to come to the place in your body-mind where you feel heat and itchy angst. Feel your desire to forgive someone or yourself. Is there resistance to this? Is punishment still necessary? Who is suffering the most from your resistance to forgiving?

Breathe deeper now into the tension and ask yourself, "Is this pride?" Let your tension guide you deeper to the root of this anger.

It's all okay. We can still be angry… until we are ready to not be angry anymore. Are you angry with God? That's okay too. We forgive when we're ready and we are only ready when our anger burns through our heart. Maybe your anger is still serving you. Is there something that your anger needs to accomplish still? Sit with these reflections, and your breath.

Betrayal is the emotion of combined Grief, Rage and Fear. The healing requires an understanding that karmic forces are a mystery, often impersonal, and that we are never abandoned by God. The healing for betrayal requires us to cultivate awareness and trust in the mystery. When we are set up by other people in our various life roles … business, relations of the heart and body, and even in the affairs of spiritual community, we are brought into the learning equation for a reason.

It may be that karma is being balanced. There are very few accidents. If our involvements with others have generated feelings of abandonment and rage, we may need to cultivate our faith and forgiveness themes. Sometimes we just need to forgive ourselves for allowing the situation that has wounded us to even happen in the first place. We didn't know at the time or we knew but acted in ignorance. Now we know, and we can place "right boundaries" around our lives and move on, free from the suffering of holding onto an old dead story.

Allow yourself to examine any dead stories.

Are you ready to bury them?

What kind of juice is an "old betrayal" still giving you?

Breathe into the tension deeper and see if there might be a deeper abiding you, that you can trust again.

See this abiding within you and sit with this part of you.

Are you trustworthy now?

All these healings: faith, forgiveness, detachment and trust, are gifts that a compassionate universe provides to all who are in pain. Through these healings, wounds dissolve and compassion for one's self, and for others, grows. When one person is wounded, it affects the condition of all people just as the wounded condition of society affects each person's capacity to heal. This same interconnectedness operates conversely — in the positive — when healing happens for one person or when social groups become more peaceful. Through the increased commitment of more people to the practices of meditation and loving touch, the healing path widens and our hearts become free.

****

Footnotes:

1. Frederick LeBoyer's book *Loving Touch* is an overview of infant massage. A variation of this approach is what I did with M.

2. From *Ecclesiastes*, in The Old Testament.

This Very Edge

"When the sun comes back again,

I will never let my arms

tire holding it up there."

—Erica Jacoby—a relative and a Holocaust survivor

And it was at that age.....Poetry arrived

In search of me. I don't know where

it came from, from winter or a river.

I don't know how or when,

no, they were not voices, they were not

words, nor silence,

but from a street I was summoned,

from the branches of night,

abruptly from the others,

among violent fires

or returning alone,

there I was without a face

and it touched me.

—Pablo Neruda

The twenty-first century is here. I don't know how long I'll be sculpting flesh. Maybe this book will sell and I can support myself writing. Maybe the old man in me will just serve tea in the garden to the mid-life me when I finish playing piano.

Many years have passed since my work with Linda and Jackie. Students have come and gone and have set up their healing arts practices, like so many seeds taken by the wind. My father's been long dead. My son, Seth will be driving any day—(Oh my God) and even today another client drove the twisting coastal highway into our driveway with his tight fearful body asking for release. This man got out of his car and noticed two huge dragons near the parking area at the top of the shallow ravine that I've terraced into an amphitheater. It's hard to miss these dragons whom I've named Zoruba and Oceana respectively after myself and Cheryl.

Oceana is about sixteen feet from head to tail; she's iridescent green with porcelain teeth and beaten copper wings; she holds a brass ball in her left claw—symbolizing creation. Abalone shells and crystals adorn her beasts and, of course, she breathes two feet of fire, thanks to a propane canister buried near her. She's from Heaven; she sits elegantly in a grounded posture inviting all comers to Dragon Breath Theater for a spiritual program of meditation, yog a and high level discourse.

Zoruba, in contrast is from Chicago. His widespread wings are enclosing for his earth landing. He claws the ground with his left front claw and holds a trombone in his right—almost like a spear. All twenty-one writhing feet of his body is burnt orange, black, red and ochre and he has beaten copper spikes emanating from his spine. Embedded in his skin is electroplated stained glass, granite and crystals. Zoruba reeks of class and danger and he breathes fire out of both his mouth and a two foot horn coming out of the top of his head. His mantra is "PARTY!"

I can tell you how it happened but you'd just think that this is what happens when grown men with too much time on their hands hit mid-life. That's sort of not true. Being Jewish and living in the country posed a unique set of circumstances for us regarding the decision to have a Bar Mitzvah for Seth. We didn't go to synagogue, though we lit candles and celebrated various holidays in the home; so it seemed silly to make a traditional thing happen when our life style was anything but traditional. And our spiritual orientation is, well, more personal. Yet I kept hearing my ancestors in my head saying, "Do It!" So when Cheryl asked who was going to drive Seth to Hebrew lessons and where were we going to hold the event, I said that we'd have Mickey the local Hebrew teacher, come and tutor him at the house, and I'd build a synagogue in the ravine.

I must have rented *Field of Dreams* at the video store around then, because I went out to the ravine and began to pick ax the beginnings of a series of roughed out terraces thinking, "Build it and they'll come." All I needed to build this outdoor synagogue was a few thousand rocks and about fifteen hundred board feet of redwood for a deck. And so I saved every penny for these raw materials.

The ground swallowed up truck load after truck load. I was working extra days in bodywork so I could buy more rocks. I was obsessed—again. This was the sand box I never had. Believe me, I did quite a bit of analysis on myself while moving these heavy suckers. Some of the boulders were the size of my head, but others were about the size of four times my chest; now we're talking at least a hundred tons of this igneous stuff hauled in from the other side of the San Andreas fault line.

My rock moving buddy, Matt, helped me a lot, especially with the big ones. And one day the initial project was complete enough to house a couple hundred people for a Bar Mitzvah service. The event went incredibly well. Seth was accompanied by our dog Star, who came onto the deck to lay by Seth's feet as he recited his Torah reading. Great food was followed by dancing in the meadow. Four days later we all took off for China for a month; Seth toured with his friend Andy and a guide while Cheryl and I taught our work in Hong Kong.

It's an old Jewish custom to send thirteen year old boys to foreign countries and leave them there for some time to see how well they adapt. Anyway, we returned home to this huge ravine transformed into a spiritual sanctuary. All it needed was a few more rocks and a theme. Now in China, there are dragons in the architecture, in the entryways and in the gardens. Also I remembered the dragon tattoo on Bob's body but, more significantly, I felt myself to be dragon energy.

One afternoon while working in my rock pile, I felt the deep trunk muscles of my lower back give in while I was trying, for the third time, to elegantly fit a large boulder into a pre-defined space. I walked away, in pain, from the rock wall I was building and did some reverse stretching to unkink my muscles. While lying on the ground and breathing through my pain, I felt three of my lower lumbar vertebrae pop back into place.

The relief was immediate but I found no interest in moving. Lying there and looking at the latest rock wall I could only smile with wonderment at this incredible project. I was alone this particular day, and as I lay there looking at the face of these rocks and imagining how old and how secure they must feel in this world of constant change, I shape-shifted into one of those rocks and felt just as insecure in geological time as my body felt in biological time.

Like blood pumping through my heart, volcanic magma formed the life force at my core. Out from behind the huge rock pile, just then, I saw what looked like smoke.

I sat up and saw, to my amazement, a twenty foot dragon. Whoa!

Now I had read about vision quests and I've had my hallucinations, but this was real. I slowly got up, discovering my body to be quite okay, and walked over to the rock pile, only to discover that there was nothing unusual except for a strange, pungent odor permeating the earth clinging to the rocks. Oddly calm, I returned to my boulder—my intimate wrestling partner. I turned it around, saw the possibility and immediately placed it, perfectly wedding both sides into the vertical wall that supported the horizontal terrace. All around me were horizontal terraces descending into the ravine. This was not an oriental hillside garden, this was DRAGONS' BREATH THEATRE—a four hundred and fifty seat amphitheater that was birthing itself with me as its human midwife.

In Chinese medicine, as I mentioned, there is The Law of Five Elements that explains the inter-relationships between the organs of the body and the seasons, the senses, sounds, the time of the day and the continuity of flow and transformation within this earthly realm. Fire, earth, metal, water and wood are the elements, and they all feed and balance one another in a healthy organism or system—fire melts metal which chops wood that penetrates the earth which contains water that extinguishes fire which melts metal and so on and so forth. This cyclical and regenerating flow is what healers tap into as they work, whether they are conscious of it or not. This flow is called Chi or Ki. In the modern vernacular we can call it "the force" as in, "May the Force Be With You!"

When this flow is blocked, excesses and deficiencies occur. Stagnation occurs upstream from the dam while starvation and lack occur downstream from the blockage. In bodies I see this situation constantly. Anger, for example, is an emotional energy of the liver and resentment is related to the gall bladder. When nice people block these natural feelings from arising, they stagnate and ferment into rage which becomes violent, whereas expressed anger reasserts dignity.

When I began my work with this new client, who finally dragged himself away from the dragons, I looked into his masked over face and studied his hard belly and crossed arms. He knew that he knew what happened to him but that it was not conscious...yet. He had already failed twice in suicide attempts which ended badly enough, and had wasted many years in avoidance and numbed out consciousness. He was desperate now to get to the other side of his wound—whatever it was—desperate enough to see me and be touched in ways that would illicit all his issues of rage and betrayal. Halfway into the session I smelled the pungent smell of dragon and flashed back to the remaining sessions with Linda and Jackie, and with that recall, I pushed my thumbs into his diaphragm and began the disarmament process.

As we know, denial is a form of pain management. There are individuals who have been abused, or who have been abusers, who cannot find their memories, and then find, unexpectedly out of nowhere, a real killer within them has been unleashed. The rehabilitation of Jackie is a story of meeting darkness with "the force" and prevailing for a noble cause. Bad things happen, but they can be restructured by acknowledging them and working with them.

The acts of Hitler's Nazi Germany opposed the natural laws of life and human dignity. His evil power required a courageous and overwhelming response by warriors who were willing to defend human dignity. The right use of force is a delicate and core issue in transformation, difficult for philosophical pacifists to look at sometimes. Stephen R. Schwartz says: "We can approach an enemy with undeviating love and raise the sword with compassion."[1]

When asked if one could bring the sword down with compassion, Schwartz's answer is: "I think so. I think that's rare, though, and one has to be very cautious about making that into a position. Gandhi said that if you keep yourself from raising the sword out of fear, then it's better to raise the sword. Nonviolence is total fearlessness."[2] Does this suggest that when we, out of fear, allow injustice to prevail, we are encouraging violence by not standing up to the darkness and evil? I think so. For every action, both taken and not taken, there is a karmic field that is generated. This is the way it is.

"To everything there is a season, and a time to every purpose under the heaven: a time to be born, and a time to die...a time to kill and a time to heal." —Ecclesiastes 3:1

Most people never thought that they would ever see, in their life times, the Israelis and Palestinians sign a peace accord with each other. Violence, hatred and historical prejudice had characterized the relationship between these people for so long that it seemed the past would always win the day.

Instead, on a beautiful day in September of 1993, these two old enemies shook hands. How this happened will be analyzed for generations, but we have a strong clue why in the sad and solemn voice of the Israeli Prime Minister, Yitzhak Rabin: "Enough of blood and tears. Enough."

When is enough enough?

As we shall see, later in this chapter, Jackie and Linda were tied to the world just like all of us, and all peace loving people experienced a part of them die when Yitzhak Rabin was assassinated by a Jewish fanatic for his efforts to end the war and bloodletting.

The dispute between the Israelis and the Palestinians extends back into the very roots of history and, therefore, fundamentally changes not only the political and psychological maps of the Mideast, but also the inner maps of everyone. If they can say "Enough to suffering," then anyone can! This event caused many people to take pause and reflect upon their own inner wars. This struggle to make the flow state of peace more desirable than the stimulating rush of conflict is an ongoing exercise for humanity and for each of us individually. And if Linda, as an individual, could say "enough", I thought, then anyone could truly heal.

The weightiness of our personal histories and all of our habituated reactions is seldom overcome by good luck alone; it usually takes self-discipline and a steadfast will to hold the vision of a better life. When people hope for better times, they often wish themselves *good luck*, but it is usually with a sense of fatalism too passive to magnetize the kind of vital energy upon which "new lives" are built upon. Sometimes healing energy comes to us and other times we have to dig in and work hard for it, especially when wounds go deep.

Until we have faced our inner enemies, we cannot truly embrace nonviolence; we are still living in separation and are thus run by fear at some level. When I see the shadow side or evil in my work, I don't judge it, but instead witness it closely and do nothing very carefully. If I have disowned my own capacity for darkness to such an extent that I have completely identified with *the light*, then I will be untrustworthy to all those still struggling with their fears and rages and feelings of betrayal. In retrospect, I realize that I could never have helped Jackie cross over his bridge if, on some level I, too, didn't have to cross my own.

The dynamic tension of living within duality with a spirit of oneness with everything, including the shadow, and the capacity for evil, is a place I visit from time to time in my work at the edge. Embracing the spirit of non-violence while totally respecting the violent urge in another person has been a great teaching for me, and I find the paradox central to our human capacity to grow beyond conflict. A ferry ship captain, in a Buddhist allegorical teaching, sees -- in his omniscience -- a robber's murderous intention to kill all of his passengers. Because he realizes that this act would torment the murderer for ages, and cause great pain to the families of his passengers, the captain kills the robber with compassion to prevent the greater karmic suffering. And still the Captain takes on karma. There is responsibility for everything.

****

After many months of integration time, Linda made an appointment to continue her healing journey. After her arrival, I realized the respite had softened my antenna as to who was *really* here. About a half hour into our session, Linda dropped down into her wounded child. As soon as I beheld her in my eyes, my heart opened, like never before. She was only a toddler, and I saw the knife that her father thrust into her little vagina. I almost bolted but was more frozen than revolted. The freeze thawed very quickly, but I was so confused by the mix of strong emotions that I was speechless and unable to do anything but hold her heart and solar plexus. Compassion interpenetrated feelings of rage and grief. I also felt compassion for the deep woundedness of Linda's father, the perpetrator. I had met others, like him, in my work, unpredictable and cruel personality fragments that *take over* a person's life for a time. These fragments are sometimes energies that a person is unable to integrate. And sometimes, they are a distinctly separate consciousness that has taken over another person.

Healing is often messy, as we have seen in some of these tales. And there is little glamour for the practitioner, lest there be any doubt at this point on our journey. So there I was with Linda, who was in a deep altered state having made a very emotional contact with her most vulnerable part. We had worked toward this possibility and there were always doubts in my mind about whether she could heal from this severe abuse in this life. I did not judge myself for not having faith in her healing process; it was just that I had seen so much and appreciated how much work it took for real healing to happen, that I felt myself to be realistic, almost practical about the entire situation. Therefore, with this mind set, I was totally unprepared for what transpired. It took me five months to integrate from the following experience.

I had finally centered myself with Linda's tortured little girl. I looked out from my studio, over the San Francisco Bay toward the Golden Gate Bridge. My eyes were very dry. Linda and I had been here before. The last time I was present with this wounded little girl, with a knife in her vagina, (and it was still stuck inside, energetically), I was struggling with my own feelings about man's inhumanity toward man. The United Nations Arms Embargo in Bosnia was depriving the Muslims from defending themselves against the vicious genocide that descended upon village after village, while western democracies lounged in platitudes and inaction. This infuriated me, and I observed my confusion about non-violence, the "right use of force" and the karma of not lifting the sword out of fear. I would read the morning news and fume inside hearing my Jewish relatives say, "Never again! we shall never forget." I never did forget what man is capable of doing, but as a child, I was looking forward, not backward. Nevertheless, I caught a glimpse of how much pain there was in war and I only wanted to make things better. On a psychic level I carried some of the post holocaust pain in my consciousness, perhaps thinking—just like a child, that if I carried some of the load maybe it would be easier for others.

I didn't even realize how much pain I was carrying, in my desire to help others who were carrying so much grief and rage from the holocaust, until....that bright, September morning, when Yitzhak Rabin said to his enemies in front of the whole world, "We say to you today in a loud and clear voice: 'Enough of blood and tears! Enough!'" At mid-life, hearing those words, I regressed back into my little boy who—before he became a "pleaser" and set out to make other people happy, was a very sensitive human being who felt incredible joy and pain and sweetness and, of course, confusion.

So I gazed down at Linda's tortured being and embraced my confusion. I was torn between wanting to kill her father, that son of a bitch, and at the same time to take him in my arms and rock him until he was loved enough to re-join the human race. And my eyes were very dry.

Rather abruptly, Linda opened her eyes and I gazed at her. "How are you doing?" I asked, with a certain neutrality and concern.

"Very well, thanks." was the reply. The tone struck me funny and I took a closer look into her eyes. It was "Jackie"—Linda's Killer sub-personality.

Oh Boy. "What are you doing here?"

"I've come to help this little wounded girl."

Hmmmm. "How so?"

"I don't know, I'm here because she needs me."

What's an outraged killer like you doing in a place like this? I'm thinking, and I'm feeling somewhat strange by the simultaneous emergence of these two sub-personalities in Linda. *How perfect though. Now what?*

It felt as if some energy vortex just swept into the room and took over; it was so much more powerful than anything I could direct or even comprehend. I immediately knew that something very large was at play, and that I could not know what it was from where I was. I also knew that the best, and only, thing I could do was to stay open, stay grounded, and stay loving

Linda's body began writhing and shaking on the table. Her energy field collapsed and then erratically over expanded, causing the room to appear distorted to me. Suddenly, Linda began screaming so damned loud, and with such incredible terror, that it was all I could do to stay standing in place and hold her body. "AM I CRAZY?!, AM I CRAZY!?" she screamed directly at me, with eyes bulging.

"What's going on? Where are you?", I blurted.

"Oh my God.....it's Kristalnacht, it's Kristalnacht. They're coming to get us, the Nazis. They will take us away. Oh my God, I must hide Johann." [At this point Linda's voice takes on a German accent; her speech pattern and syntax are that of a German woman translating her reality for me in English.]

"Who is Johann?" I ask.

"He's my twelve year old boy. They will certainly take him; I must hide him." At this point, Linda is hysterical, completely inhabiting this "other life zone," and only marginally anchored to my voice and hands. Some big wave is moving through this little room. I had never felt such terror going through my body, and frankly, I hope it never happens again.

Linda is totally unglued and speaking now with a German accent. I can't believe this is happening. There are so many levels going on simultaneously, and right in the middle of this entire catastrophe I hear this little voice inside my head go off and whisper, just to me, "You don't look Jewish." The humorous aside was very helpful; it grounded me, and I told Linda to take some slow breaths and just look all around and then describe exactly what is happening.

She squeezed my hand so tight and yelled right at my face, saliva exploding out of her mouth, "Get me out of here! Stop this NOW!!!"

So much for humor.

I felt totally responsible and totally unable to function...and totally confused. I knew there was a reason behind all this, and I knew that some insight was working its way into Linda's consciousness, and mine too. I consciously asked for help. And I got it.

A sweet liquid stillness descended down my body and a long breath followed. Some higher power had joined us and, though I've experienced this kind of support and blessing in my work before, I really needed it now. When I felt it come in I knew that something good was going to happen through all this. I am sure my sensing this calmed Linda down, at least enough to speak English and describe what was happening.

Anchored in the room, with my touch and presence, Linda drifted back into that "past-life/concurrent life" horror show. Now feeling that some part of her was here with me in 1993, in the San Francisco Bay Area, witnessing this whole incredible thing, she *really* went for it!

"Oh my God!" she started in again...and through her screams, over a period of time of not less than twenty grueling minutes, I came to understand that four Nazi soldiers stormed into her home, did not find Johann, and were furious and crazy. Then I found out that all along, throughout this entire scenario, Linda is frantically running around holding a little baby girl in her arms.

The entire scene being played out upon Linda's body at this point is totally electric. It is definitely one of the strangest places I have ever visited. I can hardly track what's happening because, as Linda is blurting out rapid-fire descriptions of the "movie", I feel that I am somehow holding on this fourth dimensional movie camera that is projecting this horror show upon her body as a screen. I am holding this "work space" as grounded as I can, but my strength to stay focused is waning.

"No, No, NO!!! Don't take my baby, oh please don't take my baby!!" Linda screams hysterically and grasps at her throat and at her abdomen in gut wrenching spasms. I can hardly maintain a moment longer, and I shout over her own wailing: "WHO'S TAKING YOUR BABY?"

Dead silence.

It seemed like an eternity. Linda's eyes became very glassy and introspective. The room became calm. There was a clarity in the room that was indescribable, as if some beautiful bell had pierced the air and cut through all of the dimensions at once.

"It's Jackie; he's a Nazi," Linda said to me very soberly, "and the one and a half year old baby that he took out of my arms is *me*!"

Linda began to cry. These cries were quieter and they seemed very, very private. For a moment, I felt embarrassed to be included in this energetic field. Linda's body just cried and cried and cried. Something very deep was being resolved, and I felt that I was in the presence of some great mystery. I felt grateful and a little scared.

Wasn't that something!

Perhaps out of desire, I proceeded as if the session was winding down and that we would just do a little integrating work, maybe around the heart or feet. This was not the case. It seems that "Jackie" had just arrived. The real work was just beginning.

Where did "Jackie" come from?

Staring at me was a cold blooded killer who I thought I had met in an earlier session. This "Jackie" was really ominous and, I noticed, Linda's body took on a peculiar odor. I stared right into his eyes, Linda was completely gone, and asked, "What are you doing here, Jackie?"

"I'm here because I need to be here. Linda needs me."

"Why?"

"To protect her from her father or anyone who tries to harm her."

"I see. Tell me, Jackie, how did you come to be the one who arrived to help Linda?"

"I was the meanest and strongest person she had ever met, and I was in debt to her."

"From the Nazi life, when you stole her as a baby?" I pressed.

"Naturally, it all balances out."

"Jackie," I asked, "how do you feel about being so close to Linda's wounded child when you had ripped her out of Linda's arms on Kristalnacht, in that other life?"

"It's my job to take care of this little baby now. It's my job. I have to do my job. She needs me."

"Jackie, you hold a lot of Linda's energy. When you're doing your job, its hard to find Linda because you've just taken her over."

"She needs me. You never know when the shit's going to roll."

"Jackie, you've done a terrific job taking care of Linda; have you considered a change, perhaps moving on from her or taking an extended vacation?"

"Fuck You! You're just trying to get rid of me. Linda needs me! I don't trust you. Go to hell!"

And so, I found myself right up against this edge. Jackie is not just a part of Linda, he is also a fragment from some other source that is completing a karmic debt toward Linda that he had incurred in Germany, two generations ago. I understood this at the time and intuitively felt that the debt had already been paid in full, and that the whole equation had been neutralized in some way. Jackie didn't agree, and he was adamant about staying in Linda's life.

As long as Linda had Jackie's energy anchored in her field, she would be unable to dis-identify and move on from her profound woundedness, regardless of how much good therapy she received. I knew this, and Jackie knew that I knew this, and we locked onto each other's eyes and maintained a very silent contact. Unbeknownst to me, at the time, something in my eyes arose to meet Jackie's stare.

Who am I in all this?

"Jackie, the war is over and Linda made it through her difficult early life, thanks to you. She always knew she could count on you. She always felt strong because you were by her side. She never knew until today that you were here, serving her cause, because you had to repay her. Right now she is still absorbing what that means to her. I can tell you that there is a completion here for you today and that you are now free of any karmic debt to Linda." I said this and felt incredibly alive and suspended somehow, wishing someone else were here to witness this with me, thinking "Who the hell do you think you are, Fred, trying to reason with this Nazi asshole?"

The session suddenly began to feel very thick to me. Linda's body was breathing heavily. Though the energy and verbal exchanges were proceeding in a cool and orderly way on one level, inside my skin there was a rising heat—chaotic, ancient and seething. (Linda later told me how calm and centered I was throughout). It is so interesting to perceive and act from the "witness" perspective and also hold these passionate feelings.

Perhaps you're in over your head here, Fred. Have you thought about that? Whose edge are you up against?

My clarity returned. I looked at Jackie, thinking that he'd always been a survivor. That's his job, he's good at it, and that's why he's here to protect Linda...and he will do this for eternity because he doesn't know how to do anything else or believe in any other possibilities...(until today, maybe).

I became quite cool and even a little social, to my surprise.

"OK Jackie, let's make that deal real. You back off and give some of this power you're holding onto back to Linda so that she can get a life, and you can still serve her but in some new and really different ways. You could learn some new stuff. How does that sound?"

"Fuck You!"

"Well Fuck you too!—you God Damned SHIT!!"

"FUCK YOU!!! Who the hell do you think you are?"

This God Damned Nazi won't go away. Linda is too scared and weak to take care of this situation. Be careful. He is a survivor, and remember, he hates Jews, like you.

Suddenly, Jackie and I were joined in this incredible energy web that had nothing to do with Linda anymore. He was, in my mind, my opposite. He was a hired killer and I was a hired healer. We play different roles in the karma dramas.

Here I was playing the role of a passing transient healer in this "Linda Movie" and Jackie believed, rightly so, that I was just trying to smoothly manipulate him right out of his role. I knew that he didn't trust me. Even though I believed he was real, and that he prevented Linda from moving on from her terrible abuse, I also knew that Jackie believed that he could take care of me by just waiting out this whole thing. After all, it wasn't my life. What did I care. The session was almost over. Jackie knew the score. And now he knew that I knew he really knew the score.

Long silence. In that long silence something happened in me.

I'm going to move *this son of a bitch because this poor bastard is just following orders, just like every Nazi bastard said in their self-defense. He's got nothing else to do. His presence evoked a subterranean reactivity in me. He's never had anything but his rage, but he's not evil, he's just following orders. He needs to know he's not alone. His stubborn arrogance is all he's got between this breath and his fear of the abyss, except.....his life with Linda. Linda is his only survival. He's never bothered to get to know her because he's never been asked to stretch; he's just mean and scared.*

I know whose fucking edge we're at now!

I'm maintaining a grounded therapeutic relationship with Linda. I feel that she is secure in the process, though at this point, the process itself is all over the place.

"Look Jackie, there is more to life than being a killer waiting for an opportunity to prove how mean you can be. I realize that you and Linda have been together a long time, but she is working very hard to grow beyond this world of survival that you thrive in. She can't jump into her joy when you're sitting all over her. In fact, your presence, the way it is, just keeps her a victim."

"FUCK YOU!!" Jackie snapped back.

And I thought he was softening. Something snapped in me.

Suddenly I was draped in black leather and screamed at him, "NO!, you listen to me!!! You think you're all alone here, the only mean tough guy in this world, or in this room, but I'll tell you right now "Jackie," there's a killer in me and he's looking you right in the eye. THIS IS LINDA'S LIFE!, Damn it!! Get out of it or make some changes. I realize you're a killer, but you're not evil. You just follow orders. You're just in a lot of pain, and you don't know what to do. I am sad for you."

After saying this, I felt completely drained. Jackie and I couldn't connect. I felt a deep futility on a lot of levels.

After a long silence Jackie said to me, "You mean I could be with Linda in a different way?"

An opening.

"Yes, Jackie, you hold a lot of Linda's passion, and power drive, her anger, her will. Since the only thing you know how to do, at this time, is kill, she really hasn't been able to use you that much except to give her a sense of protection if any really bad things happen to her. And you know, her adult life is nothing like her childhood. There's just not that much real action as a killer in Linda's daily life."

Jackie very simply asked me then, "How do you know so much about this killer stuff?"

Bingo!

My ancient black-leathered killer had amazingly returned, in this session, as the only part of me that could possibly get Jackie to transform and give Linda a chance for freedom. I was touched by the multidimensional irony and humanness of this entire exchange, realizing that Linda herself was only a fly on the wall. I remember thinking, "I hope someone is getting this down."

So there I was, explaining to this astral Nazi about my disowned child-hood rage, and how I never knew where to put it, and how frustrated I became holding it all in my body. Jackie questioned me long and hard. The conversation was like an interview for me and, in the end, I told him that the only way I finally got to the root of my rage and began to work it out of my body, was when I dug out a mountainside, pick ax by shovelful by wheelbarrow, day after day for almost five years.

"How does it look now?," Jackie asked.

I said to Jackie, "It's now a water garden with a lot of koi, five waterfalls, aquatic plants and some beautiful, but very stubborn manzanita trees growing over the edge."

"I like the edge," Jackie said. "Can I come and see it?"

To my utter dismay, I said "YES!"

Jackie settled into Linda again with thoughts of a future field trip to my home and the session with Linda continued in a remarkable way. Looking down into Linda's very clear eyes, I could see my own reflection. We both had a clarity and look of incredulity on our faces. *Did that really happen?* was the unspoken question in both of our minds. We both agreed that this experience unexpectedly opened some kind of time warp karmic wooden door," and that we both needed another session in a season or so, to understand this experience. Neither Linda nor I had much capacity for reflection at that time.

Jackie had been met and perhaps, as a result, his dangerous rage could be transformed. Perhaps Linda could be freed from her unconscious hostilities, especially the ones that were triggered by seeing happy children.

Maybe Jackie could be integrated into Linda's life. *Maybe* healing is really possible. I wondered what a fully healed Linda would look like. Would Jackie be in her life in a different way or would she be freed of his influence? I drove home along the mountainous coastline with the windows wide open, hoping the fresh ocean air would clear my head. Digging deep within my own psyche, in Linda's session—to find the violent part in me that I needed in order to meet Jackie—left me feeling strangely exhilarated and exhausted. How much effort, I mused to myself, will it really take to positively change the violent nature of Linda's psyche, or my own, or any of ours? How much unconscious energy was it taking from me to keep what came up for me contained.

Big questions.

Accessing my own "killer energy" and witnessing the positive effect that owning it had upon Jackie, threw me into deep reflection about our inherent human condition as compared to the concept of Western history as one of a civilization moving from barbaric violence to rationality and peace. This utopian vision of a civilization freed from violent instincts, noble as it is, appeared to me as unrealistic. Each hairpin turn above the crashing Pacific waves, carried me more deeply into my struggle with that paradox: *Is our ideal of a world at peace decreasing our ability to actually make peace?*

As long as we perceive violence as an aberration, a deviation from our normal condition, we will keep drawing lines between ourselves and those we fear, and add to the fragmentation and violence of our society. Perhaps a less rosy meta-belief system might actually serve our lives better. I'm sure, though, it would lack the visionary appeal of our current world steadily progressing into "a civilized society in eternal peace," the words of Immanuel Kant, an Eighteenth Century German philosopher.

Driving the highway home I had dark thoughts about the sham of European high culture, with all its lofty philosophy hiding a mean spirited underworld that was once again popping out in Bosnia. I recalled Gandhi's response to the question, "What do you think, Sir, about Western civilization?" He said, "I think that would be a good idea."

Previous to my session with Linda, I had found a nice, convenient storage place for my own "inner killer," and though I secretly felt safe in the knowledge that I could conjure up this rage in me, if I had to, I mostly subscribed to the belief that violence was an inappropriate way to resolve anything....period. After my session with Linda, I was agitated and confused by my success. Perhaps I needed a vacation, maybe another meditation retreat.

It would be another five months before Linda would rent a car, in San Francisco, drive the winding highway to my home, making good on our agreement to give Jackie his field trip. During that five month period, I would often sit in my Zen water garden imagining Linda's relationship with Jackie changing. At times I heard my mind give voice to noble thoughts I imagined sharing with a rehabilitated Jackie. Other times my cynic would emerge and shoot down any positive feelings that arose over my work with Jackie.

During that five month period Cheryl and I were invited, by some friends, to join them on a sailing vacation in the Dodecanase Islands, the southern most Greek Isles. I was able to relax and really let go. Up until this vacation, I had been wrestling with the issue of evil and the transformation of evil. The black leather force that had surfaced in my work with Jackie was rattling around in me, unable to find its old resting place. One morning, on the azure blue of the Aegean Sea, I was sitting in the "bird's nest" at the stern of the boat, lost in contemplation, when these mythic waters delivered the perfect omen.

More than a dozen dolphins joined our fifty-five foot sailboat for an hour. We all screamed with joy and delight, cheering them until we were hoarse. Their grace and freedom and power were the ultimate in perfection; a part of me joined them in their swim. A feeling of deep gratitude and exuberant joy permeated my entire being.

Remembering my experiences with the Florida dolphins and my research into their incredibly responsive behaviors and intelligence, I thought again about how they are true teachers of Flow. Dolphins move creatively and with real power within their environment. Their brains are, on average, larger than the typical human brain, "and the associational cortex, the part of the brain specialized for abstract and conceptual thinking is definitely larger than ours, [and has been this way] for at least thirty million years."[3]

Dolphins can be deadly to sharks when they are threatened. They use their sonar to hone in on the shark's sensitive liver; they circle the shark and at precisely the correct moment they ram, bludgeon and crush the shark's rib cage until the shark is dead. The creative style in which the dolphin goes about revising its strategies, whether it be in self-protection or in adapting to a changing environment is very inspiring.

Prior to sighting the dolphins I had been obsessed with the fact that I was meeting Jackie with an ancient shark consciousness that had been dormant in me. I had mixed feelings because, although the initial outcome held some promise, I was left with an uneasy feeling that these dark forces are destined to cyclically arise in our lives, if not personally, then certainly collectively. If this shark consciousness was latent in me then it was manifest in others. That is just the way it is with us humans encumbered by all the acts of violence and acts of brutality going on in every corner of the world today.

After sighting the dolphins, I reframed *who* in me met Jackie. Dolphins could kill if they needed to and in that moment with Jackie, it was appropriate to demonstrate my capability of exercising that option. When that energy appeared in my session with Linda, it was an energy released by conscious choice. I intended to demonstrate to Jackie that I could meet him toe to toe, that I would meet him there, and if necessary, prevail without apology. And he *got it*.

This willful determination was a response within a powerful and fluid situation, and it was the practical alternative to either backing down and losing or "machoing" it up and activating more of Jackie's egoic armament. Responsiveness and Flow characterized my expressions; these expressions were not feminine and nurturing but rather masculine and boundary setting. In human evolution, aggression produces victims and aggressors.

In the book *Strategy of the Dolphin*[4] human aggressiveness is metaphorically portrayed in two kinds of people, the "Carp" type and the "Shark" type. Typically, the "carps" employ only two choices: flight or freeze; whereas the "sharks," of course, fight unchallenged. All of us possess different degrees of both of these types with all of their traits and capacities.

"Carps and Sharks play finite games...within boundaries [whereas] Dolphins play infinite games by playing with the boundaries."[5] In a finite universe, scarcity beliefs predominate. In a universe where boundaries are expanded, abundance beliefs can develop and thus, fear-based perception diminishes, accordingly. "Dolphin people" are the new potential humans we have been conjuring in this exploration of *the edge* potential. "Dolphin

WOUNDS INTO BLESSINGS

people" are creative pragmatists. "They are responsible not for what happens but for how they respond to what happens." They believe in choice and the possibilities of creative transformation and it is in the cultivation of "dolphin" consciousness that our species evolution now depends. Dolphins are incredibly sensual and sexually playful creatures and are great teachers for us. They are also unafraid to create "right boundaries" in their water-world. Our challenge as a species, on both personal and social levels, is to embrace our lives in the pleasure-body and create boundaries that are respected by those who are limited and run by fear and greed.

Jackie came out of the uneducated, dispossessed, poor German working class. He was ripe for indoctrination like today's youth who have only bleak futures in their respective societies. People who are deeply wounded and abused are enraged when they see happiness and sensuality in others, particularly in children, as we saw with Linda earlier.

Wounded adults, usually close family members, who cannot witness the innocence and white-silk reveries of children fondling their hair and bodies in sweet and true ways, lash out in unconscious rage and envy, molesting and abusing those very human beings who look toward them with trust. The betrayal, of course, sets in motion the potential for further abuse. Not everyone who has been abused becomes an abuser, thank God, but all abusers, in fact, were once abused themselves. This painful cycle will keep being re-generated until these wounds are addressed and healed. And this is why engaging in healing work is the most profound endeavor for humanity. It is the only way to break through the survivalist (shark-carp) mind state and learn a whole new (dolphin) way of being. We have no viable alternative. Healing work is the Twenty-First Century's spirituality. And we have our work cut out for us.

These are the words of a Serbian (human-shark) sniper, from his prison cell in Sarajevo: "I am happy to kill a child when he is with his mother because there is something fantastic in the face of the mother."[6] This deranged satisfaction is identical to the distorted sexual turn-on that motivates child abusers like the fathers of Bob and Linda. And I believe that his mind-set is much more widespread than any of us are willing to admit.

Deep down in the cellular unconsciousness of our loins is this incredibly deep feeling of angst and betrayal. For our "white-silk" was not just taken away by wounded adults who were triggered by our natural aliveness; we have also felt our erotic impulses muted, attacked and distorted by the insidious taboos which our predominant cultures have thrown upon us.

Our vital regenerative life-force has been so repressed through the tyrannical effects of shame, guilt and sin, that what we see in the violent acts of reactive people is, at core, the explosion of all that pent-up rage. The right expression of anger establishes boundaries that have integrity while rage transgresses any boundary in order to be released. Rage knows no consciousness, no intent, and no responsibility.

Every one of us has, in some way been wounded by another and, in some way, perpetrated a wound upon another, at one time or another. What was painful might have actually passed in a brief period of time, but our reactions to the pain are what keep us living inside our private hells—unable to move on and re-establish our integrity with our selves. This is where therapy and healing work are meant to enter in, and there is no shame to admit that we need help at certain times.

We all have dolphin, shark and carp sub-personalities. In my work with clients and with myself I have seen many sub-personalities of all stripes. Frequently I've seen dis-owned parts of myself in others; I see this by noticing my strong reactions to these aspects in people. Some of these aspects in people were shark-sub-personalities looking to make amends and find forgiveness. Others were carp-sub-personalities hoping to tell their woeful stories, gain sympathy, and transform their fears into anger. Maybe they were hoping to become sharks themselves.

Learning dolphin ways has been the focus of my work with people and with myself. The ways of sharks and carps is full of perpetration and victim hood. Our personal and political landscape is littered with the endless stories of futile martyrdom, empty glory, and thinly worn pride. It is time we created new archetypes of playfulness in a world made safe by the "right use of power," and find ways to speak our truths so that we *can* be heard.

At core, human beings have this longing for body pleasure, but through their conditioning, they have developed a bio-physical incapacity to accept pleasure and freedom beyond a relatively superficial level. The dynamic tension generated by this yearning for and inability to truly receive pleasure and freedom has essentially set human beings against themselves and each other. As a result what we see in the world, instead of joy, play and loving dolphin-fun, are distorted power-drives that frequently become violent.

Is there really a difference between a rapist in Central Park, a sniper in Sarajevo, a molester in Sacramento, or a bandit in Mogadishu? Wilhelm Reich, the Great Grandfather of bodywork, was absolutely correct in his assertion that all violence is the result of repressed sexual feeling. Learn-

WOUNDS INTO BLESSINGS

ing how to heal our core sensual nature responsibly is perhaps the most important healing task for our species. Since it is such a radical idea, it will unlikely happen in any large-scale manner at this time. After all, Reich himself was imprisoned in Harrisburg Penitentiary, and died there, espousing this prescription for our human suffering.

We are not evolved enough to do this work collectively at this time. The only way we can evolve as a species is by doing this healing work personally until there are enough "dolphin people" who can lead us into the next stage of our cosmic adventure. We cannot wait for someone else to do it first or do it for us. We must seize the day and do the work of retrieving our missing pieces.

The missing pieces wait where we left them. Linda was only three years old when she dissociated in order to survive her father's sexual assaults. She did not become a multiple personality, but she did live within several sub-personalities; one of them was Jackie, her warrior from hell. Jackie's very existence in Linda's life allowed her to survive but not really live. Jackie's time was up. He knew it in that nano-second when I stared him down. It would take me another five years to realize that the eyes that met Jackie were the eyes of Zoruba, the male dragon I've built on my property.

When Linda took Jackie up the coast for his field trip, I knew that our meeting signaled that my time was up too, in some way. Linda got out of her car. I saw her from the garden before she saw me. I studied her walk, her posture, the carriage of her head upon her neck and shoulders. Something was different. I felt a strange excitement course through my nervous system. It took five months for Linda and me to create this meeting. We sat down together under the manzanita tree and silently gazed upon the smooth waters of the pond. In our silence we waited.......ready for death, rebirth, and liberation.

****

A sweet and expansive stillness permeated the garden that day; birds splashed in the water. Linda and I reflected upon our work together. I had stopped wrestling with my feelings about justice in an insane world and my confusion about the right use of force while still embracing the path of non-violence. All of these paradoxes came to a resting point, in my garden, as Linda spoke to me about the extreme pain that brought her to the point of facing the terror of her incest. She described her whole journey from the reference point, finally, of a transformed spirit. From the journal entry she wrote about our meeting in the garden, she reflects: "My pain was the pain of having closed myself off from the love of the Universe; it was the pain of knowing that what lay between my capacity for love and a life of eternal loneliness, loss and despair, was the abyss of terror from which I had fled since that fateful day in 1963. It yawned before me like the chasm of hell itself—nothing Dante could have devised could equal it in terror— the very place from which I had hidden myself, the place from which I had armored myself in bitter defiance. A black hole that ate energy and gave nothing in return. The center. The edge. My world as it had broken and remade itself around the wound, hideously malformed.

"I had known the white heat of rage, the pain of betrayal and loss. I faced these feelings when they came. But I knew the terror lay dormant within. I knew that, as much as I had 'processed' the incest experience, I had not really touched its core. I could be angry and feel strong. I could feel sad, raw, naked terror running through my three year old body...and freeze. No, it was too much. This I could not do. I told my god as much, despairing of ever crossing the abyss. I would live wounded forever, my heart closed. I would view all people as my potential enemy. I had guards, armor, tactics, reconnaissance, defensive positions. I was dying. And I knew it."

Prior to our pivotal session, Linda had walked for weeks in terror through her life, feeling herself on a battlefield. She went to work, rode the bus, tapped her keyboard, read the newspaper, the whole while dreading her imminent destruction, sure that it lurked among the common artifacts of the city. "My body walked on the city streets, but my soul walked in a no man's land, stepping gingerly to avoid the mines, crouching low, running from the shelter of one crater to the next, hoping to avoid getting hit by the artillery barrages that thundered overhead. World War 1. It ended two full generations before my birth, yet I have stalked its battlefields. How can this be?"

"Terror. Terror. The terror of a child whose father turns on her, does inexplicable, horrible things, breaking her world and, even more, break- ing something deep inside her that she never knew was gone until, after jumping into that abyss of terror thirty years later, she began to reclaim it. Terror. The terror of a child huddled all night in a bomb shelter, her world breaking outside her, wondering what would be left in the morning. Wait- ing for the all clear."

When is the war really over?

Linda brought her terror to our last session, not knowing she would leap into that abyss, with me at her side. She tried to explain her feeling of being on a battlefield to me. The images prior to our session were of the battlefields of World War 1, but once the session began, Linda's cellular

WOUNDS INTO BLESSING

memories shifted into the madness that initiated the holocaust.

"What I didn't say to Fred, was that the word that kept coming to mind was 'Kristalnacht'. 'Kristalnacht'. The beginning of the Holocaust. The beginning of the end. And I was always so drawn to the Holocaust, not a drop of Jewish blood in me, not a single Eastern European ancestor, not a reason in the world to bow my head in remembrance and murmur 'never again'. One feels an abstract rage at these things, deploring 'man's inhumanity to man', but my feelings had always cut closer, deeper. What I didn't say to Fred that day was 'Kritalnacht' because I was ashamed to equate my thirty-year-old incest experience with the unspeakable horrors of World War 2. So I didn't say it. *I'm being dramatic,* I thought.

[Linda did not remember shouting out "It's Kristalnacht!"]

"I lay on Fred's table in that familiar studio across the bay, naked, vulnerable beneath the blankets, ready to deliver myself over to Fred's ministrations and I knew not what else. Ready to deliver myself over to God. To whom else can we go with these things? To God and His agents. So I opened myself. I entered altered states in that session, becoming aware of a spirit-guide who was helping me through the recovery process. Fred worked with the guide for a while, then asked me if I was ready to go into the wound. I was. If I were ever going to be ready, now was the time.

"How it happened I don't know. I felt terror, terror unnamable, unspeakable. And then I slipped. Something shifted and I moved or passed into another place. Or, more precisely, another place inside of me rose up into my consciousness. The image of the battlefield, the word 'Kristalnacht' and the terror coalesced into a memory of breaking glass, of pounding footsteps and the sinister ring of rifle butts against a wooden door, of a desperate scramble in the dark, of a heart racing with terror and the sinking rage of betrayal drawing itself into a knot inside my gut. The police burst into my flat, even as I snatched my baby girl up into my arms and hid another child in a clothes basket. The eldest child somehow eluded me. Johann, where was he? They grabbed me, scattered my things, shouted questions at me. Caught unaware, I had no answers for them. I only knew vaguely that my husband went to secret meetings at night with other men of the intelligentsia. The meetings were political, perhaps subversive, but more I did not know, had not bothered to know. They got my husband first then came for me.

"My innocence was my punishment. Before they hauled me to the camps, they took my baby girl out of my arms and raped her, then dropped her dead onto the floor. They held me to the floor and raped me in my turn.

After that, the camps meant nothing. In my vision, I saw myself staring through a barbed wire fence, unmindful of the cold, the hunger, the cries of the dying behind me, unmindful of the children I had lost, the husband I had loved, then hated, then lost in turn. Only the gray sky and indifferent sullen wind were real to me. My only comfort was the hope of death."

"All this came to me in an instant. I saw these scenes like flashbacks in a movie (which, indeed, they were) but they were loaded with content. I was flooded with details. These were not pictures such as I had seen in memories. They were records of a lifetime. My lifetime. A past lifetime. I screamed terror in that little studio, sitting up beneath the blankets, sure I was losing my mind, sure I would get lost in that other life and never come back. Had Fred not been there, that might have been the case. The veil between the two lives, that one and this one, might have slipped away forever. Even as I knew the experience for what it was, the memory of a past life, I fought that knowledge; it bent my notion of reality too far. How had I gone from an incest survivor to a Holocaust survivor? And what did they have to do with each other?

War....War and terror....What did I know of such things?

Linda was raised in a white suburb in California in the 1960's. "Sure, I had been incested," Linda told me in the garden, "But that can hardly be equated with the scope and horror of a World War. Yet I had lived the war, in this lifetime, through the psychic pain of parents. Dissociated, locked behind walls of denial and oblivion, my parents' memories of war cast their shadow on my childhood."

Linda's father, a seventeen-year-old farm boy watched helplessly as his mother died of breast cancer at forty-one. Two days later a Japanese squadron drops its payload on a U.S. naval base. America enters the war. Within months, the farm boy, unmourning and unmourned, buries the rotting corpses of Japanese soldiers under the blazing sun of Guadalcanal. Years later in a drunken stupor he thrusts a knife into the vagina of his three-year-old daughter and rapes the two-year-old one right after. Is there a connection? What demons spawned within him out of terror and deprivation unleashed themselves upon the innocent, the helpless, whose only crime was that they were close at hand? What demons did he struggle to contain with bottle after bottle of cheap vodka?

Is he responsible? Yes. But is he to blame?

And what about Linda's mother? As a child in Northern England, she was awakened at night by the shriek of sirens and bundled off to sit shivering in a freezing shelter. Hearing the bombs explode and the rattling of the antiaircraft fire, she waited for the All Clear to sound before stumbling numbly back to bed to uneasy dreams. She never knew when it would begin again.

"Hearing of the fall of France," Linda writes, "My grandmother swore she'd gas her children rather than let the Germans have them. My mother was nine years old. Her choices in life were to be killed by her own mother or to have atrocities committed upon her by the monstrous Germans who sent their "engines of terror" over a little girl's village during the night. Yes, what about my mother, who got up and cooked breakfast and went on like the incest never happened, like she'd never seen the blood, never heard the screams. Had not the war taught her well? How had that little girl gotten up in the morning and gone to school and recited her sums? She split herself between the two realities: the world of everyday surroundings and activities and the nighttime nightmare world of the exploding bombs. When the bomb exploded in her family, she did what she knew best. She survived. She hid terror away and got on with life, pretending, denying. After this, how can I say that my life had never been touched by the war?

"And now the war came back to me in a different way. This time it was my war, too. While my mother huddled terrified in a drafty shelter and my father heaved the bodies of soldiers into a common grave, I stood empty behind a barbed wire fence and prayed for the peace of death."

"Reliving this past life showed me the banality, the universality of terror. We are all victims. We are all survivors. We are all perpetrators. What gets denied gets lived out, somewhere, some time. All the terror of all the wars that were ever waged is inside us now. The Holocausts, the pogroms, the sieges, the 'ethnic cleansings,' the Matanzas, the crackdowns, the battles, the slaughters, the raids, the conquests, the wars live inside each of us. We bear the scars. We bear the guilt.

"From this past life understanding, I have attained some measure of forgiveness for my parents. I cannot condone or approve of their actions, but I can understand them, for I too, have been caught in the web of history. We cannot easily escape the terrors. I see what my parents did, not as personal acts of hatred or neglect toward me, but as a part of history. The war came to me through my father's violence and my mother's denial. History had taught them well.

"This knowledge would seem to lessen the pain of incest. I can depersonalize it, abstract it, place it in an impersonal context and remove its sting.

Yet the reverse is true. To see my parents as evil and neglectful gives me the moral high ground; to see all of us helplessly caught up in karmic cycles of violence and terror, as victims of history, forces the weight of an awesome reality down upon my head. I cannot condemn. I cannot condone. I can only heal.

"Violence was my friend and savior, too, I must confess. For after Fred pulled me back, somehow, from the vision and experience of my past life, we both had to contend with a part of me I call Jackie. Who Jackie is, karmically or energetically, I cannot say exactly. Fred seems to be surer about this than I am. I can only say that I experienced him as an entity that was part of me yet separate. He had witnessed the incest from a vantage point outside my body, and, believe me, he seemed to feel none of the terror I did.

"Jackie was pure rage. His whole existence revolved around fantasies of power and revenge. He fueled my will to live with a steady stream of hatred. I might be ashamed to admit such a cold and pitiless sub-personality, but in truth, I loved and admired Jackie. He made me feel invincible, and a part of me needed that. True, he sapped my energy and kept me isolated from others, but these seemed a small price to pay for this protection. But after traversing the depths of terror, what need did I have of such fury? Jackie had given me the strength and will to live in the face of unspeakable violence and violation, but these were not happening in my life now. Did I need him? Did he have a purpose in all this?

"He raised his fist when Fred went to talk to him, but Fred met him head on with kindness and patience. Jackie was afraid. His task finished, his purpose fulfilled, he had nothing, nowhere to go. He expected derision and was on guard, but he needed something, too. Underneath that killer instinct was terror and an unbearable, inconsolable loneliness. Jackie lived safely, but he paid for safety with utter isolation. Fred explained to him that he was taking my energy and that I needed to do other things with my life besides hate. Jackie wanted the hope that he could go on with me, but he knew his days as my mercenary and bodyguard were over. His façade began to crumble.

"Jackie knew he faced an eternity alone if he could not somehow transform. He wanted hope of rehabilitation, but only when Fred told him of his own 'killer' did Jackie begin to hope in earnest. 'And what happened to him?' Jackie asked. 'He became a gardener,' said Fred, 'with his own two hands he carved out the side of a mountain.' 'What is there now?' asked Jackie. 'A garden. A Japanese garden,' Fred answered. 'May I see it sometime?' Jackie inquired. 'Of course,' Fred replied. And so, the cold-hearted murderer found a vision and a purpose and felt the hope of transformation. A large part of my healing was complete."

Linda had not recalled that conversation, actually, until five months later when I recounted Jackie's request for this field trip. Linda laughed a Jackie laugh. We all three laughed. We had come full circle. Jackie then said to me "Do you know what I'm going to do, Fred? I'm going to medical school. That's my garden. That's my mountain". And then Linda returned, and she began to laugh again. As she says, "I laughed lightly and freely, in a way I'd never known how to laugh before."

That day, after our conversation in the garden, I gave Linda a nurturing and very quiet massage. My hands moved knowingly over her transformed body; a light shone from her skin. Jackie was integrated into Linda, and I would find myself contemplating the significance of this for many days and weeks. The implications of human beings actually owning their shadow, their "killers", and their disowned instincts and transforming them into a will to serve, fostered great faith in me regarding our human adventure.

Long after Linda drove away, I could still feel the warmth from her light shining in my heart. I walked around my land for many days afterward filled with gratitude for all of this exploration, and awe for the mystery that draws our lives together to do this work. I also carried with me a sweet sigh of irony in the thought that Jackie had found a way to transform "a dull, serviceable" killing knife into a sharp scalpel that could help heal a world in need.

Perfect.

At the end of the year, there was a holiday greeting from Linda in my mailbox. On the card was pictured a lioness with two cubs, sitting proudly at dusk on the Serengeti plains, a snow capped Mount Kilimanjaro in the distance, with the word "Peace" in the corner. While walking up my driveway, I read her personal note inside: "Thank you for being the boatman on my journey." Linda became the lioness. If I did not know before that instant, I knew then that everything in the universe is, like the Zen masters keep reminding us, perfect just the way it is. With each step, walking up my driveway, I felt all of me come home—all of me right here, right now.

The common and universal ground of every religion, philosophy, tradition or path is this understanding: *all healing, all empowerment, and all union with the divine only happens in the present moment.*

So then, if *I* want to really live, *I* must show up.

And to really show up, I must stop running from the parts that don't "fit in." And when I do, when I flow with *all of it*, the crack in the vase, the break in my heart, becomes an unexpected blessing—an opening through which more light shines in; my disowned energies return home unafraid and without shame, and they give to me all the energy that I've been missing. All is forgiven, and now I can rekindle the flame. This healing that I extend to myself is the best contribution I can make toward a better and more loving world.

We don't do this work alone. We do this work in relationship, and it is in relationship where our learning lies. Albert Camus, my favorite existentialist, offers a useful hint about how we might proceed in embracing healthy relationship: "Don't walk in front of me, I may not follow. Don't walk behind me, I may not lead. Walk beside me, and just be my friend." In noble friendship our gifts return to us, echoing the love we extended inthe beginning. With Bob Taylor, I had used the words carpe diem in our work together because they carry the passion necessary to change a life. These poems arrived in the mail, coincidentally, as I wrote this last chapter and they carry the spirit of wounds finally healed.

Perfect.

Seize the day

When on the brink of insanity and decay,
I think of your sad smile and generous heart,
Then all the silent moments of this empty day
Take on a new and wonderful hue from the start.
I sit and bask in the flood of gifts you gave
And laugh at the things we did in a time long ago.
I move to a melody half heard half felt save
For the special, secret phrase we knew and loved so.
When I remember the beach, the surf, the birds,
The sky, the rocks—where all pain and time cease—
Our place of refuge and strength, then I lack words
To tell the story of our camaraderie and peace.
Those times—those seconds of eternity—were not for naught.
They nourish and sustain me now in thought.

Carpe Diem

When darkness falls on cliffs above the sea,
I close my eyes and travel in my head;
I hear your sad, melodic voice and dread
The painful thoughts of what will never be.
I feel the warmth of your strong hands and face
I see the magic spell within your eyes,
I hear the echo of your sullen sighs,
And then lose touch with this transparent place.
I think of many gentle moments still,
When all the tragic past had come to rest,
And nothing stood between us any more:
The time we walked in the rain and climbed the hill,
The time we studied hard and passed the test,
The time we opened wide the wooden door.

Sooner or later it becomes clear to us that it is this opening wide the "wooden door," this, our healing journey of befriending our self and making bonds of friendship with others, that is our true destination. It is grace itself. It is "the real life" and it can only be found right now in the space between this step, and this breath. Breathing and stepping, one moment at a time; this is the dance.

Gradually, as I learn to move in this dance of Grace, I must ask myself, "What is the least amount of armament I need in order to feel safe in this world?" And by remaining in this question I can discover, little by little, that awareness is my best defense. As this awareness grows I can learn to live like a warrior, vigilant in the moment, ever watchful for potential distractions, and like a dolphin, ever more open to the universe's invitation to play, to love, and to dance with more joy and more laughter.

I awaken my heart and the unnecessary armament dissolves. Imploding into the eternal present, I realize: "I am not in the body, the body is in me." I am deathless. I can feel the joy of the soul and the suffering within my life simultaneously. I can trust that my awareness and instincts will, together, guide me within the realities of the moments that arise. I have faith in this guidance.

In the great film *Dead Poet's Society*, Robin Williams, as the inspired English professor, stands on his desk and both whispers and shouts at his students: "CARPE DIEM!" This passion and love for life is the kind of energy we need to cultivate in ourselves and give to ourselves, so that we can join Lao Tzu and dance...and dance...and dance with this universe until there's nothing left.

Put on your dancing shoes!

****

Footnotes:

1. The work of Stephen R. Schwartz, "The Prayer of the Body", an interview in THE SUN MAGAZINE, with the editor, Sy Safransky

2 Ibid

3. Strategy of the Dolphin , p. 6, by Dudley Lynch and Paul Kordos, published by William Morrow and Company, Inc., New York. Copyright by Brain Technologies Corp. 1988

4. Ibid

5. Ibid

6. *Sarajevo: a War Journal,* by Zlatko Dizdarevic, Translated by Anselm Hollo, Edited by Ammiel Alcalay, Preface by Joseph Brodsky, Introduction by Robert Jay Lifton, Illustrated. Fromm International,1993, (viewed in the New York Times Book Review, December 19, 1993)

Epilogue

The next year, after our work together, Linda returned to school to fulfill her medical school pre-requisites, and two and a half years later was accepted to the medical school of her dreams. During this time she also underwent formal conversion to Judaism. "It was like taking back an identity that someone had tried to deny me," Linda writes. "When I was studying for conversion, I had a dream. I was living in Germany during the war. I had just lit Shabbat candles when a neighbor came to the door and began speaking to my husband. I was very frightened that my neighbor would see the candles and so discover that we were Jewish. When I awoke, I knew this was no dream but a memory. Now with my healing, I have come full circle, and perhaps picked up where I left off, before my world broke.

"I have continued to heal from the incest. At one point I had concluded that no one would expect me to sit down to Thanksgiving dinner with a stranger who had raped me, so why should I do so with my father? So I cut off contact with him, out of self-respect rather than anger. Forgiveness came much later, as a gift of grace, not an act of my will. I was eventually able to spend a holiday with my father and feel only love, compassion, and tenderness toward him. I also saw the love he has for me and admitted to myself that I needed it and wanted it in my life. Today we have a loving relationship."

****

Healing for most people who have endured the nightmare of sexual abuse usually does not, and perhaps should not, involve interacting with people who once harmed them. However, for those who can, it is because:

The Law of Grace surpasses the Law of Karma; and this grace is found at the edge.

finis

The Transformational Journey

In *Wounds into Blessings*, we began with my insights into healing and my own story. I then shared with you my direct experience of select clients who agreed to offer their stories in facing their deepest wounds. These are up close and personal transformational stories of healing around abandonment, sexual abuse and incest, grief, anger/rage, anxiety, fear, shame, guilt, betrayal, depression, transcendence and avoidance...all forms of human suffering. In sharing each story I attempted to reveal the universal human condition of wounding and the fact that each person's wound is a personal "hell" until it is faced and addressed. There is no coping with our wounding or avoiding the pain of it without cost. Each person who tries to avoid facing their wounding will pay a very high price, the price of a life not truly lived!

You were invited as we traveled along this path to engage in three different Awareness Exercises. Hopefully you took the opportunity to do the exercises as we went along. If you did not participate in them I invite you again to experience them. It would be beneficial to do them now so that you can have your own experience to relate to as we move forward to the next, and final step, in this journey.

Every journey needs a map; but the map should never be confused with the actual terrain you experienced. As the progenitor and practitioner of Transformational Bodywork, I felt that it was important to build a framework to capture the entire healing process so that I could share it with my students and clients. The entire map is labeled, "The Art of Personal Disarmament", and it is a full representation of the journey into wholeness (see the map on opposite page). I give this map to each client so they can track their own experience and where they are in the healing process.

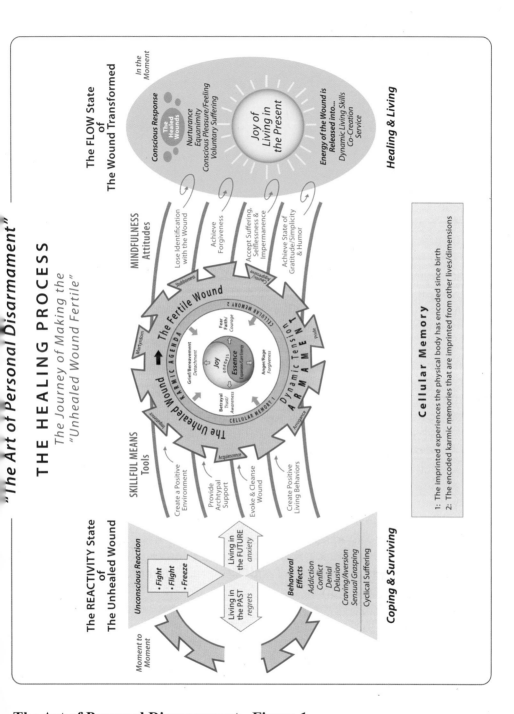

The Art of Personal Disarmament - Figure 1

In simple terms the map appears as a linear process from the "Reactivity State" (the state of the Unhealed Wound) to "The Journey of Making the Unhealed Wound Fertile". In this journey from the "Unhealed Wound" to a "Fertile Wound" is where we find the transformation from "Wounds into Blessings". The use of Skillful Means and Mindfulness are required to actually heal the wound that allows us to move into the place we all want to be "The Flow State of the Wound Transformed".

Each of the stories that I have shared with you reflected this process of healing. One very important point to make about this framework is that it appears to be a one time linear three step framework to "Joy and Living in the Present". Obviously we don't completely heal in a simple three-step linear process. This map, if it were in three dimensions, would be a spiral showing us in an ever-increasing, iterative pathway to higher levels of awareness and healing. The truth is, as humans, we are never done with our spiritual evolvement toward the maximum expression of the Divine within us. This is what makes the growth journey worth entering and it is what, once opened to it, keeps us on the path!

Don't be intimidated by the first impression of this healing map, *The Art of Personal Disarmament*. In it we use the following terms: karma, cellular memory, dynamic tension, armament and reactivity, among others. Let's review each of these terms one by one.

- *Karma* is the law of cause and effect; this translates into every day speech as, "What goes around, comes around."Lessons of the soul" are learned through the working out of karmic forces.

- *Cellular memory*, think of it as one's secretary, it records karma and produces a dynamic tension that expresses itself in the form of direct life experience. This dynamic tension causes most of us discomfort and we react by deeply armoring our bodies and/or our minds to protect us from life. In healing work of all kinds this reactive armament can be seen as a *story* that can be read, edited and re-written or released. Or, if not properly transformed, can become an endless story loop from which we never seem to escape.

- *Dynamic Tension* is perfectly natural and it is uniquely organized around each individual's karmic choices and personal history. The challenge, of course, is to develop the capacity to hold this tension and use it as concentrated awareness to gain insight, understanding, and healing. Later we'll see *who* creates this learning curriculum in the first place. For now we note that tension is created by the very nature of these two forces (karmic choices and personal history) acting upon us.

- *Armament* is the multilayered protection we create around us and within us to keep us *safe* from that which we deem harmful. On psychological levels, an insecure ego structure might deem all criticism as a threat to one's self-esteem and thereby construct the psychological armament of a *higher than thou authority* or a *caustic shamer,* for example, to silence would be critics. Armament is often constructed to hold back primitive emotions that might lead to inappropriate reactions within a person that, if expressed, might bring them negative consequences. Human biological life is filled with the inhibited urges to strike out, cave in and run away. It is armament that keeps these impulses under control and, too often, protects us from "enemies" that no longer exist or are even imaginary.

- *Reactivity* is the state of unconscious behaviors and mindsets that lack free will and the capacity to choose otherwise. It arises out of base instincts to protect against real or imagined threats and presents in at least one of three primary behaviors: fight, flight or freeze. Transforming reactivity into responsiveness is humanity's greatest collective evolutionary challenge. Non-violent ways to manage conflict and creative and loving relationships require that reactivity be transformed.

Now that you understand some of the terms we use in the map, let's look at "The Art of Personal Disarmament" map as a kind of board game. Create three markers for yourself and place each one on the map based on where you see yourself. As you look at the placement of each marker see if their position and their relationship to each other tells a version of your story. Learning how to exist in our separate selves while feeling unified with the whole is the central issue of our lives. We can either accept reality i.e., life on its own terms and *flow* with what happens, or we can react to what happens and try to *get a grip* on things. In the absence of connection with flow, with *oneness,* substitutes are sought and, for most people, alienation abounds in the reactive state.

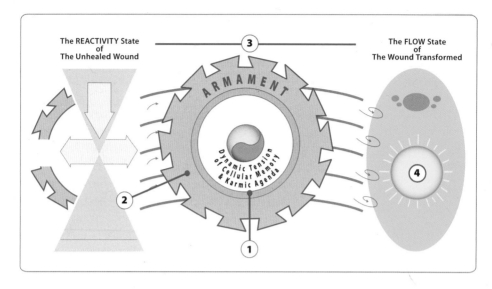

Entrance to the Transformational Journey - Figure 2

A person can enter the Transformational Journey at any one of four points:

1. Dynamic Tension

2. Armament and Reactivity State

3. The Journey of Making the Unhealed Wound Fertile

4. Yearning for Flow

So far Science has been ill equipped to investigate the plasticity of consciousness prior to form. These are the realms of pre-conception knowledge and after-death experiences. In the absence of deep scientific inquiry therefore, throughout history, we have been given information about consciousness through various religions and mystical practices.

However, in recent years, "near death experiences" have been widely recorded by researchers studying numerous cases where individuals, who had been pronounced dead (and all vital signs confirmed this), returned to life with lucid descriptions of another realm. Common to all these descriptions is the perception that this realm is a place of oneness, joy, and light.

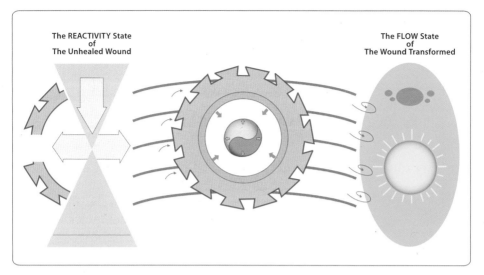

Separate-Self Existence in Duality as The Wound - Figure 3

In the heart of the map, at the core of "The Wound," is an outward expansion of core life-force energy (Figure 3). This is the manifestation of the oneness, joy and light that seeks expression and expansion. Our yearning is to experience it while here in these limited, separate, sensate formations called bodies. In the absence of this opportunity to expand, yearning for it grows, sometimes in the form of a *death wish*.

Core Life Force Expansion - Figure 4

This expansion can be observed in the natural world within the movement of single celled animals. An amoeba, for example, reaches out into its environment for its nourishment with an excited energy that expands its membrane. Conversely, when the environment attacks the membrane, the amoeba contracts. Actual experiments on amoebae were carried out and have been described in Man in the Trap, Dr. Elsworth Baker's definitive exposition of Wilhelm Reich's theories of psychiatry and the physiological realities of life in the human body (See Figure 4).

In the laboratory an amoeba was stuck with a pin and it naturally contracted. After a short time the amoeba expanded again, but after several attacks it behaved cautiously by expanding tentatively, and staying within its cellular memory of hostile territory. After further attacks, the amoeba stayed contracted and existed in an anxious and armored state. "It has defended itself from its environment by reduction in size, but at the expense of lowered motility and increased inner pressure," Dr. Baker tells us. Continued attacks, at this point would prevent the amoeba from expanding and its life force would diminish causing the amoeba to gradually shrink and die (like a human depression or cancer case)," Dr. Baker concludes. This is a sad story and we can certainly empathize with our single celled friend, because its experience in the laboratory resembles some of the basic mechanisms we have seen in human emotional disorders.

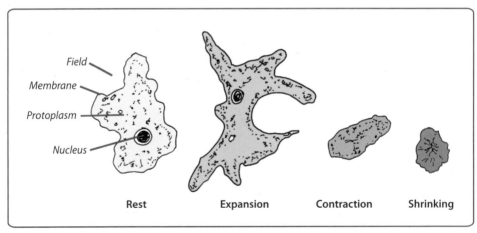

Field
Membrane
Protoplasm
Nucleus

Rest   Expansion   Contraction   Shrinking

Amoeba in four states - Figure 5

A young child, ecstatic to see daddy, comes running with open arms to greet him; because daddy has been drinking and is depressed he rejects her, or worse, hits her or abuses her. The little girl emotionally contracts, and over time, her light dims and her sparkling joy sours into a rage. She deserves better and hopefully, in the future, she will find a way to disarm her armored protective wall and melt her fury.

Human beings experience pinprick attacks in many ways. Sometimes these attacks are extreme; but for most of us, more subtle events and energies impact our psyches and frame the expression of our individual life force. We can view our lives as expressions of the dynamic relationship between the expanding nature of our *core essential life force* interacting within the limitations, boundaries and qualifiers that arise from *cellular memories* of our own pasts, and from the challenges we have chosen to explore in our lives as represented by our *karmic agendas* (See Fig. 6).

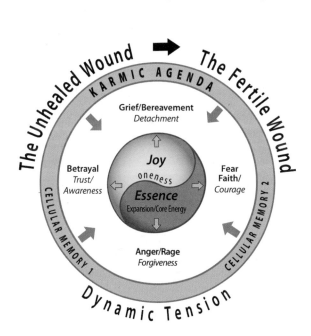

Dynamic Tension - Figure 6

The dynamic tension, which results from the interplay of these two polar forces, usually occurs in human life on a sub-conscious plane. Change can begin when one chooses to become aware of the motivational impetus behind his or her life experience.

Each individual's karmic choices and personal history form their particular form of dynamic tension. It is part of the price we pay for living in our wonderful sensate bodies. In other words, our life experiences are generated by the dynamics that ensue from our own core yearning to expand within environments that are inherently limited by form, gravity and time.

Because our bodies have delicate and exquisitely sensitive nervous systems, we must create various filters so that we can tolerate the magnitude of sensory input and the functional demands of living in a physical body. Our essence becomes shrouded in the protection of our personalities that form around our early conditioning, cultural cues and personal inclinations. Our bodies become alert to potential threats from those around us. We leave the security of having our mother's care, if it ever existed in the first place, and find that our needs have powerful energies all their own.

Depending upon whether or not we have come to believe that there is either abundance or scarcity, (a BUN dance or Scare-City), we form patterns of behavior around the meeting of these needs. It can be a sticky mess. We may find that this pursuit to satisfy our desires creates further tension. We may find that others want what we want and because they perceive the world through a lens of scarcity, they position us in a competitive frame. We are no longer who we are. We become scripted as their adversaries.

All of these things, along with the impermanent nature of life, make it very difficult to creatively hold the tension without feeling overwhelmed. Most of us reach our overwhelm threshold quite young and discover that psyche and our soma (body) can merge together and deal with this "overwhelm" by creating a defensive network of body based armament and psychological defense mechanisms. This network insulates us somewhat from a variety of dents—wounds from the rough and tumble of life in this physical plane. We've put on an armament that affords us protection in this strange world.

Life is easier with this protection in place. Or is it?

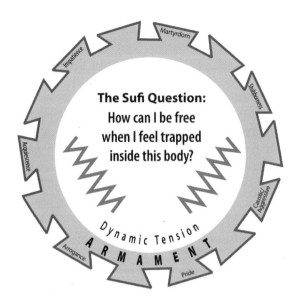

The Armament Ring - Figure 7

Nisargadatta (Sufi-teacher) answers: "You are not in the body, the body is in you."

It seems that the very reality of armament focuses our minds upon our wounds and our vulnerabilities. We may feel safer in relation to other people; but the armament has also served to distance us from our own core essences, where feelings of joy and timelessness abide. Overwhelmed people make this trade off and, at some later point, often re-evaluate whether it is still worth the price. "There must be another way to feel safe in this world," they may come to think. There is, but it is not found until the journey is undertaken. Our motivations for our journeys, ironically, come from our discontents, our yearnings and our tensions—all of which we'll call *our wounds*.

The force contained in this wound can unlock deep, karmic complexes that one has carried forward from other lives or dimensions. For now, we will call this...*The Mystery*. The soul wants reconciliation and deepening whereas the socially conditioned parts of us want safety and protection. The body has to balance these opposing forces and does a masterful job considering the mixed messages it gets. But in time, as we're seeing throughout the human species, there is a breakdown in immune functioning. This is a symptom of the body's inability to balance out, integrate and process many conflicting demands. When the balance is lost and the symptoms grow too painful to tolerate and suicide has been ruled out, one begins his search for a map to bring us back home to a balanced state.

Rather than reacting and then having to deal with the negative side effects of our disowned shadow selves that painfully pop out of our manicured lives when we're over stressed, it makes sense to be proactive and learn from our bodies' polarities, contrasts, and tensions. We *can* learn to dance with these realities in creative and realistic ways. How do we begin?

The first requirement to healing the imbalances in our lives is to feel our pains and befriend them. So if alienation, denial and enslavement to socially sanctioned roles really bug you, then diving in and being really bugged is essential to healing. It sounds counterintuitive to the ego but our soul knows to embrace the wound in order to transform it.
The second requirement for healing to occur is to realize that a healing process must happen. Many people struggle with the commitment to heal because they see the outer shell of anxiety around the actual pains rather than simply seeing the pain itself. The reaction to the pain is a major problem to be addressed in healing and accounts for all the addictive behaviors that go with our human predicament.

The third requirement of the healing process is the courageous journey into the heart of the wounded territory. The healing of the wound never lies at its periphery, though many fascinating diversions seem to congregate there. While involved in these diversions, people spend enormous amounts of time and energy absorbed in their "personality-stories" and are always seeking ways to tell them and explain them to themselves and others.

As we go into the heart of our wounded territories we discover that our body based muscular armaments are woven together with psychological defenses and emotional reactions. With these insightful discoveries our perceptions grow dramatically and we begin to metabolize the wound.

We see that when our armaments are in place, we function better even though we are still in the reactive state. We hear our little selves, our ego structures, thinking, "If we can't satisfy our most core yearnings, we can at least satisfy all these other desires." We see that in reactivity, our orientations are focused upon coping by gaining and acquiring; *our desires eclipse our joys* and our getting by and surviving well is more important than simply living in balance. The reactive life-style is about highs and lows rather than the middle ground. Most of all, the Reactivity State is about unconscious reactions.

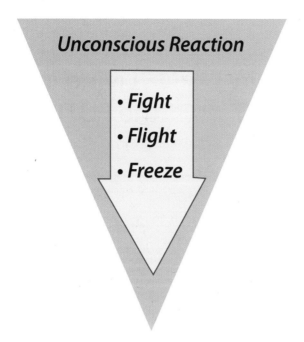

Unconscious Reaction to the Unhealed Wound - Figure 8

In Figure 8 we see three possible ways an overwhelmed person can react. These reactions may be unconsciously learned in formative years or they may be genetically predisposed, but they are definitely unconscious. As a reactive person *responds* to a situation, there is a reflective pause between perception and action. When *reacting*, however, the person automatically, without reflection, goes into fight, flight or freeze behaviors.

In the reactive state, the present moment is abandoned. Time is split into Past and Future frames wherein the overwhelmed person survives by either projecting onto his future or falling into routinized past solutions. The present is, thus, by passed with outworn and inefficient beliefs and actions. Experience is organized into linear, moment-to-moment, increments based on past fears/regrets or anxieties about the future. The body synchronizes its heartbeat and breath to match this fear/anxiety based rhythm.

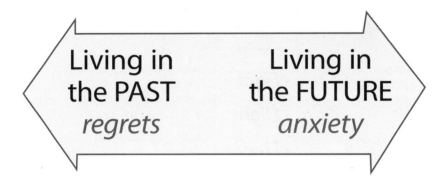

Splitting time into past and Future - Figure 9

You'll notice that in anxiety or fear reactions, the body holds its breath—that is, it stops time in order to get a grip on what is happening. The neuro-musculature freezes movement and sensations, attempting to stabilize a universe that is, inherently, in constant flux. Held breath and tight muscles can foster the illusion of stability, but what a price to pay! This illusion of security becomes, for the reactive person, the focus in life. The effort to control and dominate internal environments (the body) and the external environment (other people, our culture and the natural world) runs rampant. This effort encourages grasping, denial, and materialistic values that further our attachments to security and control, leaving the *conditioned human* habituated in body and fragmented in mind.

Past and future are safe havens for the reactive life, because in the present exists a breathing body filled with natural passions, vulnerabilities, pain and a hunger for intimacy—all forces too intense for the conditioned mind to tolerate. The body moves instinctually into its unconscious reactions to handle this intensity. Instead of recognizing, respecting and utilizing the energies of these feelings of rage, betrayal, fear and grief—not to mention the soft nature of human sensuality undulating upward from the pelvis—we often choose to abandon our bodies. Pretty grim. I try to share my sense of humor about this predicament with my clients.

When greeting a new client, as you have witnessed in this journey we have taken together, I maintain a certain gravity about the nature of healing work. I share a version of the "Art of Personal Disarmament" map, which I have referenced here, with my clients. I ask them to refer to the map between our sessions. Because I've grounded my clients with my commitment to them and the process, I can proceed with a kind of lightness that is never frivolous, but can sometimes be quite humorous.

In all of my years of practice, I've never felt that a moment of humor, when it arose naturally, was wasted time. In this light, I share with my clients' brief descriptions of some of the body's physiological personality types. This invites them to lighten up a little and suspend their self-judgment. Here is a synopsis of some typical physiological mindsets:

• The *Ass & Should-ers Types* relate to authority with rage and complain of things being unfair. The pain in the ass types say, "I'm okay!" like a rebel. The pain in the neck types ask, "Am I okay?" like the good child wanting approval.

• The *I Hurt Therefore I Am Types* relate to being self-contained in their own intimacy and the grief of being all alone. These types include: The "Wound lickers" (including thumb suckers), The Bellyachers, The Swallowers and The Teeth Grinders.

• The *"What me Worry"? Types* relate to fear by managing their fear-based reactions.

These types include: The Space Cadets, The Mack Truck Types, and The Girl or Boy on the Run. Most of these types sabotage the good things that happen to them just as life begins to show some promise. The heroic familiarity of the problematic is just *so* stimulating. Who cares about relaxing into the experience of good fortune?

I invite my clients to record their personal reflections, of their work with me, in a journal. If they live mostly in their heads, I sometimes ask them to keep a "From Head to Toe Body Assessment Journal." This can be very grounding and affords them a multi dimensional mirror in which they can witness their transformations. I ask them to use non-judgmental awareness in recording their thoughts and feelings about their bodies, especially the following areas: Neck and Shoulders, Pelvis, Mouth, Gut, Heart, Arms, Legs, and Psyche (mental dissociation). The insight gained from this writing is helpful in leveraging unresolved material out of the unconscious. The objectivity gained from the discipline of writing also diminishes the sense of intensity and overwhelm that usually accompanies transformational work. Life in the body does not have to be *too* intense. We *can* learn how to live here meaningfully. We can wake up! This is what transformation is about. But before we can live in response to natural rhythms, we must first understand our conditionings and our relationships to both our sensual lives and to the emotional material we are carrying.

Theoretically, most of us are ready to let go of our familiar "personal world orders" if we are either sick and tired of being stuck in a mess or if we are inspired to embrace a richer life style. Either the carrot or stick is what moves us, but usually it is the stick of our discomfort with ourselves that is the more powerful motivation.

My job is to help my clients get comfortable with the discomforts of their feeling life. In the early sessions, I work with my client's bodies in ways that afford them a pleasurable flow experience, enough sweetness to meet their bitter feelings with some equanimity. Here are some basic principles I work with, internally as a practitioner and verbally with my clients:

- Balance gravity with lightness and humor.

- Suspend self-judgment and judgment of others and the entire situation.

- Perceive that despair and disgust can be tools for change, and not just symptoms of hopelessness.

- Maintain patience.

- Note that perceptual filters are cellular identities within consciousness.

- See the pain of holding on as greater than the pain of letting go.

- Perceive that resistance to healing is not necessarily negative.

- Understand that we have to rescue ourselves.

Not everyone I see in my practice is ripe for my work even though they think they are, or their referring therapist, friend or family member is so convinced. Perhaps they want a quick "cure" or they want me to rescue them, or they need their pain as motivation to *do* their life still—all contraindications for me to consider in opening someone up. Similar to the Gallo wine commercial, I remind myself: "Open no-one before their time." So, I invite my new clients into a relationship with the principles stated above; and if there is a lack of receptivity, I modulate my work into an easy, rejuvenating massage. By the next session, a shift may have occurred; and if not, I patiently introduce them again to their feeling life by actively interpreting some of what I see their body expressing to me. Patience with process is what this work with the body teaches us.

To appreciate the challenge of transformation, consider the seductive obstacles that the reactive life has generated as substitutes for natural passion and emotional aliveness. When the body receives a fear signal, a very potent, quick "hit" of adrenaline permeates the nervous system with a compressed and distorted sense of immediacy, resulting in a false sense of aliveness. It is "moment to moment" life and resembles "life in the moment" but it is linear, not multi-dimensional. The hit we derive from reacting to fear feels desirable and it is this desire that becomes the source of our addiction to the reactive life. It is also the home of our ambivalence toward healing.

Behavioral Effects of the Reactivity States - Figure 10

We want to heal, but we are afraid to heal. "Yes, please help me heal!" "No, I'm too afraid of losing what I have!" This perpetual cycle of reactivity (Figure 10), keeps creating cravings, aversions and us wanting, and not wanting, to experience the actual healing process. In craving we greedily hold onto pleasurable experiences or furtively seek out fresh pleasures. In aversion we build walls to keep out unpleasantness in our lives or else we procure the psychic equipment to either numb out (freeze), transcend (flight), or bulldoze away (fight) unpleasantness that has found entry into our consciousness. Busy, busy.

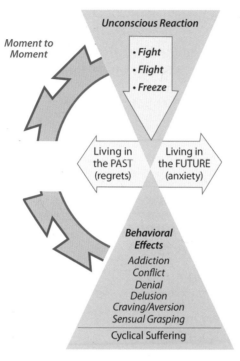

The REACTIVITY State
of
The Unhealed Wound

Unconscious Reaction

Moment to Moment

- *Fight*
- *Flight*
- *Freeze*

Living in the PAST (regrets)   Living in the FUTURE (anxiety)

Behavioral Effects

Addiction
Conflict
Denial
Delusion
Craving/Aversion
Sensual Grasping

Cyclical Suffering

Coping & Surviving

The Reactivity State of the Unhealed Wound - Figure 11

The unpleasantness is, of course, the messy business of our unhealed wounds. If we are ever to get off this merry-go-round of reactivity, we must make friends with our wounds and heal them.

Why is this so difficult?

Ultimately, if we heal our wounds they will no longer have dominance in our lives. No more quick hit adrenaline; no more drama. If I am identified with my wounds and my reactions to these wounds, then healing means *no more me.* Death of ego is the big threshold in the transformational journey. The armament based ego (see the Armament Ring—Figure 7) dissolves; in its place is born an aware ego capable of navigating conventional reality while affording us connection to our feelings. We begin to flow with

WOUNDS INTO BLESSINGS

life. In contrast to the state of cyclical suffering, existence in the present is not about moving from moment to moment, but rather about being in the moment. Here we experience the dynamic flow between the artificial boundaries of *self*, and the rest of the world that is interpenetrating the self. This flow state is timeless and transcendent. The spontaneous flow of life is not too intense. The flow of feelings, like water, can arise and recede; its waves with crests and troughs are not problems. It is not so strange. We can look at our pains and just be with them until they flow beyond us. We don't have to fix them, or pretend we don't have them or run away from them. We can just be and observe them.

Just being, without agenda or preferences, opens up a new window within the mind. The view from this window is spacious; there is fresh air. We look out with neutrality. In the absence of judgment there is a freedom and a flowing sweetness. This does not mean we live without concerns or discernment; rather it means we can harmonize with what's in front of us—regardless of what it is; we have equanimity.

Sounds pretty good to me. Where can I get some of this flow stuff? That's the paradox! You can't get it. You've already got it; you just forgot. There's no getting or gaining here; it's all about *sculpting away excess to reveal essence*.

The essence in all of us exists within the domain of universal natural laws. The capacity to access our personal essence, our True Nature, is universally inherent in all human beings; and bodywork and meditation are well suited to the task of discovering, establishing and maintaining access to the True Self and the universal natural laws. The experience of tapping into the universal presents the possibility of an alternate lifestyle than the reactive way. Tasting these new freedoms, a person becomes motivated to pursue his healing. Suddenly, all those old hurts—the angers, the fears, the betrayals and the grievances don't appear so large and looming. Offering these healings to other people is often easier than giving them to yourself. But by giving healing to others, you cannot but be opened to your own healing.

The journey from reactivity to flow follows a pathway. The pathway leads directly into the heart of our wounded territories. How could it be otherwise? The Transformational Journey is an invitation to go directly into our woundedness rather than attempt to overcome it, transcend it or find a way around it. The pathway goes directly into the armament that was created to handle all of the difficult history.

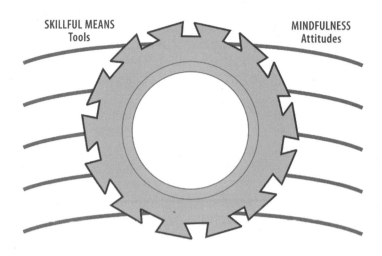

The Journey of Making the Unhealed Wound Fertile - Figure 12

You must accept your armament if you are to succeed in disarmament. Armament is necessary on this planet. How much one needs is debatable. To elect to drop degrees of armament, we need to become intimately familiar with the way we have armored ourselves. Through healing we learn to flow, and we learn that we can choose to put on or take off "appropriate armament" as we would choose to dress appropriately for an occasion. Understanding the *Reactivity State*, on a personal level, is a prerequisite to outgrowing its hold on us. How attractive do we find our buffering addictions? Are we intimidated by descending into our wounds to find wholeness and integration despite our deep yearnings for it? Big questions.

I ask each client to consider his or her beliefs about death and dying and I ask him or her to explore what feels incomplete within his or her life. I explore with each client the wisdom in this Zen phrase:

> *To die but not to perish is to be eternal.*

Who in us is ready to die? Is it just an aspect of my experience that I'm identified with? If I dis-identify, will that be the death of "ME"? Which Me? We can see our ego personality traits as defensive filters that afford us appropriate buffers between the world and our vulnerable sensitivities. The self can be seen as light; the personality can be seen as filters, or filter gels that go over the light. When we feel the need for protection we employ a defense mechanism. The primary defense mechanisms I explore with my clients are:

Stubbornness and Caustic-Aggressiveness for those who Fight; these defenses are anger based. Acquiescence and Impatience for those who Run-Away; these are fear-based defenses. Pride and Martyrdom are the defenses for those who Freeze up. These constellate around the emotion of grief. Arrogance is an all-purpose defense mechanism that can cover up fear, anger and grief with equal effectiveness.

Interesting combinations of defenses can occur when one of the freeze filters joins with a fight or flight reaction. Frozen fight might result in an arm immobility such as bursitis. Frozen flight can cause a physical symptom of leg immobility like sciatica, or a psychological reaction of frozen feet when one has an urge to run away. In all frozen movement one is stuck because the muscles armor up to hold back the expression of an impulse.

When one of these defensive filters arises while I'm working with a client, I ask him to feel into it and to identify it so that he knows what it is he is experiencing. This allows him the objectivity to *not* identify with that defensive reaction. This transformation of awareness allows for disengagement of identification; that is, a filter has been removed. The more filters we remove the brighter the lighting gets. Makes sense.

Can we allow it? Can we move on it now?

We can. We can really let go. But when?

HOW ABOUT NOW? Why wait?

Let's die now and avoid the June rush.

Everybody wants to go to heaven but no one wants to die!

Why not? Is there more story that needs to be played out before the insight is gained?

The ego filters and structures are cellular identities that have their own DNA territory in our energy fields. They have their own beliefs, value systems and versions of our personal histories, and their own karmic propensities that they share with us until they transform—that is, until they heal and die. All our CELLULAR IDENTITIES are literally REACTIONS TO WOUNDS and negative conditions. When we stop reacting, the identity begins to die and lose power over us.

Healing can be seen as a deliberate effort to allow our wounded identities the death of benign neglect. This process of allowing also involves the complete feeling and expression of grief. We just let those parts of us die completely, have our funeral pyres or burials and let our bodies have their releases. This can be very brief but it needs to be complete. Transformational healing work is the art of midwifing the conscious death of illusory identities.

All of these perspectives I share with my clients and students so that healing and freedom can happen. Two of the great motivations for healing are despair and disgust; emotions associated with the stomach, as in, "I just can't stomach it any longer." Sometimes we have to get extremely *fed up* with ourselves before we'll budge from the passive acquiescence of our lives. When our difficulties are seen as just extensions of tired stories—our precious versions of reality—real changes happen. Up until this shift in perception, reality is defined by our unhealed wounds. I try to help my clients feel that the pain in holding on is a greater suffering than the fear of letting go. *"Me die. You've got to be kidding...I've got plans, this pain is nothing."*

A significant aspect of healing work is resistance. All scabs itch as they heal. The tendency to scratch that scab, re-infect it and keep the war going, one more fix for the wound addict to manage, is aimed at avoiding the pain of the wound itself. My job is to dispassionately accompany the "wounded self" at the edge of despair and not rescue her from the pain's teaching like so many of her well intentioned family members and friends may have done. Each person must, ultimately, rescue himself or herself. When my client is ready to do that I am right there, for him or her, driving the ambulance or the get away car and I am ready to uncork the champagne. But until that point, I keep letting air out of her sails and adding ballast to her experience so she can't float above her despair anymore. My client can't paste a smile back on for conventions sake just to keep everyone happy in the waiting room...indefinitely. Once my client lands into her despair, she can do a lot of unhooking quickly.

We all do a disservice to ourselves and the people we try to help when we encourage a *get better faster* approach by adopting various positive behaviors. If these behaviors are not grown from the inside out—by personally working through the challenges and gifts of the wounds—they can only last until the glue dries up. So, I wait at the threshold quietly; I neither push nor coax them through. And when they're ready, they move on with their journeys.

An effective dis-identification exercise, in this regard, is to go into your basement, attic or secret storage area and find something you've held onto that has a special meaning for you. Sacrifice it. Own it by giving it away or throwing it away. Notice any resistance and observe who in you still does not want to let go. Build on this exercise and start letting go of all your relationships that no longer serve your essential life anymore.

This letting go is a lightening up process and can sustain us in our continual evolving enlightenment as we go on metabolizing our ego-filters except for those we choose to employ *only as needed.*

Now that we're ready to heal we need *Skillful Means* to gain entry into the wounded territory. We need the tools and attitudes shown in the graphic of the Skillful Means (see Figure13) to make safe and fruitful journeys into our wounded realms and to succeed in *The Art of Personal Disarmament.* We enter the pathways into our armaments through skillful means.

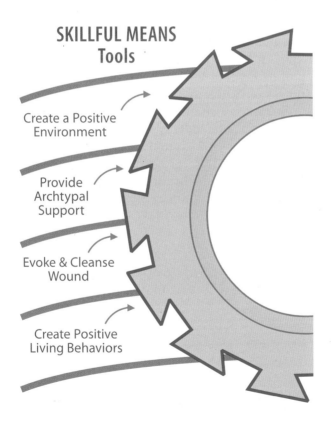

SKILLFUL MEANS Tools

Create a Positive Environment

Provide Archtypal Support

Evoke & Cleanse Wound

Create Positive Living Behaviors

Skillful Means - Figure 13

Skillful Means allows us access into our armament. The process of gaining access is supportive, friendly and nourishing. There are many attributes within a "Positive Environment" and in "Healthy Living Behaviors," and many methods of evoking the wound to come out of hiding. In the holistic health movement, therapeutic practices abound to this end and there are always supports for healing that can be tapped into from archetypal sources including: shamans, the magical child, Buddha, Christ's Love, the warrior, the Black Madonna or the wise woman are examples of these archetypes available to us.

Once we are inside the wound—with intent to heal—we no longer perceive old angers, fears, betrayals and grievances as negative afflictions, enemies or burdens we'd rather deny or avoid. They can prompt our growth, as in the analogy of an oyster making its pearl from an irritating grain of sand. Our wounds, viewed this way, can be seen as the catalyst for us to reclaim our affinity with the creator. What began as anger can become forgiveness and leave us bigger and wiser beings.

Once inside the wound we explore the healings. We meet each of these places and are transformed by what transpires. We grieve one last time before perceiving our losses with a new healing detachment. We experience the sting of betrayal or the guilt of having betrayed again; and then we invite awareness of the karmic play into consciousness and find we can trust again. Finally, we visit our fears and we shake, perhaps like never before, and then slowly, or suddenly, we awaken with faith. With these healings we welcome ourselves into the present.

Where skillful means opens us to the healing process, mindfulness allows us to accomplish the healing. In addition to these healings, mindfulness allows us to enter and remain within the Flow State.

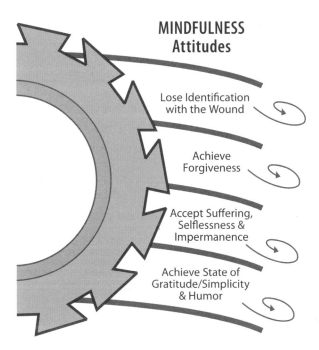

**MINDFULNESS
Attitudes**

Lose Identification
with the Wound

Achieve
Forgiveness

Accept Suffering,
Selflessness &
Impermanence

Achieve State of
Gratitude/Simplicity
& Humor

Mindfulness - Figure 14

In contrast to the Reactivity State, the Flow State is an experience of soft boundaries that can disappear and reveal the seamless unity that pervades all things. The Flow State is often arrived at, in a person's life, during periods of gratitude or in activities that nourish the soul such as gardening, massage, lovemaking or meditation. A flow state can also be achieved through exhilarating activity as well. It is possible to sustain Flow State consciousness and behaviors within the realm of human relations but it requires a fundamental change in perception. Mindfulness sets the stage and invites this change of perception.

Mindfulness alters what we see as well as the way we see it because of a change of awareness within the perceiver. For example, in our conditioned world, we are raised to see through a separate-self awareness filter. This mentality centers around gaining. What can I gain from this experience?

How can I become more attractive, wealthy, secure or spiritual? In contrast to this gaining mentality, which underlies reactivity, there is the flow state awareness, which is about unfolding, simplicity, and relaxation. Mindfulness is the mechanism by which perception is transformed from gaining into unfolding and it is one of the major goalless goals of a meditation practice. This separate-self window of perception is the core of what needs to be transformed. It is the source of our loneliness and suffering and it is encouraged by antiquated, mechanistic, Newtonian science and by the dominant cultures of the world.

Beginning with Einstein's Theory of Relativity and expanding rapidly in the decades since, a new scientific paradigm has emerged which explains physical reality at the sub-atomic level. Quantum physicists describe their findings in terms that sound similar to the experiential insights of ancient mystics, as well as to modern day explorers of consciousness. Revealed within the micro-universe of protons, neutrons and electrons is a strange world where hundreds of kinds of sub-atomic particles behave, not as discrete entities, but rather as waves of energy that disappear and reappear sometimes as particles and sometimes as waves.

The cosmos, from this updated model, appears to be a manifestation of energetic webs and unified relationships that are constantly in motion. Interestingly, the consciousness of the observing scientist seems to have an effect upon what is being observed (this phenomenon is called the Heisenberg Uncertainty Principle). This dynamic relationship between the observer and that, which is being observed, has generated the understanding that consciousness creates reality and that the mind is interactive with physical reality.

This is not news to anyone who has worked with psychosomatic illness or who has explored his own consciousness through a regular meditation practice. What is new and exciting is that this new scientific reality-model has subconsciously affected enough people on earth today that the transformation of separate-self identity into unity-self identity is a distinct possibility for human beings. The shift from separate-self modes of perception to unity-self modes of perception invites flow into our lives.

Mindfulness is the careful mental examination of experience similar to the scientific examination of observable phenomena. The concentrated and focused mental energy of a meditating person cuts through the field of observation (which could be body based experience or mental patterns or emotional fixations, to name a few) and breaks the hold of "separate-self identification" with that which is being observed. For example, a woman who has identified with her wound all her life (i.e. "he abused me") is, with mindfulness, able to disengage her identity from that wound. She can see the event of the wound as an arising which wants to pass away if it were not for her consciousness that has become attached to the wound. The attachment of identity to the wound only re-enforces the woundedness.
Dis-identification allows the energetic web of the wound to pass away.

This dis-identification happens as the consciousness of the person unites with the insight that the wound carries. Without insight there is no detachment, and therefore no freedom. You might say that the whole purpose of a wound is to deliver an important message. It seems that we pay more attention when we are in pain than when we are riding high on waves of joy.

The easiest way to evolve into Flow State experience is to allow the separate-self identity to gradually dissolve. This dissolving of the protective ego is the by-product of healing and, conversely, healing is the result of ego-deactivation. When we heal, there is no longer an activated wound to protect. If we were identified with our wounds, the healing signifies the loss of placement for our wounded egos. In essence, we outgrow the need for protection because there is no longer an "I" that is hurting. In its place an aware ego is birthed. The warrior who's *Battle is Over,* lays down his arms and opens himself to love. Personal disarmament opens us, finally, to "the real life" we've always yearned for—a life of love.

Through mindful observation of our inner reactions, we can come to see that no amount of guru blessing, intimate love, private therapy or communion with nature will ever satisfy our yearning for true release into wholeness. If we cannot let go of our identification with our wounds, we will always be busy upgrading our symbolic substitutes, whether they are centered around money, fame, food, knowledge, sex or power. The bottom line is that we cannot open to this strange new life of spiritual promise until we stop fearing death.

Healing work creates a transformed observer. Gradually, by observing the transient nature of thoughts, feelings and sensations, one gets the distinct impression that this entire self-identity construct is also arising and passing away. *What self?* Without a self to suffer, the "end of suffering" becomes a possibility.

Outgrowing the self is kinder than plotting the death of ego, which only sounds like more gaining anyway. In fact, the outgrowing process can be an antidote to the peril on the path that is spiritual materialism. The conventional self transforms into an aware selflessness by virtue of the shift in the perception of the perceiver. How we arrive at this inner shift in perception is through examination of our wounds. One could make a case that we could get a similar shift in perception by examining our joys and pleasures, but for the most part pain grabs attention more thoroughly. Pain focuses our consciousness on our mortality and on our spiritual edges. Focusing upon our difficulties transforms those suffering places into opportunities to investigate our souls' curriculums. This investigation immediately grabs our attention. Suddenly we intuit what we came here to learn and experience; we tap into a universal place that has always existed within us and transcends the mortality of the body. We come to realize that God created suffering so that we would be dissatisfied with everything but him/her/it. This is the punch line to the big cosmic joke.

In the heart of our pains we see the humor of God's view of existence. The pain humbles us and in the space that is created from this humility, God comes to visit us. This soulful regeneration at the core of our wounds and heartbreaks is the surest sign that we are held within the arms of a compassionate universe. Albert Camus, the great French existentialist, spoke to this most eloquently: "In the midst of winter, I found in me, that there was an invincible summer."

When healing intent meets our unhealed wounds, the stage is set for spiritual alchemy. We are now poised for disarmament.

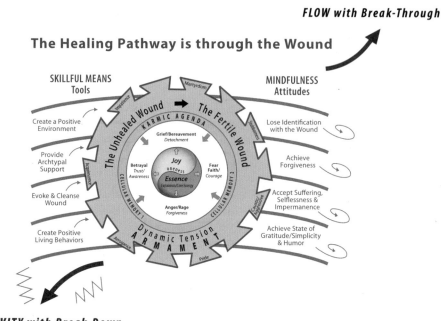

The Healing Process - Figure 15

The skillful means and the mindfulness we have cultivated and brought to our lives is the best we can do. We may wait for a long time as we continue to ripen; something deep and internal must still happen. During this period of ripening, many would-be liberated people experience their existential tensions and choose to return to their reactions. They lose patience. Without patience there can be a regression back to reactivity; with patience, there can be a breakthrough to Flow.

Before transformation our small self experiences *break-down*; after transformation our large Self experiences *break-through* into Flow. There is no intrinsic difference in the phenomena of transformation; there is only a different perceiver. And our large Self-perceiver is infinitely patient. Patience is the child of faith; when you realize that you've never been abandoned, you can allow yourself to just be still within the realm of "not knowing." In this stillness a knowing comes; now a mysterious ripening can occur. This is what is meant by the aphorism, "Time heals all wounds." The divine comes to harvest us when we finally stop trying to be ripe.

Disarmament - Figure 16

As we disarm, the wounds dissipate as our bodies and minds naturally integrate. There is not an end to this process. The journey continues in ever more subtle ways, with occasional periods of slippage back into less skillful modes of behavior. This slippage reminds us of our commitments to wholeness by demonstrating to us, again, the un-satisfactoriness of our earlier ways. For some people, backsliding into old reactions is seen as an ominous sign of their inherent inadequacies; others may see it as a fall from grace and live their days "waiting for the other shoe to drop." I call this mindset "the tyranny of perfection." It is fear based and drives people into performance mode, affecting everything from their diets to their exercise and meditation practices. It is kinder to just notice that we have strayed from our "true heart's desire" and simply return to a more mindful way of being in our lives—being especially mindful of how much our inner critic has taken to posturing conventional or new age sentiments.

Disarmament is not about being inappropriately vulnerable. Personal disarmament is an art and it requires attentiveness. By cultivating awareness, we're able to perceive real threats and distinguish them from imaginary ones. With this discernment we no longer put fears into our bodies, or project hostilities or become easy targets. The old, reactive self-perceived the world in a rear-view mirror mode, moving forward while looking backward, never being present right now. With disarmament we are able to be aware and to live in the present, and as a result we are able, like a martial artist, to flow with personal adversaries or dangerous situations.

Awareness is the best defense because, by keeping us within the moment, it allows us to be spontaneous. This is the understanding behind tai chi and aikido, two very potent, oriental martial arts that aim at blending the spirits of both the practitioner and the attacker. "The Japanese word for the martial arts as a whole is *budo*. It means literally, 'the way to stop the spear.' [Pragmatically]... it means to *stop fighting*, as does the Chinese word for the martial arts, *wushu*. Psychological studies have confirmed [that] the more advanced students have much less aggressive personalities than the average person." [2] This means that *as we become more aware, grounded, sensitive and spontaneous, we also can become gentle without compromising our security.* Kabir, the Sufi poet, tells us, "Gentleness is a divine trait. There is nothing stronger than gentleness; and there is nothing more gentle than real strength."

With this transformation of consciousness, self-absorption dissipates; other people's needs and challenges come to your attention. Service to others is a natural outgrowth of self-healing. We voluntarily find ourselves opening to the suffering of others and find that compassion leads to *right action*. Pain is not avoided in the flow state, and pleasures can be wonderful and conscious. There is no resistance; there are no preferences. The weather changes; it's all okay. We can be pretty certain the scabs have fallen away when our sensitivities feel like blessings rather than burdens. We don't erase history, we just unplug from it. When we've truly forgiven ourselves and others and have found our lost parts, we move on from the weight of identifying with those stories. At this point transformational work goes beyond healing. It becomes the work of self-cultivation and spiritual growth. This is where all the hard work involved in healing our wounds starts to pay us back dividends.

We no longer need the wounds as excuses to get attention, to access our depths or to mobilize our energies. A higher-octane fuel energizes us, we're as deep as we want to be without getting heavy, and we don't need excuses because we already accept our imperfections. Now we can be of service to others for all the right reasons.

This transformation of consciousness can help us flow in harmony with our lives and make possible a more peaceful world. As we can see in Figure 17, the arrows going from the path of mindfulness into the *flow state* circulate back and forth. Essentially, mindfulness and flow are different aspects of the same phenomena.

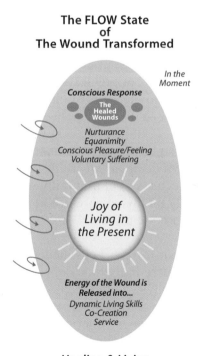

The FLOW State of The Wound Transformed

In the Moment

Conscious Response

The Healed Wounds

Nurturance
Equanimity
Conscious Pleasure/Feeling
Voluntary Suffering

Joy of Living in the Present

Energy of the Wound is Released into...
Dynamic Living Skills
Co-Creation
Service

Healing & Living

The Flow State - Figure 17

Notice the porousness of the egg shaped FLOW State symbol; appreciate how the center is expansive and filled with joy. This joy is the same joy we met in the beginning [of this chapter (in Figure 3)]. We reclaim our essential resonance with creation again and, like the egg suggests, we are reborn. On our transformational journey, we have learned how to die in order to truly live. We have learned how to do this through our investigation of ourselves and have found, through this exploration, that there is truly no death, only a change of form.

"This dance of existence," that Lao Tzu describes, permeates all things and describes a constantly moving realm of impermanence. Therefore, the concept of security, which is the constant pre-occupation of most human beings, presents an amusing paradox. Since the entire universe is in a constant state of flux, the only realistic security can be achieved through changing at the same rate as the universe is moving. Since this is impossible to predict, the best we can do is to learn how to flow with this dynamic reality. *Security then, it appears, lies in our ability to flow;* and this is quite difficult when one is burdened with the heaviness of unhealed wounds.

Since human beings are social animals, real security can be defined by our relationships with other human beings. In fact, the loving bonds we form with other people can be seen as our greatest security. The art of friendship, the skills of parenting, and the tools of building community are examples of human capacities that can offer security.

On an existential level, security can be seen as a human being's ability to live at peace with his or her own death, as we've discussed. There is nothing that provides greater security than true faith; and organized religion does not hold a monopoly on this experience at all, nor is it the gatekeeper on this road of existence we all travel on.

The road signs guiding us along our life journeys include the ways we behave, the emotions that characterize individual consciousness and the patterns of tension that define our physical and mental experiences. When we have a map, being aware of these road signs is very useful, because, awareness allows us to be in choice. We can choose to drop a degree of armament, and when we do, we will notice to that same degree, feelings of increased freedom and vulnerability. Vulnerability is not necessarily a negative, especially if one is defended by a keen awareness of what is happening around them. Consciousness is our best defense. The martial arts, as metaphor, demonstrate how awareness of the here and now affords true perception of potential danger. This awareness allows us to make conscious choices regarding the degree of our vulnerabilities. Bear in mind the definition of *vulnerable*: "Liable to an increased penalty if defeated or to an *increased benefit*, if successful." A person who has created elaborate defenses for himself, or herself, has chosen to perceive experience through the lens of unhealed wounds and has proportionately limited his/her capacity to utilize awareness, itself, to foster security.

Real security flows from our harmony with the laws of nature and it is cultivated through loving relationships with other human beings. The ultimate security is the fruit we harvest by living with a faith that befriends death. These kinds of securities are the "increased benefits" we win by exploring our vulnerabilities. This experimentation with dropping armament by degrees is precisely the invitation that healing and transformation offer.

The complete map of the "Art of Personal Disarmament" at the beginning of this chapter has four major tributaries:

   1) The dynamic tension of the Unhealed Wound;

   2) The Armament Ring and the Reactivity State;

   3) The Journey of Making the Unhealed Wound Fertile—including tools and attitudes, or *skillful means* and *mindfulness* respectively;

   4) The Flow State.

All of these tributaries wind around and come together just as rivers flow into the ocean. Each one comes together and arrives at the ocean of FLOW. Regardless of where one starts, whether it be letting go of reactivity and armament or by opening to flow and *higher mind*, the destination remains the same: *a life based on self-acceptance, loving behaviors, and a harmony with natural law.* A life imbued with these qualities is both the journey and the destination.

The "Art of Personal Disarmament" map that we have investigated appears to be one linear healing process. It suggests that you begin with Reactivity, move into Disarmament and healing which results in entering the FLOW State. This is true at the Meta level and we spend our whole lives repeating this process of metabolizing our wounds over and over again…especially since we gather new wounds of loss, abandonment, etc as we go. The truth is we are never done as long as we are alive in this human body. We are always arriving at a new level and state of FLOW. With each passing through the "Art of Personal Disarmament" we reach ever-greater levels of joy and FLOW! It is a beautiful thing!

"And the end of all our exploring. Will be to arrive where we started. And know the place for the first time. "
— *T.S. Eliot, The Little Gidding (the last of his Four Quartets)*

Every traveler takes this circular, sacred and epic journey alone; no one can travel this path for you. There is, however, nurturance, support, and excellent company for every traveler upon this path. When two or more people gather together, nurture, support and provide companionship for one another on this journey to the sea, the divine becomes ordinary, and the ordinary becomes divine.

****

Footnotes:

1. *Man In The Trap,* by Elsworth Baker, M.D., (Avon Books copyright 1967). p.33

2 *A way to stop the spear,* The Economist magazine, May 15th, 1993 (p.114) Appendix II 219

Appendix

1. The Work

Transformational work of any kind is not for everyone. It is about waking up, not about finding a better psychological pillow. Transformational Bodywork is not a coping therapy; it is a radical alteration of sheer perception. Readiness, and desire, to change one's perception of his or her world is how I gauge whether my work is appropriate for someone. Simply put, if someone is emotionally numb or tactile defensive or spiritually cynical, they will most likely not be a candidate for Transformational Bodywork, at least not until they have reached a crisis state. In this case, particularly, the individual would also need to be in some form of psychotherapy so that he or she has an ongoing support system outside of our work.

I have always had many clients who value good, nurturing bodywork and are not dealing with heavy issues—just the normal stresses of modern life. They make up about thirty percent of my clientele. Another twenty percent involve the clinical cases that revolve around neuro-muscular dysfunction. Working with these people affords me a base line understanding that I naturally use as a benchmark in working with my "edge" clients. These clients, and their stories in *Wounds into Blessings,* represent a cross section of the transformational context I, and others, regularly visit in our work.

Deep, healing therapeutic relationships require that a comfortable meeting ground be sustained. Some clients quit after a session or two with me, not because they completed their healing work but because our energies were not a good match. This happens on both sides of any therapeutic relationship. When I feel this "mis-match" on my end, I refer this client to another bodyworker or therapist more temperamentally compatible with this person, and make every attempt to graciously communicate my impressions so as not to create any sense of rejection in them. I have found that I am more respectful to myself and the people I work with when I accept my limitations, inclinations and boundaries.

I have not always felt successful with clients that *work* a situation too much. Perhaps they remind me of a part of myself. Nevertheless, when I get bored or impatient with a client now, I initiate an honorable closure to our work together. Often these same clients return a couple of years later to finish the "piece" that was not yet ripe in our earlier meeting.

The transformational meeting ground is arrived at through a dance of trial and error until an understanding comes into play, just like in any learning activity. Those of us who practice this kind of work come to this understanding through *practice*. There is no magical formula. Often I wished I had a mentor. Now I know the work itself is my teacher.

2. For the Client of Transformational Bodywork

Transformational Bodywork[sm] is an exploration of self through conscious touch. It can be viewed as the art of "peace making" between the inner human being and the physical body. Unlike massage and most styles of bodywork which have physical goals as their primary focus, this approach is aimed at awareness itself. The focus is upon the causal place in the physical body where unconscious beliefs, repressed memory and charged unresolved emotional experience co-exist. The reactivity and dynamic tension are accessed through the breath, subtle energy fields and deep tissue manipulation of the musculature.

The dynamic tension leads us into a healing zone I refer to as "The Fertile Wound". Within this zone, perceptions are more clear, meaningfulness grows deeper and a spirit of lightness and confidence establishes itself within the structures of the individual's body and psyche.

The Five Phase Journey

Phase One: Establish a communicative *working relationship* between client and practitioner. Through the building of trust and confidence in the quality of touch an understanding of the core issue emerges.

Phase Two: *Unveiling.* The issue and unhealed wound are revealed along with the associative thinking that has grown around the wound-experience. The work touches the core of the wound and invites a release to occur and an opening for life energy, 'chi', to flow throughout the body.

Phase Three: *Commitment to heal:* the inner dynamic that has emerged is made more conscious. Through manipulation of the musculature and testing, the connection between inner emotion and outer armament is apparent. The client can see the relationship between body and mind and own the issue in order to heal. Healing moves us from unclaimed anger, fear and grief to forgiveness, faith and detachment.

Phase Four: *Relinquishment.* The wound is cleansed with archetypal support, selflove and a spirit of dis-identification. Client assumes responsibility for letting go of the habituated armament that has evolved around the wound for protection.

Phase Five: *Integration.* The capacity to feel deeply one's experience, cultivate a compassionate life and feel safe in a world of impermanence is the ultimate value of this process. Changes in life-style, self-image, and tools for appropriate self-defense are explored as the journey into the Flow State deepens.

3. Transformational Bodywork for the Healing Artist

The ancient masters were
profound and subtle.
Their wisdom was unfathomable.
There is no way to describe it;
all we can describe is their appearance.
They were careful as
someone crossing an iced-over stream.
Alert as a warrior in enemy territory.
Courteous as a guest.
Fluid as melting ice.
Shapeable as a block of wood.
Receptive as a valley.
Clear as a glass of water.

~ Tao Te Ching

Practitioner Training Program

The teachings of Transformational Bodywork revolve around a simple premise: We are spiritual beings having a human experience on Earth. The ideal candidate for this style of healing bodywork is someone who resonates with the understanding that healing experiences invite themselves into our lives as touchstones to higher-self learning. A Transformational Bodyworker is a skilled practitioner who is comfortable exploring the questions: "Why am I feeling this way?" and "What is the deeper meaning of this experience?" Someone who has embraced their own suffering and transcends it enough to know deeply the qualities of compassion, humor, gratitude and humility is essentially capable of facilitating another person on the path of metaphorical dying in order to truly come alive.

This seven level professional training program in depth-healing and personal transformation embraces a curriculum that invites mature practitioners in the healing arts, psychotherapy, spiritual disciplines and the bodywork fields. Education specific to the breath, musculature, cellular memory, biological defense mechanisms and the nature of armament is explored in relationship to free will, the karmic agenda and the journey of the self into love and freedom.

The seminar series cultivates perspectives and pragmatic interventions that are designed to offer both an organic *uncovering* to human problems and a grounded approach to *integrating* into daily life the healing understandings gained through the work.

All instruction occurs in groups of 8 to 12 participants, is taught in residential retreat, often video-taped and is designed to meet the needs and requirements of each individual student. For example, if a person has years of bodywork experience but no meditation practice they would design a different program than an individual who has had extensive background as a psychotherapist with a minimum of hands-on training in touch modalities. The following outline is a breakdown of the seven level offerings:

Level One:

Perspective and Application. Understanding the Reactive and Flow States; 40 movement sequences and their appropriate usage.

Level Two

Healing the Wound. Personal Growth for the practitioner. Videotaped sessions documenting the relationship dynamic between the personal identity and its belief structures and karmic agenda.

Level Three

Technique. Musculo-skeletal manipulation strategies. Organ-Muscle associations. Energetic Repatterning Approaches to the bio-field in transition.

Level Four

Apprenticeship. Students individually contract supervised time with their clients, and observe and are observed in their practicum. Personal ownership of the strategy, technique and perspective.

Level Five

Yoga-Massage* and Meditation**. Integrating the expanded body with the expanded mind.

Levels Six and Seven

Seminars in Voice Dialogue***, Self-Transformation with Cheryl Mitouer and courses in meditation are individually arranged; a research project and a personal health assessment complete the requirements.

* *Yoga-Massage* as designed by Transformational Bodywork Seminars is a series of specific asanas that, along with deep massage while the asana is in effect, creates in the body expanded possibilities.

** *Meditation* is an essential and core foundation in the life of someone choosing to assist other people in the transformational process. There are many paths to enlightenment; each avenue can provide an opportunity for the cultivation of peace and harmony in this life.

*** *Voice Dialogue* is an internationally acclaimed approach to the psychology of selves created by Hal Stone Ph.D. and Sidra Stone Ph.D. The balancing of sub-personalities within the matrix of identity is considered a primary characteristic of healthy psychological functioning and personal fulfillment.

4. Biography

Fred Mitouer, Ph.D., is internationally known for his groundbreaking somatic therapy: Transformational Bodywork^sm and as the founder of Dragons' Breath Theatre--a forum for cultural experiments in consciousness and irreverent play. He created Pacific School of Massage in 1978 and Transformational Bodywork in 1989. Fred has been a featured presenter at many International Conferences, including the International Somatics Congresses -- which he co-sponsored with the Association of Humanistic Psychology, The State of the World Forum and the 9th International Conference on Conflict Resolution, in ST. Petersburg, Russia. His writings

have appeared in *Perspective, Massage Magazine, Common Ground* and *Yoga Journal*. He is a co-author of the award winning book, *Healing the Heart of the World*, Elite Press, 2005 (http://www.bodyworkmassage.com/writings/tamingdragon/tamingdragon.html)

Fred Mitouer, 2012

Fred has presented his work in Paris, Hong Kong, and throughout the United States and has maintained a private practice in Northern California for nearly 40 years that has transformed the consciousness of countless individuals in diverse arenas spanning the creative arts through the shamanic depths to the corporate world. The New York Times has called him, "The Hollywood A list's favorite guru...a master." He is a father and grandfather and lives with his wife, Cheryl, on California's Mendocino Coast where he sculpts in metal and stone and rides his dragons. He can be found at: http://www.transformationalbodywork.org

Notes